BEACON LIGHTS OF HISTORY

VOLUME IV

IMPERIAL ANTIQUITY

HISTORICAL FIGURES

Additional books and e-books in this series can be found
on Nova's website under the Series tab.

BEACON LIGHTS OF HISTORY

VOLUME IV

IMPERIAL ANTIQUITY

JOHN LORD

Copyright © 2019 by Nova Science Publishers, Inc.

NOTICE TO THE READER

Library of Congress Cataloging-in-Publication Data

ISBN: 978-1-53615-185-5

Published by Nova Science Publishers, Inc. † New York

CONTENTS

List of Illustrations   ix

Preface   xi

Chapter 1   Cyrus the Great: Asiatic Supremacy   1

Chapter 2   Julius Caesar: Imperialism   23

Chapter 3   Marcus Aurelius: The Glory of Rome   47

Chapter 4   Constantine the Great: Christianity Enthroned   65

Chapter 5   Paula: Woman as Friend   85

Chapter 6   Chrysostom: Sacred Eloquence   107

Chapter 7   Saint Ambrose: Episcopal Authority   129

Chapter 8   Saint Augustine: Christian Theology   151

Chapter 9   Theodosius the Great: Latter Days of Rome   173

Chapter 10   Leo the Great: Foundation of the Papacy   195

Index   219

Figure 1. The Conversion of Paula by St. Jerome. *After the painting by L. Alma-Tadema.*

LIST OF ILLUSTRATIONS

Figure 1. The Conversion of Paula by St. Jerome.
After the painting by L. Alma-Tadema. **vii**

Figure 2. Archery Practice of a Persian King.
After the painting by F.A. Bridgman. **7**

Figure 3. Tomyris Plunges the Head of the Dead Cyrus
into a Vessel of Blood.
After the painting by Henri Motte. **19**

Figure 4. Julius Caesar.
From the bust in the National Museum, Rome. **26**

Figure 5. Surrender of Vercingetorix, the Last Chief of Gaul.
After the painting by Henri Motte. **34**

Figure 6. Marcus Aurelius.
From a photograph of the statue at the Capitol, Rome. **49**

Figure 7. Persecution of Christians in the Roman Arena.
After the painting by G. Mantegazza. **66**

Figure 8. St. Jerome in His Cell.
After the painting by J.L. Gérôme. **91**

Figure 9. St. Chrysostom Condemns the Vices
of the Empress Eudoxia.
After the painting by Jean Paul Laurens. **124**

Figure 10. St. Ambrose Refuses the Emperor Theodosius
          Admittance to His Church.
          After the painting by Gebhart Fügel.   **145**
Figure 11. St. Augustine and His Mother.
          After the painting by Ary Scheffer.   **157**
Figure 12. Invasion of the Goths into the Roman Empire.
          After the painting by O. Fritsche.   **179**
Figure 13. Invasion of the Huns into Italy.
          After the painting by V. Checa.   **203**

PREFACE[*]

Beacon Lights of History is a 14-volume set first published in 1902. This collection of John Lord's lectures spans 6,000 years of European and American history. The first 12 volumes are all Lord's work; the 13th was completed from his notes and the 14th is follow-ups by other authors.

---

[*] This is an edited, reformatted and augmented version of *Beacon Lights of History. Volume IV: Imperial Antiquity* by John Lord, originally published by New York, J Clarke and Co., dated 1883-1902. The views, opinions, and nomenclature expressed in this book are those of the authors and do not reflect the views of Nova Science Publishers, Inc.

Chapter 1

CYRUS THE GREAT: ASIATIC SUPREMACY

559-529 B.C.

One of the most prominent and romantic characters in the history of the Oriental world, before its conquest by Alexander of Macedon, is Cyrus the Great; not as a sage or prophet, not as the founder of new religious systems, not even as a law-giver, but as the founder and organizer of the greatest empire the world has seen, next to that of the Romans. The territory over which Cyrus bore rule extended nearly three thousand miles from east to west, and fifteen hundred miles from north to south, embracing the principal nations known to antiquity, so that he was really a king of kings. He was practically the last of the great Asiatic emperors, absorbing in his dominions those acquired by the Assyrians, the Babylonians, and the Lydians. He was also the first who brought Asia into intimate contact with Europe and its influences, and thus may be regarded as the link between the old Oriental world and the Greek civilization.

It is to be regretted that so little is really known of the Persian hero, both in the matter of events and also of exact dates, since chronologists differ, and can only approximate to the truth in their calculations. In this lecture, which is in some respects an introduction to those that will follow on the heroes and sages of Greek, Roman, and Christian antiquity, it is of more importance to present Oriental countries and institutions than any particular character, interesting as he may be, – especially since as to biography one is obliged to sift historical facts from a great mass of fables and speculations.

Neither Herodotus, Xenophon, nor Ctesias satisfy us as to the real life and character of Cyrus. This renowned name represents, however, the Persian power, the last of the great monarchies that ruled the Oriental world until its conquest by the Greeks. Persia came suddenly into prominence in the middle of the seventh century before Christ. Prior to this time it was comparatively unknown and unimportant, and was one of the dependent provinces of Media, whose religion, language, and customs were not very dissimilar to its own.

Persia was a small, rocky, hilly, arid country about three hundred miles long by two hundred and fifty wide, situated south of Media, having the Persian Gulf as its southern boundary, the Zagros Mountains on the west separating it from Babylonia, and a great and almost impassable desert on the east, so that it was easily defended. Its population was composed of hardy, warlike, and religious people, condemned to poverty and incessant toil by the difficulty of getting a living on sterile and unproductive hills, except in a few favored localities. The climate was warm in summer and cold in winter, but on the whole more temperate than might be supposed from a region situated so near the tropics, – between the twenty-fifth and thirtieth degrees of latitude. It was an elevated country, more than three thousand feet above the sea, and was favorable to the cultivation of the fruits and flowers that have ever been most prized, those cereals which constitute the ordinary food of man growing in abundance if sufficient labor were spent on their cultivation, reminding us of Switzerland and New England. But vigilance and incessant toil were necessary, such as are only found among a hardy and courageous peasantry, turning easily from agricultural labors to the fatigues and dangers of war. The real wealth of the country was in the flocks and herds that browsed in the valleys and plains. Game of all kinds was abundant, so that the people were unusually fond of the pleasures of the chase; and as they were temperate, inured to exposure, frugal, and adventurous, they made excellent soldiers. Nor did they ever as a nation lose their warlike qualities, – it being only the rich and powerful among them who learned the vices of the nations they subdued, and became addicted to luxury, indolence, and self-indulgence. Before the conquest of Media the whole nation was distinguished for temperance, frugality, and bravery. According to Herodotus, the Persians were especially instructed in three things, – "to ride, to draw the bow, and to speak the truth." Their moral virtues were as conspicuous as their warlike qualities. They were so poor that their ordinary dress was of leather. They could boast of no large city, like the Median Ecbatana, or like Babylon, – Pasargadae, their ancient capital, being comparatively small and deficient in architectural monuments. The people lived chiefly in villages and hamlets, and were governed, like the Israelites under the Judges, by independent chieftains, none of whom attained the rank and power of kings until about one hundred years before the birth of Cyrus. These pastoral and hunting people, frugal from necessity, brave from exposure, industrious from the difficulty of subsisting in a dry and barren country, for the most sort were just such a race as furnished a noble material for the foundation of a great empire.

Whence came this honest, truthful, thrifty race? It is generally admitted that it was a branch of the great Aryan family, whose original settlements are supposed to have been on the high table-lands of Central Asia east of the Caspian Sea, probably in Bactria. They emigrated from that dreary and inhospitable country after Zoroaster had proclaimed his doctrines, after the sacred hymns called the Gathas were sung, perhaps even after the Zend-Avesta or sacred writings of the Zoroastrian priests had been begun, – conquering or driving away Turanian tribes, and migrating to the southwest in search of more fruitful fields and fertile valleys, they found a region which has ever since borne a name – Iran – that evidently commemorated the proud title of the Aryan race. And this great movement took place about the time that another branch of their race also migrated southeastwardly to the valleys of the Indus. The Persians and the Hindus therefore had common ancestors, – the same indeed, as those of the Greeks, Romans, Sclavonians, Celts, and Teutons, who migrated to the northwest and settled in Europe. The Aryans in all their branches were the noblest of the primitive races, and have in their later developments produced the highest civilization ever attained. They all had similar elements of character, especially love of personal independence, respect for woman, and a religious tendency of mind. We see a considerable similarity of habits and customs between the Teutonic races of Germany and Scandinavia and the early inhabitants of Persia, as well as great affinity in language. All branches of the Aryan family have been warlike and adventurous, if we may except the Hindus, who were subjected to different influences, – especially of climate, which enervated their bodies if it did not weaken their minds.

When the migration of the Iranians took place it is difficult to determine, but probably between fifteen hundred and two thousand years before our era, although it may have been even five hundred years earlier than that. All theories as to their movements before their authentic history begins are based on conjecture and speculation, which it is not profitable to pursue, since we can settle nothing in the present state of our knowledge.

It is very singular that the Iranians should have had, after their migrations and settlements, religious ideas and systems so different from those of the Hindus, considering that they had common ancestors. The Iranians, including the Medes as well as Persians, accepted Zoroaster as their prophet and teacher, and the Zend-Avesta as their sacred books, and worshipped one Supreme Deity, whom they called Ahura-Mazda (Ormazd), – the Lord Omniscient, – and thus were monotheists; while the Hindus were practically poly-theists, governed by a sacerdotal caste, who imposed gloomy austerities and sacrifices, although it would seem that the older Vedistic hymns of the Hindus were theistic in spirit. The Magi – the priests of the Iranians – differed widely in their religious views from the Brahmans, inculcating a higher morality and a loftier theological creed, worshipping the Supreme Being without temples or shrines or images, although their religion ultimately degenerated into a worship of the powers of Nature, as the recognition of Mithra the sun-god and the mysterious fire-altars would seem to indicate. But even in spite of the corruptions introduced by the Magi when they became a powerful sacerdotal body, their doctrine remained purer and more elevated than the religions of the surrounding nations.

While the Iranians worshipped a supreme deity of goodness, they also recognized a supreme deity of evil, both ruling the world – in perpetual conflict – by unnumbered angels, good and evil; but the final triumph of the good was a conspicuous article of their faith. In close logical connection with this recognition of a supreme power in the universe was the belief of a future state and of future rewards and punishments, without which belief there can be, in my opinion, no high morality, as men are constituted.

In process of time the priests of the Zoroastrian faith became unduly powerful, and enslaved the people by many superstitions, such as the multiplication of rites and ceremonies and the interpretation of dreams and omens. They united spiritual with temporal authority, as a powerful priesthood is apt to do, – a fact which the Christian priesthood of the Middle Ages made evident in the Occidental world.

In the time of Cyrus the Magi had become a sort of sacerdotal caste. They were the trusted ministers of kings, and exercised a controlling influence over the people. They assumed a stately air, wore white and flowing robes, and were adept in the arts of sorcery and magic. They were even consulted by kings and chieftains, as if they possessed prophetic power. They were a picturesque body of men, with their mystic wands, their impressive robes, their tall caps, appealing by their long incantations and frequent ceremonies and prayers to the eye and to the ear. "Pure Zoroastrianism was too spiritual to coalesce readily with Oriental luxury and magnificence when the Persians were rulers of a vast empire, but Magism furnished a hierarchy to support the throne and add splendor and dignity to the court, while it blended easily with previous creeds."

In material civilization the Medes and Persians were inferior to the Babylonians and Egyptians, and immeasurably behind the Greeks and Romans. Their architecture was not so imposing as that of the Egyptians and Babylonians; it had no striking originality, and it was only in the palaces of great monarchs that anything approached magnificence. Still, there were famous palaces at Ecbatana, Susa, and Persepolis, raised on lofty platforms, reached by grand staircases, and ornamented with elaborate pillars. The most splendid of these were erected after the time of Cyrus, by Darius and Xerxes, decorated with carpets, hangings, and golden ornaments. The halls of their palaces were of great size and imposing effect. Next to palaces, the most remarkable buildings were the tombs of kings; but we have no remains of marble statues or metal castings or ivory carvings, not even of potteries, which at that time in other countries were common and beautiful. The gems and signet rings which the Persians engraved possessed much merit, and on them were wrought with great skill the figures of men and animals; but the nearest approach to sculpture were the figures of colossal bulls set to guard the portals of palaces, and these were probably borrowed from the Assyrians.

Nor were the Persians celebrated for their textile fabrics and dyes. "So long as the carpets of Babylon, the shawls of India, the fine linen of Egypt, and the coverlets of Damascus poured continually into Persia in the way of tribute and gifts, there was no stimulus to manufacture." The same may be said of the ornamental metal-work of the Greeks, and the glass manufacture of the Phoenicians. The Persians were soldiers, and gloried in being so, to the disdain of much that civilization has ever valued.

It may as well be here said that the Iranians, both Medes and Persians, were acquainted with the art of writing. Harpagus sent a letter to Cyrus concealed in the belly of a hare, and Darius signed a decree which his nobles presented to him in writing. In common with the Babylonians they used the same alphabetic system, though their languages were unlike, – namely, the cuneiform or arrow-head or wedge-shaped characters, as seen in the celebrated inscriptions of Darius on the side of a high rock thirty feet from the ground. We cannot determine whether the Medes and Persians brought their alphabet from their original settlements in Central Asia, or derived it from the Turanian and Semitic nations with which they came in contact. In spite of their knowledge of writing, however, they produced no literature of any account, and of science they were completely ignorant. They made few improvements even in military weapons, the chief of which, as among all the nations of antiquity, were the bow, the spear, and the sword. They were skillful horsemen, and made use of chariots of war. Their great occupation, aside from agriculture, was hunting, in which they were trained by exposure for war. They were born to conquer and rule, like the Romans, and cared for little except the warlike virtues.

Such were the Persians and the rugged country in which they lived, with their courage and fortitude, their love of freedom, their patriotism, their abhorrence of lies, their self-respect allied with pride, their temperance and frugality, forming a noble material for empire and dominion when the time came for the old monarchies to fall into their hands, – the last and greatest of all the races that had ruled the Oriental world, and kindred in their remote ancestry with those European conquerors who laid the foundation of modern civilization.

Figure 2. Archery Practice of a Persian King. *After the painting by F.A. Bridgman.*

Of these Persians Cyrus was the type-man, combining in himself all that was admirable in his countrymen, and making so strong an impression on the Greeks that he is presented by their historians as an ideal prince, invested with all those virtues which the mediaeval romance-writers have ascribed to the knights of chivalry.

The Persians were ruled by independent chieftains, or petty kings, who acknowledged fealty to Media; so that Persia was really a province of Media, as Burgundy was of France in the Middle Ages, and as Babylonia at one period was of Assyria. The most prominent of these chieftains or princes was Achaemenes, who is regarded as the founder of the Persian monarchy. To this royal family of the Achaemenidae Cyrus belonged. His father Cambyses, called by some a satrap and by others a king, married, according to Herodotus, a daughter of Astyages, the last of the Median monarchs.

The youth and education of Cyrus are invested with poetic interest by both Herodotus and Xenophon, but their narratives have no historical authority in the eyes of critics, any more than Livy's painting of Romulus and Remus: they belong to the realm of romance rather than authentic history. Nevertheless the legend of Cyrus is beautiful, and has been repeated by all succeeding historians.

According to this legend, Astyages – a luxurious and superstitious monarch, without the warlike virtues of his father, who had really built up the Median empire – had a dream that troubled him, which being interpreted by the Magi, priests of the national religion, was to the effect that his daughter Mandanê (for he had no legitimate son) would be married to a prince whose heir should seize the supreme power of Media.

To prevent this, he married her to a prince beneath her rank, for whom he felt no fear, – Cambyses, the chief governor or king of Persia, who ruled a territory to the South, about one fifth the size of Media, and which practically was a dependent province. Another dream which alarmed Astyages still further, in spite of his precaution, induced him to send for his daughter, so that having her in his power he might easily destroy her offspring. As soon as Cyrus was born therefore in the royal palace at Ecbatana, the king intrusted the infant prince to one of the principal officers of his court, named Harpagus, with peremptory orders to destroy him. Harpagus, although he professed unconditional obedience to his monarch, had scruples about taking the life of one so near the throne, the grandson of the king and presumptive heir of the monarchy. So he, in turn, intrusted the royal infant to the care of a herdsman, in whom he had implicit confidence, with orders to kill him. The herdsman had a tender-hearted and conscientious wife who had just given birth to a dead child, and she persuaded her husband – for even in Media women virtually ruled, as they do everywhere, if they have tact – to substitute the dead child for the living one, deck it out in the royal costume, and expose it to wild beasts. This was done, and Cyrus remained the supposed child of the shepherd. The secret was well kept for ten years, and both Astyages and Harpagus supposed that Cyrus was slain.

Cyrus meanwhile grew up among the mountains, a hardy and beautiful boy, exposed to heat and cold, hunger and fatigue, and thus was early inured to danger and hardship. Added to personal beauty was remarkable courage, frankness, and brightness, so that he took the lead of other boys in their amusements. One day they played king, and Cyrus was chosen to represent royalty, which he acted so literally as to beat the son of a Median nobleman for disobedience. The indignant and angry father complained at once to the king, and Astyages sent for the herdsman and his supposed son to attend him in his palace. When the two mountaineers were ushered into the royal presence, Astyages was so struck with the beauty, wit, and boldness of the boy that he made earnest inquiries of the herdsman, who was forced to tell the truth, and confessed that the youth was not his son, but had been put into his hands by Harpagus with orders to destroy him. The royal origin of Cyrus was now apparent, and the king sent for Harpagus, who corroborated the statement of the herdsman. Astyages dissembled his wrath, as Oriental monarchs can, who are trained to dissimulation, and the only punishment he inflicted on Harpagus was to set before him at a banquet a dish made of the arms and legs of a dead infant. This the courtier in turn professed to relish, but henceforth became the secret and implacable enemy of the king.

Herodotus tells us that Astyages took the boy, unmistakably his grandson and heir, to his palace to be educated according to his rank. Cyrus was now brought up with every honor and the greatest care, taught to hunt and ride and shoot with the bow like the highest nobles. He soon distinguished himself for his feats in horsemanship and skill in hunting wild animals, winning universal admiration, and disarming envy by his tact, amiability, and generosity, which were as marked as his intellectual brilliancy, – being altogether a model of reproachless chivalry.

For some reason, however, the fears and jealousy of Astyages were renewed, and Cyrus was sent to his father in Persia with costly gifts. Possibly he was recalled by Cambyses himself, for a father by all the Eastern codes had a right to the person of his son.

No sooner was Cyrus established in Persia, – a country which it would seem he had never before seen, – than he was sought by the discontented Persians to head a revolt against their masters, and he availed himself of the disaffection of Harpagus, the most influential of the Median noblemen, for the dethronement of his grandfather. Persia arose in rebellion against Media. A war ensued, and in a battle between the conflicting forces Astyages was defeated and taken prisoner, but was kindly treated by his magnanimous conqueror. This battle ended the Median ascendency, and Cyrus became the monarch of both Media and Persia.

Since the Medes belonged to the same Aryan family as the Persians, and had the same language, religion, and institutions, with slight differences, and lived among the mountains exposed to an uncongenial climate with extremes of heat and cold, and were doomed to hard and incessant labors for a subsistence, and were therefore – that is, the ordinary people – frugal, industrious, and temperate, it will be seen that what we have said of Persia equally applies to Media, except the possession by the latter of political power as wielded by the sovereign of a larger State.

Before a central power was established in Media, the country had been – as in all nations in their formative state – ruled by chieftains, who acknowledged as their supreme lord the King of Assyria, who reigned in Nineveh. Among these chieftains was a remarkable man called Deioces, so upright and able that he was elected king. Deioces reigned fifty-three years wisely and well, bequeathing the kingdom he had founded to his son Phraortes, under whom Media became independent of Assyria. His son and successor Cyaxares, who died 593 B.C., was a successful warrior and conqueror, and was the founder of Median greatness. With the assistance of Nabopolassar, a Babylonian general who had also revolted against the Assyrian monarch, Cyaxares succeeded, after repeated failures, in taking Nineveh and destroying the great Assyrian Empire which had ruled the Eastern world for several centuries. The northern and eastern provinces were annexed to Media, while the Babylonian valley of the Euphrates in the south fell to the share of Nabopolassar, who established the Babylonian ascendency. This in its turn was greatly augmented by his son Nebuchadnezzar, one of the most famous conquerors of antiquity, whose empire became more extensive even than the Assyrian. He reigned in Babylon with unparalleled splendor, and made his capital the wonder and the admiration of the world, enriching and ornamenting it with palaces, temples, and hanging gardens, and strengthening its defences to such a marvellous degree that it was deemed impregnable.

Cyaxares the Median meanwhile raised up in Ecbatana a rival power to that of Babylon, although he devoted himself to warlike expeditions more than to the adornment of his capital. He penetrated with his invincible troops as far to the west as Lydia in Asia Minor, then ruled by the father of Croesus, and thus became known to the Ionian cities which the Greeks had colonized. After a brilliant reign, Cyaxares transmitted his empire to an unworthy son, – Astyages, the grandfather of Cyrus, whose loss of the throne has been already related. With Astyages perished the Median Empire, which had lasted only about one hundred years, and Media was incorporated with Persia. Henceforth the Medes and Persians are spoken of as virtually one nation, similar in religion and customs, and furnishing equally the best cavalry in the world. Under Cyrus they became the ascendent power in Asia, and maintained their ascendency until their conquest by Alexander. The union between Media and Persia was probably as complete as that between Burgundy and France, or that of Scotland with England. Indeed, Media now became the residence of the Persian kings, whose palaces at Ecbatana, Susa, and Persepolis nearly rivalled those of Babylon. Even modern Persia comprises the ancient Media.

The reign of Cyrus properly begins with the conquest of Media, or rather its union with Persia, B.C. 549. We know, however, but little of the career of Cyrus after he became monarch of both Persia and Media, until he was forty years of age. He was probably engaged in the conquest of various barbaric hordes before his memorable Lydian campaign. But we are in ignorance of his most active years, when he was exposed to the greatest dangers and hardships, and when he became perfected in the military art, as in the case of Caesar amid the marshes and forests of Gaul and Belgium. The fame of Caesar rests as much on his conquests of the Celtic barbarians of Europe as on his conflict with Pompey; but whether Cyrus obtained military fame or not in his wars against the Turanians, he doubtless proved himself a benefactor to humanity more in arresting the tide of Scythian invasion than by those conquests which have given him immortality.

When Cyrus had cemented his empire by the conquest of the Turanian nations, especially those that dwelt between the Caspian and Black seas, his attention was drawn to Lydia, the most powerful kingdom of western Asia, whose monarch, Croesus, reigned at Sardis in Oriental magnificence. Lydia was not much known to distant States until the reign of Gyges, about 716

B.C., who made war on the Dorian and Ionian Greek colonies on the coast of Asia Minor, the chief of which were Miletus, Smyrna, Colophon, and Ephesus. His successor Ardys continued this warfare, but was obliged to desist because of an invasion of the Cimmerians, – barbarians from beyond the Caucasus, driven away from their homes by the Scythians. His grandson Alyattes, greatest of the Lydian monarchs, succeeded in expelling the Cimmerians from Lydia. After subduing some of the maritime cities of Asia Minor, this monarch faced the Medes, who had advanced their empire to the river Halys, the eastern boundary of Lydia, which flows northwardly into the Euxine. For five years Alyattes fought the Medes under Cyaxares with varying success, and the war ended by the marriage of the daughter of the Lydian king with Astyages. After this, Alyattes reigned forty-three years, and was buried in a tomb whose magnificence was little short of the grandest of the Egyptian monuments.

Croesus, his son, entered upon a career which reminds us of Solomon, the inheritor of the conquests of David. Like the Jewish monarch, Croesus was rich, luxurious, and intellectual. His wealth, obtained chiefly from the mines of his kingdom, was a marvel to the Greeks. His capital Sardis became the largest in western Asia, and one of the most luxurious cities known to antiquity, whither resorted travelers from all parts of the world, attracted by the magnificence of the court, among whom was Solon himself, the great Athenian law-giver. Croesus continued the warfare on the Greek cities of Asia, and forced them to become his tributaries. He brought under his sway most of the nations to the west of the Halys, and though never so great a warrior as his father, he became very powerful. He was as generous in his gifts as he was magnificent in his tastes. His offerings to the oracle at Delphi were unprecedented in their value, when he sought advice as to the wisdom of engaging in war with Cyrus. Of the three great Asian empires, Croesus now saw his father's ally, Babylon, under a weak and dissolute ruler; Media, absorbed into Persia under the power of a valiant and successful conqueror; and his own empire, Lydia, threatened with attack by the growing ambition of Persia. Herodotus says he "was led to consider whether it were possible to check the growing power of that people."

It was the misfortune of Croesus to overrate his strength, – an error often seen in the career of fortunate men, especially those who enter upon a great inheritance. It does not appear that Croesus desired war with Persia, but he did not dread it, and felt confident that he could overcome a man whose chief conquests had been made over barbarians. Perhaps he felt the necessity of contending with Cyrus before that warrior's victories and prestige should become overwhelming, for the Persian monarch obviously aimed at absorbing all Asia in his empire; at any rate, when informed by the oracle at Delphi that if he fought with the Persians he would destroy a mighty empire, Croesus interpreted the response in his own favor.

Croesus made great preparations for the approaching contest, which was to settle the destiny of Asia Minor. The Greeks were on his side, for they feared the Persians more than they did the Lydians. With the aid of Sparta, the most warlike of the Grecian States, he advanced to meet the Persian conqueror, not however without the expostulation of some of his wisest counsellors. One of them, according to Herodotus, ventured to address him with these plain words: "Thou art about, O King, to make war against men who wear leather trousers and other garments of leather; who feed not on what they like, but on what they can get from a soil which is sterile and unfriendly; who do not indulge in wine, but drink water; who possess no figs, nor anything which is good to eat. If, then, thou conquerest them, what canst thou get from them, seeing that they have nothing at all? But if they conquer thee, consider how much that is precious thou wilt lose; if they once get a taste of our pleasant things, they will keep such a hold of them that we never shall be able to make them lose their grasp." We cannot consider Croesus as utterly infatuated in not taking this advice, since war had become inevitable, It was "either anvil or hammer," as between France and Prussia in 1870-72, – as between all great powers that accept the fortune of war, ever uncertain in its results. The only question seems to have been who should first take the offensive in a war that had been long preparing, and in which defeat would be followed by the utter ruin of the defeated party.

The Lydians began the attack by crossing the Halys and entering the enemy's territory. The first battle took place at Pteria in Cappadocia, near Sinope on the Euxine, but was indecisive. Both parties fought bravely, and the slaughter on both sides was dreadful, the Lydians being the most numerous, and the Persians the most highly disciplined. After the battle of Pteria, Croesus withdrew his army to his own territories and retired upon his capital, with a view of augmenting his forces; while Cyrus, with the instinct of a conqueror, ventured to cross the Halys in pursuit, and to march rapidly on Sardis before the enemy could collect another army. Prompt decision and celerity of movement characterize all successful warriors, and here it was that Cyrus showed his military genius. Before Croesus was fully prepared for another fight, Cyrus was at the gates of Sardis. But the Lydian king rallied what forces he could, and led them out to battle. The Lydians were superior in cavalry; seeing which, Cyrus, with that fertility of resource which marked his whole career, collected together the camels which transported his baggage and provisions, and placed them in the front of his array, since the horse, according to Herodotus, has a natural dread of the camel and cannot abide his sight or his smell. The result was as Cyrus calculated; the cavalry of the Lydians turned round and galloped away. The Lydians fought bravely, but were driven within the walls of their capital. Cyrus vigorously prosecuted the siege, which lasted only fourteen days, since an attack was made on the side of the city which was undefended, and which was supposed to be impregnable and unassailable. The proud city fell by assault, and was given up to plunder. Croesus himself was taken alive, after a reign of fourteen years, and the mighty Lydia became a Persian province.

There is something unusually touching in the fate of Croesus after so great prosperity. Saved by Cyrus from an ignominious and painful death, such as the barbarous customs of war then made common, the unhappy Lydian monarch became, it is said, the friend and admirer of the Conqueror, and was present in his future expeditions, and even proved a wise and faithful counsellor. If some proud monarchs by the fortune of war have fallen suddenly from as lofty an eminence as that of Croesus, it is certain that few have yielded with nobler submission than he to the decrees of fate.

The fall of Sardis, – B.C. 546, according to Grote, – was followed by the submission of all the States that were dependent on Lydia. Even the Grecian colonies in Asia Minor were annexed to the Persian Empire.

The conquest of the Ionian cities, first by Croesus and then by Cyrus, was attended with important political consequences. Before the time of Croesus the Greek cities of Asia were independent. Had they combined together for offence and defence, with the assistance of Sparta and Athens, they might have resisted the attacks of both Lydians and Persians. But the autonomy of cities and states, favorable as it was to the development of art, literature, and commerce, as well as of individual genius in all departments of knowledge and enterprise, was not calculated to make a people politically powerful. Only a strong central power enables a country to resist hostile aggressions on a great scale. Thus Greece herself ultimately fell into the hands of Philip, and afterward into those of the Romans.

The conquest of the Ionian cities also introduced into Asia Minor and perhaps into Europe Oriental customs, luxuries, and wealth hitherto unknown. Certainly when Persia became an irresistible power and ruled the conquered countries by satraps and royal governors, it assimilated the Greeks with Asiatics, and modified the forms of social life; it brought Asia and Europe together, and produced a rivalry which finally ended in the battle of Marathon and the subsequent Asiatic victories of Alexander. While the conquests of the Persians introduced Oriental ideas and customs into Greece, the wars of Alexander extended the Grecian sway in Asia. The civilized world opened toward the East; but with the extension of Greek ideas and art, there was a decline of primitive virtues in Greece herself. Luxury undermined power.

The annexation of Asia Minor to the empire of Cyrus was followed by a protracted war with the barbarians on his eastern boundaries. The imperfect subjugation of barbaric nations living in Central Asia occupied Cyrus, it is thought, about twelve years. He pushed his conquests to the Iaxartes on the north and Afghanistan on the east, reducing that vast country which lies between the Caspian Sea and the deserts of Tartary.

Cyrus was advancing in years before he undertook the conquest of Babylon, the most important of all his undertakings, and for which his other conquests were preparatory. At the age of sixty, Cyrus, 538 B.C., advanced against Narbonadius, the proud king of Babylon, – the only remaining power in Asia that was still formidable. The Babylonian Empire, which had arisen on the ruins of the Assyrian, had lasted only about one hundred years. Yet what wonders and triumphs had been seen at Babylon during that single century! What progress had been made in arts and sciences! What grand palaces and temples had been erected! What a multitude of captives had added to the pomp and wealth of the proudest city of antiquity! Babylon the great, – -"the glory of kingdoms," "the praise of the whole earth," the centre of all that was civilized and all that was corrupting in the Oriental world, with its soothsayers, its magicians, its necromancers, its priests, its nobles, – was now to fall, for its abominations cried aloud to heaven for punishment.

This great city was built on both sides of the Euphrates, was fifteen miles square, with gardens and fields capable of supporting a large population, and was stocked with provisions to maintain a siege of indefinite length against any enemy. The accounts of its walls and fortifications exceed belief, estimated by Herodotus to be three hundred and fifty feet in height, with a wide moat surrounding them, which could not be bridged or crossed by an invading army. The soldiers of Narbonadius looked with derision on the veteran forces of Cyrus, although they were inured to the hardships and privations of incessant war. To all appearance the city was impregnable, and could be taken only by unusual methods. But the genius of the Persian conqueror, according to traditional accounts, surmounted all difficulties. Who else would have thought of diverting the Euphrates from its bed into the canals and gigantic reservoirs which Nebuchadnezzar had built for purposes of irrigation? Yet this seems to have been done. Taking advantage of a festival, when the whole population were given over to bacchanalian orgies, and therefore off their guard, Cyrus advanced, under the cover of a dark night, by the bed of the river, now dry, and easily surprised the drunken city, slaying the king, with a thousand of his lords, as he was banqueting in his palace. The slightest accident or miscarriage would have defeated so bold an operation. The success of Cyrus had all the mystery and solemnity of a Providential event. Though no miracle was wrought, the fall of Babylon – so strong, so proud, so defiant – was as wonderful as the passage of the Israelites across the Red Sea, or the crumbling walls of Jericho before the blasts of the trumpets of Joshua.

However, this account is to be taken with some reserve, since by the discoveries of historical "cylinders," – the clay books whereon the Chaldaean priests and scribes recorded the main facts of the reigns of their monarchs, – and especially one called the "Proclamation Cylinder," prepared for Cyrus after the fall of Babylon, it would seem that dissension and treachery within had much to do with facilitating the entrance of the invader. Narbonadius, the second successor of Nebuchadnezzar, had quarreled with the priesthood of Babylon, and neglected the worship of Bel-Marduk and Nebo, the special patron gods of that city. The captive Jews also, who had been now nearly fifty years in the land, had grown more zealous for their own God and religion, more influential and wealthy, and even had become in some sort a power in the State. The invasion of Cyrus – a monotheist like themselves – must have seemed to them a special providence from Jehovah; indeed, we know that it did, from the records in II. Chronicles xxxvi. 22, 23: "The Lord stirred up the spirit of Koresh, King of Persia, that he made a proclamation throughout all his kingdom, and put it also in writing." The same words occur in the beginning of the Book of Ezra, both referring to the sending home of the Jews after the fall of Babylon; the forty-sixth chapter of Isaiah also: "The Lord saith of Koresh, He is my shepherd, and shall perform all my pleasure."

Babylon was not at that time levelled with the ground, but became one of the capitals of the Persian Empire, where the Persian monarch resided for more than half the year. Although the Babylonian Empire began with Nabopolassar, B.C. 625, on the destruction of Nineveh, yet Babylon was a very ancient city and the capital of the ancient Chaldaean monarchy, which lasted under various dynasties from about 2400 B.C. to 1300 B.C., when it was taken by the Assyrians under Tig Vathi-Nin. The great Assyrian Empire, which thus absorbed ancient Babylonia, lasted between six and seven hundred years, according to Herodotus, although recent discoveries and inscriptions make its continuance much longer, and was the dominant power of Asia during the most interesting period of Jewish history, until taken by Cyaxares the Median. The limits of the empire varied at different times, for the conquered States which composed it were held together by a precarious tenure. But even in its greatest strength it was inferior in size and power to the Empire of Cyrus. To check rebellion, – a source of constant trouble and weakness, – the warlike monarchs were obliged to reconquer, imposing not only tribute and fealty, but overrunning the rebellious countries with fire and sword, and carrying away captive to distant cities a large part of the population as slaves. Thus at one time two hundred thousand Jews were transported to Assyria, and the "Ten Tribes" were scattered over the Eastern world, never more to return to Palestine.

On the rebellion of Nabopolassar, in 625 B.C., Babylon recovered not only its ancient independence, but more than its ancient prestige; yet the empire of which it was the capital lasted only about the same length of time as Media and Lydia, – the most powerful monarchies existing when Cyrus was born. Babylon, however, during its brief dominion, after having been subject to Assyria for seven hundred years, reappeared in unparalleled splendor, and was probably the most magnificent capital the ancient world ever saw until Rome arose. Even after its occupancy by the Persian monarchs for two hundred years, it called out the admiration of Herodotus and Alexander alike. Its arts, its sciences, its manufactures, to say nothing of its palaces and temples, were the admiration of travelers. When the proud conqueror of Palestine beheld the magnificence he had created, little did he dream that "this great Babylon which he had built" would become such a desolation that its very site would be uncertain, – a habitation for dragons, a dreary waste for owls and goats and wild beasts to occupy.

We should naturally suppose that Cyrus, with the kings of Asia prostrate before his satraps, would have been contented to enjoy the fruits of his labors; but there is no limit to man's ambition. Like Alexander, he sought for new worlds to conquer, and perished, as some historians maintain, in an unsuccessful war with some unknown barbarians on the northeastern boundaries of his empire, – even as Caesar meditated a war with the Parthians, where he might have perished, as Crassus did. Unbounded as is human ambition, there is a limit to human aggrandizement. Great conquerors are raised up by Providence to accomplish certain results for civilization, and when these are attained, when their mission is ended, they often pass away ingloriously, – assassinated or defeated or destroyed by self-indulgence, as the case may be. It seems to have been the mission of Cyrus to destroy the ascendency of the Semitic and Hamitic despotisms in western Asia, that a new empire might be erected by nobler races, who should establish a reign of law. For the first time in Asia there was, on the accession of Cyrus to unlimited power, a recognition of justice, and the adoration of one supreme deity ruling in goodness and truth.

Figure 3. Tomyris Plunges the Head of the Dead Cyrus into a Vessel of Blood. *After the painting by Henri Motte.*

This may be the reason why Cyrus treated the captive Jews with so great generosity, since he recognized in their Jehovah the Ahura-Mazda, – the Supreme God that Zoroaster taught. No political reason will account for sending back to Palestine thousands of captives with imperial presents, to erect once more their sacred Temple and rebuild their sacred city. He and all the Persian monarchs were zealous adherents of the religion of Zoroaster, the central doctrine of which was the unity of God and Divine Providence in the world, which doctrine neither Egyptian nor Babylonian nor Lydian monarchs recognized. What a boon to humanity was the restoration of the Jews to their capital and country! We read of no oppression of the Jews by the Persian monarchs. Mordecai the Jew became the prime minister of such an effeminate monarch as Xerxes, while Daniel before him had been the honored minister of Darius.

Of all the Persian monarchs Cyrus was the best beloved. Xenophon made him the hero of his philosophical romance. He is represented as the incarnation of "sweetness and light." When a mere boy he delights all with whom he is brought into contact, by his wit and valor. The king of Media accepts his reproofs and admires his wisdom; the nobles of Media are won by his urbanity and magnanimity. All historians praise his simple habits and unbounded generosity. In an age when polygamy was the vice of kings, he was contented with one wife, whom he loved and honored. He rejected great presents, and thought it was better to give than to receive. He treated women with delicacy and captives with magnanimity. He conducted war with unknown mildness, and converted the conquered into friends. He exalted the dignity of labor, and scorned all baseness and lies. His piety and manly virtues may have been exaggerated by his admirers, but what we do know of him fills us with admiration. Brilliant in intellect, lofty in character, he was an ideal man, fitted to be the guide of a noble nation whom he led to glory and honor. Other warriors of world-wide fame have had, like him, great excellencies, marred by glaring defects; but no vices or crimes are ascribed to Cyrus, such as stained the characters of David and Constantine. The worst we can say of him is that he was ambitious, and delighted in conquest; but he was a conqueror raised up to elevate a religious race to a higher plane, and to find a field for the development of their energies, whatever may be said of their subsequent degeneracy. "The grandeur of his character is well rendered in that brief and unassuming inscription of his, more eloquent in its lofty simplicity than anything recorded by Assyrian and Babylonian kings: 'I am Kurush [Cyrus] the king, the Achaemenian.'" Whether he fell in battle, or died a natural death in one of his palaces, he was buried in the ancient but modest capital of the ancient Persians, Pasargadae; and his tomb was intact in the time of Alexander, who visited it, – a sort of marble chapel raised on a marble platform thirty-six feet high, in which was deposited a gilt sarcophagus, together with Babylonian tapestries, Persian weapons, and rare jewels of great value. This was the inscription on his tomb: "O man, I am Kurush, the son of Kambujiya, who founded the greatness of Persia and ruled Asia; grudge me not this monument."

Cyrus was succeeded by his son Cambyses, who though not devoid of fine qualities was jealous and tyrannical. He caused his own brother Smerdis to be put to death. He completed the conquests of his father by adding Egypt to his empire. In a fit of remorse for the murder of his brother he committed suicide, and the empire was usurped by a Magian impostor, called Gaumata, who claimed to be the second son of Cyrus. His reign, however, was short, he being slain by Darius the son of Hystaspes, belonging to another branch of the royal family. Darius was a great general and statesman, who reorganized the empire and raised it to the zenith of its power and glory. It extended from the Greek islands on the west to India on the east. This monarch even penetrated to the Danube with his armies, but made no permanent conquest in Europe. He made Susa his chief capital, and also built Persepolis, the ruins of which attest its ancient magnificence. It seems that he was a devout follower of Zoroaster, and ascribed his successes to the favor of Ahura-Mazda, the Supreme Deity.

It was during the reign of Darius that Persia came in contact with Greece, in consequence of the revolt of the Ionian cities of Asia Minor, which, however, was easily suppressed by the Persian satrap. Then followed two invasions of Greece itself by the Persians under the generals of Darius, and their defeat at Marathon by Miltiades.

Darius was succeeded by Xerxes, the Ahasuerus of the Hebrew Scriptures, whose invasion of Greece with the largest army the world ever

saw properly belongs to Grecian history. It was reserved for the heroes of
Plataea to teach the world the lesson that the strength of armies is not in
multitudes but in discipline, – a lesson confirmed by the conquests of
Alexander and Caesar.

On the fall of the Persian Empire three hundred years after the fall of
Babylon, and the establishment of the Greek rule in Asia under the generals
of Alexander, Persia proper did not cease to be formidable. Under the
Sassanian princes the ambition of the Achaemenians was revived. Sapor
defied Rome herself, and dragged the Emperor Valerian in disgraceful
captivity to Ctesiphon, his capital. Sapor II was the conqueror of the
Emperor Julian, and Chrosroes was an equally formidable adversary. In the
year 617 A.D. Persian warriors advanced to the walls of Constantinople, and
drove the Emperor Heraclius to despair.

Thus Persia never lost wholly its ancient prestige, and still remains, after
the rise and fall of so many dynasties, and such great vicissitudes from Greek
and Arab conquests, a powerful country twice the size of Germany, under
the rule of an independent prince. There seems no likelihood of her ever
again playing so grand a part in the world's history as when, under the great
Cyrus, she prepared the transfer of empire from the Orient to the Occident.
But "what has been, has been, and she has had her hour."

AUTHORITIES

Herodotus and Xenophon are our main authorities, though not to be fully
relied upon. Of modern works Rawlinson's *Ancient Monarchies* and
Rawlinson's *Herodotus* are the most valuable. Ragozin has written
interesting books on Media, Persia, Assyria, and Chaldaea, making special
note of the researches of European travelers in the East. Fergusson, Layard,
Sayce, and George Smith have shed light on all this ancient region. Johnson's
work is learned but indefinite. Benjamin is the latest writer on the history of
Persia; but a satisfactory life of Cyrus has yet to be written.

Chapter 2

JULIUS CAESAR: IMPERIALISM

100-44 B.C.

The most august name in the history of the old Roman world, and perhaps of all antiquity, is that of Julius Caesar; and a new interest has of late been created in this extraordinary man by the brilliant sketch of his life and character by Mr. Froude, who has whitewashed him, as is the fashion with hero-worshippers, like Carlyle in his history of Frederick II. But it is not an easy thing to reverse the verdict of the civilized world for two thousand years, although a man of genius can say many interesting things and offer valuable suggestions.

In his Life of Caesar Mr. Froude seems to vindicate Imperialism, not merely as a great necessity in the corrupt times which succeeded the civil wars of Marius and Sulla, but as a good thing in itself. It seems to me that while there was a general tendency to Imperialism in the Roman world for one or two hundred years before Christ, the whole tendency of modern governments is against it, and has been since the second English Revolution. It still exists in Russia and Turkey, possibly in Germany and Austria; yet constitutional forms of government seem to be gradually taking its place. What a change in England, France, Italy, and Spain during the last hundred years! – what a breaking up of the old absolutism of the Bourbons! Even the imperialism of Napoleon is held in detestation by a large class of the French nation.

It may have been necessary for such a man as Caesar to arise when the Romans had already conquered a great part of the civilized world, and when the various provinces which composed the Empire needed a firm, stable, and uniform government in the hands of a single man, in order to promote peace and law, – the first conditions of human society. But it is one thing to recognize the majesty of divine Providence in furnishing a remedy for the peculiar evils of an age or people, and quite another thing to make this remedy a panacea for all the future conditions of nations. If we believe in the moral government of this world by a divine and supreme Intelligence whom we call God, then it is not difficult to see in Julius Caesar, after nearly two thousand years, an instrument of Providence like Constantine, Charlemagne, Richelieu, and Napoleon himself. It matters nothing whether Caesar was good or bad, whether he was a patriot or a usurper, so far as his ultimate influence is concerned, if he was the instrument of an overruling Power; for God chooses such instruments as he pleases. Even in human governments it is sometimes expedient to employ rogues in order to catch rogues, or to head off some peculiar evil that honest people do not know how to manage. But because a bad man is selected by a higher power to do some peculiar work, it does not follow that this bad man should be praised for doing it, especially if the work is good only so far as it is overruled. Both human consciousness and Christianity declare that it is a crime to shed needless and innocent blood. If ambition prompts a man to destroy his rivals and fill the world with miseries in order to climb to supreme power, then it is an insult to the human understanding to make this ambition synonymous with patriotism. A successful conqueror may be far-sighted and enlightened, whatever his motives for conquest; but because he is enlightened, it does not follow that he fights battles with the supreme view of benefiting his country, like William III and George Washington. He may have taken the sword chiefly to elevate himself; or, after having taken the sword with a view of rendering important services, and having rendered these services, he may have been diverted from his original intentions, and have fought for the gratification of personal ambition, losing sight utterly of the cause in which he embarked.

Now this is the popular view which the world has taken of Caesar. Shakspeare may have been unjust in his verdict; but it is a verdict which has been sustained by most writers and by popular sentiment during the last three hundred years. It was also the verdict of Cicero, of the Roman Senate, and of ancient historians. It is one of my objects to show in this lecture how far this verdict is just. It is another object to point out the services of Caesar to the State, which, however great and honestly to be praised, do not offset crime.

Caius Julius Caesar belonged to one of the proudest and most ancient of the patrician families of Rome, – a branch of the *gens Julia*, which claimed a descent from Jules, the son of Aeneas. His father, Caius Julius, married Aurelia, a noble matron of the Cotta family, and his aunt Julia married the great Marius; so that, though he was a patrician of the purest blood, his family alliances were either plebeian or on the liberal side in politics. He was born one hundred years before Christ, and received a good education, but was not precocious, like Cicero. There was nothing remarkable about his childhood. "He was a tall and handsome man, with dark, piercing eyes, sallow complexion, large nose, full lips, refined and intellectual features, and thick neck." He was particular about his appearance, and showed a studied negligence of dress. His uncle Marius, in the height of his power, marked him out for promotion, and made him a priest of Jupiter when he was fourteen years old. On the death of his father, a man of praetorian rank, and therefore a senator, at the age of seventeen Caesar married Cornelia, the daughter of Cinna, which connected him still more closely with the popular party. He was only a few years younger than Cicero and Pompey. When he was eighteen he attracted the notice of Sulla, then dictator, who wished him to divorce his wife and take such a one as he should propose, – which the young man, at the risk of his life, refused to do. This boldness and independence of course displeased the Dictator, who predicted his future. "In this young Caesar," said he, "there are many Mariuses;" but he did not kill him, owing to the intercession of powerful friends.

Figure 4. Julius Caesar. *From the bust in the National Museum, Rome.*

The career of Caesar may be divided into three periods, during each of which he appeared in a different light: the first, until he began the conquest of Gaul, at the age of forty-three; the second, the time of his military exploits in Gaul, by which he rendered great services and gained popularity and fame; and the third, that of his civil wars, dictatorship, and imperial reign.

In the first period of his life, for about twenty-five years, he made a mark indeed, but rendered no memorable services to the State and won no especial fame. Had he died at the age of forty-three, his name would probably not have descended to our times, except as a leading citizen, a good lawyer, and powerful debater. He saw military service, almost as a matter of course; but he was not particularly distinguished as a general, nor did he select the military profession. He was eloquent, aspiring, and able, as a young patrician; but, like Cicero, it would seem that he sought the civil service, and made choice of the law, by which to rise in wealth and power. He was a politician from the first; and his ambition was to get a seat in the Senate, like all other able and ambitious men. Senators were not hereditary, however nobly born, but gained their seats by election to certain high offices in the gift of the people, called curule offices, which entitled them to senatorial position and dignity. A seat in the Senate was the great object of Roman ambition; because the Senate was the leading power of the State, and controlled the army, the treasury, religious worship, and the provinces. The governors and ambassadors, as well as the dictators, were selected by this body of aristocrats. In fact, to the Senate was intrusted the supreme administration of the Empire, although the source of power was technically and theoretically in the people, or those who had the right of suffrage; and as the people elected those magistrates whose offices entitled them to a seat in the Senate, the Senate was virtually elected by the people. Senators held their places for life, but could be weeded out by the censors. And as the Senate in its best days contained between three and four hundred men, not all the curule magistrates could enter it, unless there were vacancies; but a selection from them was made by the censors. So the Senate, in all periods of the Roman Republic, was composed of experienced men, – of those who had previously held the great offices of State.

To gain a seat in the Senate, therefore, it was necessary to be elected by the people to one of the great magistracies. In the early ages of the Republic the people were incorruptible; but when foreign conquest, slavery, and other influences demoralized them, they became venal and sold their votes. Hence only rich men, ordinarily, were elected to high office; and the rich men, as a rule, belonged to the old families. So the Senate was made up not only of experienced men, but of the aristocracy. There were rich men outside the Senate, – successful plebeians, men who had made fortunes by trade, bankers, monopolists, and others; but these, if ambitious of social position or political influence, became gradually absorbed among the senatorial families. Those who could afford to buy the votes of the people, and those only, became magistrates and senators. Hence the demagogues were rich men and belonged to the highest ranks, like Clodius and Catiline.

It thus happened that, when Julius Caesar came upon the stage, the aristocracy controlled the elections. The people were indeed sovereign; but they abdicated their power to those who would pay the most for it. The constitution was popular in name; in reality it was aristocratic, since only rich men (generally noble) could be elected to office. Rome was ruled by aristocrats, who became rich as the people became poor. The great source of senatorial wealth was in the control of the provinces. The governors were chosen by the Senate and from the Senate; and it required only one or two years to make a fortune as a governor, like Verres. The ultimate cause which threw power into the hands of the rich and noble was the venality of the people. The aristocratic demagogues bought them, in the same way that rich monopolists in our day control legislatures. The people are too numerous in this country to be directly bought up, even if it were possible, and the prizes they confer are not high enough to tempt rich men, as they did in Rome.

A man, therefore, who would rise to power at Rome must necessarily bribe the people, must purchase their votes, unless he was a man of extraordinary popularity, – some great orator like Cicero, or successful general like Marius or Sulla; and it was difficult to get popularity except as a lawyer and orator, or as a general.

Caesar, like Cicero and Hortensius, chose the law as a means of rising in the world; for, though of ancient family, he was not rich. He must make money by his profession, or he must borrow it, if he would secure office. It seems he borrowed it. How he contrived to borrow such vast sums as he spent on elections, I do not know. He probably made friends of rich men like Crassus, who became security for him. He was in debt to the amount of $1,500,000 of our money before he held office. He was a bold political gambler, and played for high stakes. It would seem that he had very winning and courteous manners, though he was not distinguished for popular oratory. His terse and pregnant sentences, however, won the admiration of his friend

Cicero, a brother lawyer, and he was very social and hospitable. He was on the liberal side in politics, and attacked the abuses of the day, which won him popular favor. At first he lived in a modest house with his wife and mother, in the Subarra, without attracting much notice. The first office to which he was elected was that of a Military Tribune, soon after his sojourn of two years in Rhodes to learn from Apollonius the arts of oratory. His next office was that of Quaestor, which enabled him to enter the Senate, at the age of thirty-two; and his third office, that of Aedile, which gave him the control of the public buildings: the Aediles were expected to decorate the city, and this gave him opportunities of cultivating popularity by splendor and display. The first thing which brought him into notice as an orator was a funeral oration he pronounced on his Aunt Julia, the widow of Marius. The next fortunate event of his life was his marriage with Pompeia, a cousin of Pompey, who was then the foremost man in Rome, having distinguished himself in Spain and in putting down the slave insurrection under Spartacus; but Pompey's great career in the East had not yet commenced, so that the future rivals at that time were friends. Caesar glorified Pompey in the Senate, which by virtue of his office he had lately entered. The next step to greatness was his election by the people – through the use of immense amounts of borrowed money – to the great office of Pontifex Maximus, which made him the pagan Pope of Rome for life, with a grand palace to live in. Soon after he was made Praetor, which office entitled him to a provincial government; and he was sent by the Senate to Spain as Pro-praetor, completed the conquest of the peninsula, and sent to Borne vast sums of money. These services entitled him to a triumph; but, as he presented himself at the same time as a candidate for the consulship, he was obliged to forego the triumph, and was elected Consul without opposition: his vanity ever yielded to his ambition.

Thus far there was nothing remarkable in Caesar's career. He had risen by power of money, like other aristocrats, to the highest offices of the State, showing abilities indeed, but not that extraordinary genius which has made him immortal. He was the leader of the political party which Sulla had put down, and yet was not a revolutionist like the Gracchi. He was an aristocratic reformer, like Lord John Russell before the passage of the Reform Bill, whom the people adored. He was a liberal, but not a radical. Of course he was not a favorite with the senators, who wished to perpetuate abuses. He was intensely disliked by Cato, a most excellent and honest man, but narrow-minded and conservative, – a sort of Duke of Wellington without his military abilities. The Senate would make no concessions, would part with no privileges, and submit to no changes. Like Lord Eldon, it "adhered to what was established, because it was established."

Caesar, as Consul, began his administration with conciliation; and he had the support of Crassus with his money, and of Pompey as the representative of the army, who was then flushed with his Eastern conquests, – pompous, vain, and proud, but honest and incorruptible. Cicero stood aloof, – the greatest man in the Senate, whose aristocratic privileges he defended. He might have aided Caesar "in the speaking department;" but as a "new man" he was jealous of his prerogatives, and was always conservative, like Burke, whom he resembled in his eloquence and turn of mind and fondness for literature and philosophy. Failing to conciliate the aristocrats, Caesar became a sort of Mirabeau, and appealed to the people, causing them to pass his celebrated "Leges Juliae," or reform bills; the chief of which was the "land act," which conferred portions of the public lands on Pompey's disbanded soldiers for settlement, – a wise thing, which senators opposed, since it took away their monopoly. Another act required the provincial governors, on their return from office, to render an account of their stewardship and hand in their accounts for public inspection. The Julian Laws also were designed to prevent the plunder of the public revenues, the debasing of the coin, the bribery of judges and of the people at elections. There were laws also for the protection of citizens from violence, and sundry other reforms which were enlightened and useful. In the passage of these laws against the will of the Senate, we see that the people were still recognized as sovereign in *legislation*. The laws were good. All depended on their execution; and the Senate, as the administrative body, could practically defeat their operation when Caesar's term of office expired; and this it unwisely determined to do. The last thing it wished was any reform whatever; and, as Mr. Froude thinks, there must have been either reform or revolution. But this is not so clear to me. Aristocracy was all-powerful when money could buy the people, and when the people had no virtue, no ambition, no intelligence. The struggle at Rome in the latter days of the Republic was not between the people and the aristocracy, but between the aristocracy and the military chieftains on one side, and those demagogues whom it feared on the other. The result showed that the aristocracy feared and distrusted Caesar; and he used the people only to advance his own ends, – of course, in the name of reform and patriotism. And when he became Dictator, he kicked away the ladder on which he climbed to power. It was Imperialism that he established; neither popular rights nor aristocratic privileges. He had no more love of the people than he had of those proud aristocrats who afterwards murdered him.

But the empire of the world – to which Caesar at that time may, or may not, have aspired: who can tell? but probably not – was not to be gained by civil services, or reforms, or arguments in law courts, or by holding great offices, or haranguing the people at the rostrum, or making speeches in the Senate, – where he was hated for his liberal views and enlightened mind, rather than from any fear of his overturning the constitution, – but by military services and heroic deeds and the devotion of a tried and disciplined regular army. Caesar was now forty-three years of age, being in the full maturity of his powers. At the close of his term as Consul he sought a province where military talents were indispensable, and where he could have a long term of office. The Senate gave him the "woods and forests," – an unsubdued country, where he would have hard work and unknown perils, and from which it was probable he would never return. They sent him to Gaul. But this was just the field for his marvellous military genius, then only partially developed; and the second period of his career now began.

It was during this second period that he rendered his most important services to the State and earned his greatest fame. The dangers which threatened the Empire came from the West, and not the East. Asia was already-subdued by Sulla, Lucullus, and Pompey, or was on the point of being subdued. Mithridates was a formidable enemy; but he aimed at establishing an Asiatic empire, not conquering the European provinces. He was not so dangerous as even Pyrrhus had been. Moreover, the conquest of the East was comparatively easy, – over worn-out races and an effete civilization; it gave *éclat* to Sulla and Pompey, – as the conquest of India, with a handful of British troops, made Clive and Hastings famous; it required no remarkable military genius, nor was it necessary for the safety of Italy. Conquest over the Oriental monarchies meant only spoliation. It was prompted by greed and vanity more than by a sense of danger. Pompey brought back money enough from the East to enrich all his generals, and the Senate besides, – or rather the State, which a few aristocrats practically owned.

But the conquest of Gaul would be another affair. It was peopled with hardy races, who cast their greedy eyes on the empire of the Romans, or on some of its provinces, and who were being pushed forward to invasion by a still braver people beyond the Rhine, – races kindred to those Teutons whom Marius had defeated. There was no immediate danger from the Germans; but there was ultimate danger, as proved by the union they made in the time of Marcus Antoninus for the invasion of the Roman provinces. It was necessary to raise a barrier against their inundations. It was also necessary to subdue the various Celtic tribes of Gaul, who were getting restless and uneasy. There was no money in a conquest over barbarians, except so far as they could be sold into slavery; but there was danger in it. The whole country was threatened with insurrections, leagues, and invasion, from the Alps to the ocean. There was a confederacy of hostile kings and chieftains; they commanded innumerable forces; they controlled important posts and passes. The Gauls had long made fixed settlements, and had built bridges and fortresses. They were not so warlike as the Germans; but they were yet formidable enemies. United, they were like "a volcano giving signs of approaching eruption; and at any moment, and hardly without warning, another lava stream might be poured down Venetia and Lombardy."

To rescue the Empire from such dangers was the work of Caesar; and it was no small undertaking. The Senate had given him unlimited power, for five years, over Gaul, – then a *terra incognita*, – an indefinite country, comprising the modern States of France, Holland, Switzerland, Belgium, and a part of Germany. Afterward the Senate extended the governorship five years more; so difficult was the work of conquest, and so formidable were the enemies. But it was danger which Caesar loved. The greater the obstacles the better was he pleased, and the greater was the scope for his genius, – which at first was not appreciated, for the best part of his life had been passed in Rome as a lawyer and orator and statesman. But he had a fine constitution, robust health, temperate habits, and unbounded energies. He was free to do as he liked with several legions, and had time to perfect his operations. And his legions were trained to every kind of labor and hardship. They could build bridges, cut down forests, and drain swamps, as well as march with a weight of eighty pounds to the man. They could make their own shoes, mend their own clothes, repair their own arms, and construct their own tents. They were as familiar with the axe and spade as they were with the lance and sword. They were inured to every kind of danger and difficulty, and not one of them was personally braver than the general who led them, or more skillful in riding a horse, or fording a river, or climbing a mountain. No one of them could be more abstemious. Luxury is not one of the peculiarities of successful generals in barbaric countries.

To give a minute sketch of the various encounters with the different tribes and nations that inhabited the vast country he was sent to conquer and govern, would be impossible in a lecture like this. One must read Caesar's own account of his conflicts with Helvetii, Aedui, Remi, Nervii, Belgae, Veneti, Arverni, Aquitani, Ubii, Eubueones, Treveri, and other nations between the Alps, the Pyrenees, the Rhine, and the sea. Their numbers were immense, and they were well armed, and had cavalry, military stores, efficient leaders, and indomitable courage. When beaten in one place they sprang up in another, like the Saxons with whom Charlemagne contended. They made treaties only to break them. They fought with the desperation of heroes who had their wives and children, firesides and altars, to guard; yet against them Caesar was uniformly successful. He was at times in great peril, yet he never lost but one battle, and this through the fault of his generals. Yet he had able generals, whom he selected himself, – Labienus, who afterwards deserted him, Antony, Publius Crassus, Cotta, Sabinus, – all belonging to the aristocracy. They made mistakes, but Caesar never. They would often have been cut off but for Caesar's timely aid.

Figure 5. Surrender of Vercingetorix, the Last Chief of Gaul. *After the painting by Henri Motte.*

When we consider the dangers to which he was constantly exposed, the amazing difficulties he had to surmount, the hardships he had to encounter, the fears he had to allay, the murmurs he was obliged to silence, the rivers he was compelled to cross in the face of enemies, the forests it was necessary to penetrate, the swamps and mountains and fortresses which impeded his marches, we are amazed at his skill and intrepidity, to say nothing of his battles with forces ten times more numerous than his own. His fertility of resources, his lightning rapidity of movement, his sagacity and insight, his perfection of discipline, his careful husbandry of forces, his ceaseless diligence, his intrepid courage, the confidence with which he inspired his soldiers, his brilliant successes (victory after victory), with the enormous number of captives by which he and the State became enriched, – all these things dazzled his countrymen, and gave him a fame such as no general had ever earned before. He conquered a population of warriors to be numbered by millions, with no aid from charts and maps, exposed perpetually to treachery and false information. He had to please and content an army a thousand miles from home, without supplies, except such as were precarious, – living on the plainest food, and doomed to infinite labors and drudgeries, besides attacking camps and assaulting fortresses, and fighting pitched battles. Yet he won their love, their respect, and their admiration, – and by an urbanity, a kindness, and a careful protection of their interests, such as no general ever showed before. He was a hero performing perpetual wonders, as chivalrous as the knights of the Middle Ages. No wonder he was adored, like a Moses in the wilderness, like a Napoleon in his early conquests.

This conquest of Gaul, during which he drove the Germans back to their forests, and inaugurated a policy of conciliation and moderation which made the Gauls the faithful allies of Rome, and their country its most fertile and important province, furnishing able men both for the Senate and the Army, was not only a great feat of genius, but a great service – a transcendent service – to the State, which entitled Caesar to a magnificent reward. Had it been cordially rendered to him, he might have been contented with a sort of perpetual consulship, and with the éclat of being the foremost man of the Empire. The people would have given him anything in their power to give, for he was as much an idol to them as Napoleon became to the Parisians after the conquest of Italy. He had rendered services as brilliant as those of Scipio, of Marius, of Sulla, or of Pompey. If he did not save Italy from being subsequently overrun by barbarians, he postponed their irruptions for two hundred years. And he had partially civilized the country he had subdued, and introduced Roman institutions. He had also created an army of disciplined veterans, such as never before was seen. He perfected military mechanism, that which kept the Empire together after all vitality had fled. He was the greatest master of the art of war known to antiquity. Such transcendent military excellence and such great services entitled him to the gratitude and admiration of the whole Empire, although he enriched himself and his soldiers with the spoils of his ten years' war, and did not, so far as I can see, bring great sums into the national treasury.

But the Senate was reluctant to give him the customary rewards for ten years' successful war, and for adding Western Europe to the Empire. It was jealous of his greatness and his renown. It also feared him, for he had eleven legions in his pay, and was known to be ambitious. It hated him for two reasons: first, because in his first consulship he had introduced reforms, and had always sided with the popular and liberal party; and secondly, because military successes of unprecedented brilliancy had made him dangerous. So, on the conclusion of the conquest of Gaul, it withdrew two legions from his army, and sought to deprive him of his promised second consulate, and even to recall him before his term of office as governor was expired. In other words, it sought to cripple and disarm him, and raise his rival, Pompey, over him in the command of the forces of the Empire.

It was now secret or open war, not between Caesar and the Roman people, but between Caesar and the Senate, – between a great and triumphant general and the Roman oligarchy of nobles, who, for nearly five hundred years, had ruled the Empire. On the side of Caesar were the army, the well-to-do classes, and the people; on the side of the Senate were the forces which a powerful aristocracy could command, having the prestige of law and power and wealth, and among whom were the great names of the republic.

Mr. Froude ridicules and abuses this aristocracy, as unfit longer to govern the State, as a worn-out power that deserved to fall. He uniformly represents them as extravagant, selfish, ostentatious, luxurious, frivolous, Epicurean in opinions and in life, oppressive in all their social relations, haughty beyond endurance, and controlling the popular elections by means of bribery and corruption. It would be difficult to refute these charges. The Patricians probably gave themselves up to all the pleasures incident to power and unbounded wealth, in a corrupt and wicked age. They had their palaces in the city and their villas in the country, their parks and gardens, their fish-ponds and game-preserves, their pictures and marbles, their expensive furniture and costly ornaments, gold and silver vessels, gems and precious works of art. They gave luxurious banquets; they travelled like princes; they were a body of kings, to whom the old monarchs of conquered provinces bowed down in fear and adulation. All this does not prove that they were incapable, although they governed for the interests of their class. They were all experienced in affairs of State, – most of them had been quaestors, aediles, praetors, censors, tribunes, consuls, and governors. Most of them were highly educated, had travelled extensively, were gentlemanly in their manners, could make speeches in the Senate, and could fight on the field of battle when there was a necessity. They doubtless had the common vices of the rich and proud; but many of them were virtuous, patriotic, incorruptible, almost austere in morals, dignified and intellectual, whom everybody respected, – men like Cato, Brutus, Cassius, Cicero, and others. Their sin was that they wished to conserve their powers, privileges, and fortunes, like all aristocracies, – like the British House of Lords. Nor must it be forgotten that it was under their régime that the conquest of the world was made, and that Rome had become the centre of everything magnificent and glorious on the earth.

It was doubtless shortsighted and ungrateful in these nobles to attempt to deprive Caesar of his laurels and his promised consulship. He had earned them by grand services, both as a general and a statesman. But their jealousy and hatred were not unnatural. They feared, not unreasonably, that the successful general – rich, proud, and dictatorial from the long exercise of power, and seated in the chair of supremest dignity – would make sweeping changes; might reduce their authority to a shadow, and elevate himself to perpetual dictatorship; and thus, by substituting imperialism for aristocracy, subvert the Constitution. That is evidently what Cicero feared, as appears in his letters to Atticus. That is what all the leading Senators feared, especially Cato. It was known that Caesar – although urbane, merciful, enlightened, hospitable, and disposed to govern for the public good – was unscrupulous in the use of tools; that he had originally gained his seat in the Senate by bribery and demagogic arts; that he was reckless as to debts, regarding money only as a means to buy supporters; that he had appropriated vast sums from the spoils of war for his own use, and, from being poor, had become the richest man in the Empire; that he had given his daughter Julia in marriage to Pompey from political ends; that he was long-sighted in his ambition, and would be content with nothing less than the gratification of this insatiate passion. All this was known, and it gave great solicitude to the leaders of the aristocracy, who resolved to put him down, – to strip him of his power, or fight him, if necessary, in a civil war. So the aristocracy put themselves under the protection of Pompey, – a successful but overrated general, who also aimed at supreme power, with the nobles as his supporters, not perhaps as Imperator, but as the agent and representative of a subservient Senate, in whose name he would rule.

This contest between Caesar and the aristocracy under the lead of Pompey, its successful termination in Caesar's favor, and his brilliant reign of about four years, as Dictator and Imperator, constitute the third period of his memorable career.

Neither Caesar nor Pompey would disband their legions, as it was proposed by Curio in the Senate and voted by a large majority. In fact, things had arrived at a crisis: Caesar was recalled, and he must obey the Senate, or be decreed a public enemy; that is, the enemy of the power that ruled the State. He would not obey, and a general levy of troops in support of the Senate was made, and put into the hands of Pompey with unlimited command. The Tribunes of the people, however, sided with Caesar, and refused confirmation of the Senatorial decrees. Caesar then no longer hesitated, but with his army crossed the Rubicon, which was an insignificant stream, but was the Rome-ward boundary of his province. This was the declaration of civil war. It was now "'either anvil or hammer." The admirers of Caesar claim that his act was a necessity, at least a public benefit, on the ground of the misrule of the aristocracy. But it does not appear that there was anarchy at Rome, although Milo had killed Clodius. There were aristocratic feuds, as in the Middle Ages. Order and law – the first conditions of society – were not in jeopardy, as in the French Revolution, when Napoleon arose. The people were not in hostile array against the nobles, nor the nobles against the people. The nobles only courted and bribed the people; but so general was corruption that a change in government was deemed necessary by the advocates of Caesar, – at least they defended it. The gist of all the arguments in favor of the revolution is: better imperialism than an oligarchy of corrupt nobles. It is not my province to settle that question. It is my work only to describe events.

It is clear that Caesar resolved on seizing supreme power, in taking it away from the nobles, on the ground probably that he could rule better than they, – the plea of Napoleon, the plea of Cromwell, the plea of all usurpers.

But this supreme power he could not exercise until he had conquered Pompey and the Senate and all his enemies. It must need be that "he should wade through slaughter to his throne." This alternative was forced on him, and he accepted it. He accepted civil war in order to reign. At best, he would do evil that good might come. He was doubtless the strongest man in the world; and, according to Mr. Carlyle's theory, the strongest ought to rule.

Much has been said about the rabble, – the democracy, – their turbulence, corruption, and degradation, their unfitness to rule, and all that sort of thing, which I regard as irrelevant, so far as the usurpation of Caesar is concerned; since the struggle was not between them and the nobles, but between a fortunate general and the aristocracy who controlled the State. Caesar was not the representative of the people or of their interests, as Tiberius Gracchus was, but the representative of the Army. He had no more sympathy with the people than he had with the nobles: he probably despised them both, as unfit to rule. He flattered the people and bought them, but he did not love them. It was his soldiers whom he loved, next to himself; although, as a wise and enlightened statesman, he wished to promote the great interests of the nation, so far as was consistent with the enjoyment of imperial rule. This friend of the people would give them spectacles and shows, largesses of corn, – money, even, – and extension of the suffrage, but not political power. He was popular with them, because he was generous and merciful, because his exploits won their admiration, and his vast public works gave employment to them and adorned their city.

It is unnecessary to dwell on the final contest of Caesar with the nobles, with Pompey at their head, since nothing is more familiar in history. Plainly he was not here rendering public services, as he did in Spain and Gaul, but taking care of his own interests. I cannot see how a civil war was a service, unless it were a service to destroy the aristocratic constitution and substitute imperialism, which some think was needed with the vast extension of the Empire, and for the good administration of the provinces, – robbed and oppressed by the governors whom the Senate had sent out to enrich the aristocracy. It may have been needed for the better administration of justice, for the preservation of law and order, and a more efficient central power. Absolutism may have proved a benefit to the Empire, as it proved a benefit to France under Cardinal Richelieu, when he humiliated the nobles. If so, it was only a choice of evils, for absolutism is tyranny, and tyranny is not a blessing, except in a most demoralized state of society, which it is claimed was the state of Rome at the time of the usurpation of Caesar. It is certain that the whole united strength of the aristocracy could not prevail over Caesar, although it had Pompey for its defender, with his immense prestige and experience as a general.

After Caesar had crossed the Rubicon, and it was certain he would march to Rome and seize the reins of government, the aristocracy fled precipitately to Pompey's wing at Capua, fearing to find in Caesar another Marius. Pompey did not show extraordinary ability in the crisis. He had no courage and no purpose. He fled to Brundusium, where ships were waiting to transport his army to Durazzo. He was afraid to face his rival in Italy. Caesar would have pursued, but had no navy. He therefore went to Rome, which he had not seen for ten years, took what money he wanted from the treasury, and marched to Spain, where the larger part of Pompey's army, under his lieutenants, were now arrayed against him. These it was necessary first to subdue. But Caesar prevailed, and all Spain was soon at his feet. His successes were brilliant; and Gaul, Italy, Sicily, and Sardinia were wholly his own, as well as Spain, which was Pompey's province. He then rapidly returned to Rome, was named Dictator, and as such controlled the consular election, and was chosen Consul. But Pompey held the East, and, with his ships, controlled the Mediterranean, and was gathering forces for the invasion of Italy. Caesar allowed himself but eleven days in Rome. It was necessary to meet Pompey before that general could return to Italy. It was mid-winter, – about a year after he had crossed the Rubicon. He had with him only thirty thousand men, but these were veterans. Pompey had nine full Roman legions, which lay at Durazzo, opposite to Brundusium, besides auxiliaries and unlimited means; but he was hampered by senatorial civilians, and his legions were only used to Eastern warfare. He also controlled the sea, so that it was next to impossible for Caesar to embark without being defeated. Yet Caesar did cross the sea amid overwhelming obstacles, and the result was the battle of Pharsalia, – deemed one of the decisive battles of the world, although the forces of the combatants were comparatively small. It was gained by the defeat of Pompey's cavalry by a fourth line of the best soldiers of Caesar, which was kept in reserve. Pompey,

on the defeat of his cavalry, upon whom he had based his hopes, lost heart
and fled. He fled to the sea, – uncertain, vacillating, and discouraged, – and
sailed for Egypt, relying on the friendship of the young king; but was
murdered treacherously before he set foot upon the land. His fate was most
tragical. His fall was overwhelming.

This battle, in which the flower of the Roman aristocracy succumbed to
the conqueror of Gaul, with vastly inferior forces, did not end the desperate
contest. Two more bloody battles were fought – one in Africa and one in
Spain – before the supremacy of Caesar was secured. The battle of Thapsus,
between Utica and Carthage, at which the Roman nobles once more rallied
under Cato and Labienus, and the battle of Munda, in Spain, the most bloody
of all, gained by Caesar over the sons of Pompey, settled the civil war and
made Caesar supreme. He became supreme only by the sacrifice of half of
the Roman nobility and the death of their principal leaders, – Pompey,
Labienus, Lentulus, Ligarius, Metellus, Scipio Afrarius, Cato, Petreius, and
others. In one sense it was the contest between Pompey and Caesar for the
empire of the world. Cicero said, "The success of the one meant massacre,
and that of the other slavery," – for if Pompey had prevailed, the aristocracy
would have butchered their enemies with unrelenting vengeance; but Caesar
hated unnecessary slaughter, and sought only power. In another sense it was
the struggle between a single man – with enlightened views and vast designs
– and the Roman aristocracy, hostile to reforms, and bent on greed and
oppression. The success of Caesar was favorable to the restoration of order
and law and progressive improvements; the success of the nobility would
have entailed a still more grinding oppression of the people, and possibly
anarchy and future conflicts between fortunate generals and the aristocracy.
Destiny or Providence gave the empire of the world to a single man, although
that man was as unscrupulous as he was able.

Henceforth imperialism was the form of government in Rome, which
lasted about four hundred years. How long an aristocratic government would
have lasted is a speculation. Caesar, in his elevation to unlimited power, used
his power beneficently. He pardoned his enemies, gave security to property
and life, restored the finances, established order, and devoted himself to
useful reforms. He cut short the grant of corn to the citizen mob; he repaired

the desolation which war had made; he rebuilt cities and temples; he even endeavored to check luxury and extravagance and improve morals. He reformed the courts of law, and collected libraries in every great city. He put an end to the expensive tours of senators in the provinces, where they had appeared as princes exacting contributions. He formed a plan to drain the Pontine Marshes. He reformed the calendar, making the year to begin with the first day of January. He built new public buildings, which the enlargement of business required. He seemed to have at heart the welfare of the State and of the people, by whom he was adored. But he broke up the political ascendancy of nobles, although he did not confiscate their property. He weakened the Senate by increasing its numbers to nine hundred, and by appointing senators himself from his army and from the provinces, – those who would be subservient to him, who would vote what he decreed.

Caesar's ruling passion was ambition, – thirst of power; but he had no great animosities. He pardoned his worst enemies, – Brutus, Cassius, and Cicero, who had been in arms against him; nor did he reign as a tyrant. His habits were simple and unostentatious. He gave easy access to his person, was courteous in his manners, and mingled with senators as a companion rather than as a master. Like Charlemagne, he was temperate in eating and drinking, and abhorred gluttony and drunkenness, – the vices of the aristocracy and of fortunate plebeians alike. He was indefatigable in business, and paid attention to all petitions. He was economical in his personal expenses, although he lavished vast sums upon the people in the way of amusing or bribing them. He dispensed with guards and pomps, and was apparently reckless of his life: anything was better to him than to live in perpetual fear of conspirators and traitors. There never was a braver man, and he was ever kind-hearted to those who did not stand in his way. He was generous, magnanimous, and unsuspicious. He was the model of an absolute prince, aside from laxity of morals. In regard to women, of their virtue he made little account. His favorite mistress was Servilia, sister of Cato and mother of Brutus. Some have even supposed that Brutus was Caesar's son, which accounts for his lenity and forbearance and affection. He was the high-priest of the Roman worship, and yet he believed neither in the gods nor in immortality. But he was always the gentleman, – natural, courteous, affable, without vanity or arrogance or egotism. He was not a patriot in the sense that Cicero and Cato were, or Trajan and Marcus Aurelius, since his country was made subservient to his own interests and aggrandizement. Yet he was a very interesting man, and had fewer faults than Napoleon, with equally grand designs.

But even he could not escape a retribution, in spite of his exalted position and his great services. The leaders of the aristocracy still hated him, and could not be appeased for the overthrow of their power. They resolved to assassinate him, from vengeance rather than fear. Cicero was not among the conspirators; because his discretion could not be relied upon, and they passed him by. But his heart was with them. "There are many ways," said he, "in which a man may die." It was not a wise thing to take his life; since the Constitution was already subverted, and somebody would reign as imperator by means of the army, and his death would necessarily lead to renewed civil wars and new commotions and new calamities. But angry, embittered, and passionate enemies do not listen to reason. They will not accept the inevitable. There was no way to get rid of Caesar but by assassination, and no one wished him out of the way but the nobles. Hence it was easy for them to form a conspiracy. It was easy to stab him with senatorial daggers. Caesar was not killed because he had personal enemies, nor because he destroyed the liberties of Roman citizens, but because he had usurped the authority of the aristocracy.

Yet he died, perhaps at the right time, at the age of fifty-six, after an undisputed reign of only three or four years, – about the length of that of Cromwell. He was already bending under the infirmities of a premature old age. Epileptic fits had set in, and his constitution was undermined by his unparalleled labors and fatigues; and then his restless mind was planning a new expedition to Parthia, where he might have ingloriously perished like Crassus. But such a man could not die. His memory and deeds lived. He filled a role in history, which could not be forgotten. He inaugurated a successful revolution. He bequeathed a policy to last as long as the Empire lasted; and he had rendered services of the greatest magnitude, by which he is to be ultimately judged, as well as by his character. It is impossible for us to settle whether or not his services overbalanced the evils of the imperialism he established and of the civil wars by which he reached supreme command. Whatever view we may take of the comparative merits of an aristocracy or an imperial despotism in a corrupt age, we cannot deny to Caesar some transcendent services and a transcendent fame. The whole matter is laid before us in the language of Cicero to Caesar himself, in the Senate, when he was at the height of his power; which shows that the orator was not lacking in courage any more than in foresight and moral wisdom: –

> "Your life, Caesar, is not that which is bounded by the union of your soul and body. Your life is that which shall continue fresh in the memory of ages to come, which posterity will cherish and eternity itself keep guard over. Much has been done by you which men will admire; much remains to be done which they can praise. They will read with wonder of empires and provinces, of the Rhine, the ocean, and the Nile, of battles without number, of amazing victories, of countless monuments and triumphs; but unless the Commonwealth be wisely re-established in institutions by you bestowed upon us, your name will travel widely over the world, but will have no fixed habitation; and those who come after you *will dispute about you* as we have disputed. Some will extol you to the skies; others will find something wanting, and the most important element of all. Remember the tribunal before which you are to stand. The ages that are to be will try you, it may be with minds less prejudiced than ours, uninfluenced either by the desire to please you or by envy of your greatness."

Thus spoke Cicero with heroic frankness. The ages have "disputed about" Caesar, and will continue to dispute about him, as they do about Cromwell and Napoleon; but the man is nothing to us in comparison with the ideas which he fought or which he supported, and which have the same force to-day as they had nearly two thousand years ago. He is the representative of imperialism; which few Americans will defend, unless it becomes a necessity which every enlightened patriot admits. The question is, whether it was or was not a necessity at Rome fifty years before Christ was born. It is not easy to settle in regard to the benefit that Caesar is supposed by some – including Mr. Froude and the late Emperor of the French – to have rendered to the cause of civilization by overturning the aristocratic Constitution, and substituting, not the rule of the people, but that of a single man. It is still one of the speculations of history; it is not one of its established facts, although the opinions of enlightened historians seem to lean to the necessity of the Caesarian imperialism, in view of the misrule of the aristocracy and the abject venality of the citizens who had votes to sell. But it must be borne in mind that it was under the aristocratic rule of senators and patricians that Rome went on from conquering to conquer; that the governing classes were at all times the most intelligent, experienced, and efficient in the Commonwealth; that their very vices may have been exaggerated; and that the imperialism which crushed them, may also have crushed out original genius, literature, patriotism, and exalted sentiments, and even failed to have produced greater personal security than existed under the aristocratic Constitution at any period of its existence. All these are disputed points of history. It may be that Caesar, far from being a national benefactor by reorganizing the forces of the Empire, sowed the seeds of ruin by his imperial policy; and that, while he may have given unity, peace, and law to the Empire, he may have taken away its life. I do not assert this, or even argue its probability. It may have been, and it may not have been. It is an historical puzzle. There are two sides to all great questions. But whether or not we can settle with the light of modern knowledge such a point as this, I look upon the defence of imperialism in itself, in preference to constitutional government with all its imperfections, as an outrage on the whole progress of modern civilization, and on whatever remains of dignity and intelligence among the people.

AUTHORITIES

Caesar, *Commentaries*
Curtius *History of Rome.*
Froude, *Caesar: A Sketch*
Leges Juliae, Appian, Plutarch, Suetonius, Dion Cassius, and Cicero, *Letters to Atticus*
Merivale's *History of the Empire*

Napoleon III, *Life of Caesar*
Niebuhr, *Lectures on the History of Rome*
Rollin, *Ancient History*

Chapter 3

MARCUS AURELIUS: THE GLORY OF ROME

A.D. 121-180.

Marcus Aurelius is immortal, not so much for what he *did* as for what he *was*. His services to the State were considerable, but not transcendent. He was a great man, but not pre-eminently a great emperor. He was a meditative sage rather than a man of action; although he successfully fought the Germanic barbarians, and repelled their fearful incursions. He did not materially extend the limits of the Empire, but he preserved and protected its provinces. He reigned wisely and ably, but made mistakes. His greatness was in his character; his influence for good was in his noble example. When we consider his circumstances and temptations, as the supreme master of a vast Empire, and in a wicked and sensual age, he is a greater moral phenomenon than Socrates or Epictetus. He was one of the best men of Pagan antiquity. History furnishes no example of an absolute monarch so pure and spotless and lofty as he was, unless it be Alfred the Great or St. Louis. But the sphere of the Roman emperor was far greater than that of the Mediaeval kings. Marcus Aurelius ruled over one hundred and twenty millions of people, without check or hindrance or Constitutional restraint. He could do what he pleased with their persons and their property. Most sovereigns, exalted to such lofty dignity and power, have been either cruel, or vindictive, or self-indulgent, or selfish, or proud, or hard, or ambitious, – men who have been stained by crimes, whatever may have been their services to civilization. Most of them have yielded to their great temptations. But Marcus Aurelius, on the throne of the civilized world, was modest, virtuous, affable, accessible, considerate, gentle, studious, contemplative, stained by novices, – a model of human virtue. Hence he is one of the favorite characters of history. No Roman emperor was so revered and loved as he, and of no one have so many monuments been preserved. Everybody had his picture or statue in his house. He was more than venerated in his day, and his fame as a wise and good man has increased with the flight of ages.

This illustrious emperor did not belong to the family of the great Caesar. That family became extinct with Nero, the sixth emperor. Like Trajan and Hadrian, Marcus Aurelius derived his remote origin from Spain, although he was born in Rome. His great-grandfather was a Spaniard, and yet attained the praetorian rank. His grandfather reached the consulate. His father died while praetor, and when he himself was a child. He was adopted by his grandfather Annius Verus. But his marvellous moral beauty, even as a child, attracted the attention of the Emperor Hadrian, who bestowed upon him the honor of the aequestrian rank, at the age of six. At fifteen he was adopted by Antoninus Pius, then, as we might say, "Crown Prince." Had he been older, he would have been adopted by Hadrian himself. He thus, a mere youth, became the heir of the Roman world. His education was most excellent. From Fronto, the greatest rhetorician of the day, he learned rhetoric; from Herodes Atticus he acquired a knowledge of the world; from Diognotus he learned to despise superstition; from Apollonius, undeviating steadiness of purpose; from Sextus of Chaeronea, toleration of human infirmities; from Maximus, sweetness and dignity; from Alexander, allegiance to duty; from Rusticus, contempt of sophistry and display. This stoical philosopher created in him a new intellectual life, and opened to him a new world of thought. But the person to whom he was most indebted was his adopted father and father-in-law, the Emperor Antoninus Pius. For him he seems to have had the greatest reverence. "In him," said he, "I noticed mildness of manner with firmness of resolution, contempt of vain-glory, industry in business, and accessibility of person. From him I learned to acquiesce in every fortune, to exercise foresight in public affairs, to rise superior to vulgar praises, to serve mankind without ambition, to be sober and steadfast, to be content with little, to be practical and active, to be no dreamy bookworm, to be temperate, modest in dress, and not to be led away by novelties." What a picture of an emperor! What a contrast to such a man as Louis XIV!

Figure 6. Marcus Aurelius. *From a photograph of the statue at the Capitol, Rome.*

We might draw a parallel between Marcus Aurelius and David, when he was young and innocent. But the person in history whom he most resembled was St. Anselm. He was a St. Anselm on the throne. Philosophical meditations seem to have been his delight and recreation; and yet he could issue from his retirement and engage in active pursuits. He was an able general as well as a meditative sage, – heroic like David, capable of enduring great fatigue, and willing to expose himself to great dangers.

While his fame rests on his "Meditations," as that of David rests upon his Psalms, he yet rendered great military services to the Empire. He put down a dangerous revolt under Avidius Cassius in Asia, and did not punish the rebellious provinces. Not one person suffered death in consequence of this rebellion. Even the papers of Cassius, who aimed to be emperor, were burned, that a revelation of enemies might not be made, – a signal instance of magnanimity. Cassius, it seems, was assassinated by his own officers, which assassination Marcus Aurelius regretted, because it deprived him of granting a free pardon to a very able but dangerous man.

But the most signal service he rendered the Empire was a successful resistance to the barbarians of Germany, who had formed a general union for the invasion of the Roman world. They threatened the security of the Empire, as the Teutons did in the time of Marius, and the Gauls and Germans in the time of Julius Caesar. It took him twenty years to subdue these fierce warriors. He made successive campaigns against them, as Charlemagne did against the Saxons. It cost him the best years of his life to conquer them, which he did under difficulties as great as Julius surmounted in Gaul. He was the savior and deliverer of his country, as much as Marius or Scipio or Julius. The public dangers were from the West and not the East. Yet he succeeded in erecting a barrier against barbaric inundations, so that for nearly two hundred years the Romans were not seriously molested. There still stands in "the Eternal City" the column which commemorates his victories, – not so beautiful as that of Trajan, which furnished the model for Napoleon's column in the Place Vendôme, but still greatly admired. Were he not better known for his writings, he would be famous as one of the great military emperors, like Vespasian, Diocletian, and Constantine. Perhaps he did not add to the art of war; that was perfected by Julius Caesar. It was with the mechanism of former generals that he withstood most dangerous enemies, for in his day the legions were still well disciplined and irresistible.

The only stains on the reign of this good and great emperor – for there were none on his character – were in allowing the elevation of his son Commodus as his successor, and his persecution of the Christians.

In regard to the first, it was a blunder rather than a fault. Peter the Great caused *his* heir to be tried and sentenced to death, because he was a sot, a liar, and a fool. He dared not intrust the interests of his Empire to so unworthy a son; the welfare of Russia was more to him than the interest of his family. In that respect this stern and iron man was a greater prince than Marcus Aurelius; for the law of succession was not established at Rome any more than in Russia. There was no danger of civil war should the natural succession be set aside, as might happen in the feudal monarchies of Europe. The Emperor of Rome could adopt or elect his successor. It would have been wise for Aurelius to have selected one of the ablest of his generals, or one of the wisest of his senators, as Hadrian did, for so great and responsible a position, rather than a wicked, cruel, dissolute son. But Commodus was the son of Faustina also, – an intriguing and wicked woman, whose influence over her husband was unfortunately great; and, what is common in this world, the son was more like the mother than the father. (I think the wife of Eli the high-priest must have been a bad woman.) All his teachings and virtues were lost on such a reprobate. She, as an unscrupulous and ambitious woman, had no idea of seeing her son supplanted in the imperial dignity; and, like Catherine de'Medici and Agrippina, probably she connived at and even encouraged the vices of her children, in order more easily to bear rule. At any rate, the succession of Commodus to the throne was the greatest calamity that could have happened. For five reigns the Empire had enjoyed peace and prosperity; for five reigns the tide of corruption had been stayed: but the flood of corruption swept all barriers away with the accession of Commodus, and from that day the decline of the Empire was rapid and fatal. Still, probably nothing could have long arrested ruin. The Empire was doomed.

The other fact which obscured the glory of Marcus Aurelius as a sovereign was his persecution of the Christians, – for which it is hard to account, when the beneficent character of the emperor is considered. His reign was signalized for an imperial persecution, in which Justin at Rome,

Polycarp at Smyrna, and Ponthinus at Lyons, suffered martyrdom. It was not the first persecution. Under Nero the Christians had been cruelly tortured, nor did the virtuous Trajan change the policy of the government. Hadrian and Antoninus Pius permitted the laws to be enforced against the Christians, and Marcus Aurelius saw no reason to alter them. But to the mind of the Stoic on the throne, says Arnold, the Christians were "philosophically contemptible, politically subversive, and morally abominable." They were regarded as statesmen looked upon the Jesuits in the reign of Louis XV., as we look upon the Mormons, – as dangerous to free institutions. Moreover, the Christians were everywhere misunderstood and misrepresented. It was impossible for Marcus Aurelius to see the Christians except through a mist of prejudices. "Christianity grew up in the Catacombs, not on the Palatine." In allowing the laws to take their course against a body of men who were regarded with distrust and aversion as enemies of the State, the Emperor was simply unfortunate. So wise and good a man, perhaps, ought to have known the Christians better; but, not knowing them, he cannot be stigmatized as a cruel man. How different the fortunes of the Church had Aurelius been the first Christian emperor instead of Constantine! Or, had his wife Faustina known the Christians as well as Marcia the mistress of Commodus, perhaps the persecution might not have happened, – and perhaps it might. Earnest and sincere men have often proved intolerant when their peculiar doctrines have been assailed, – like Athanasius and St. Bernard. A Stoical philosopher was trained, like a doctor of the Jewish Sandhedrim, in a certain intellectual pride.

The fame of Marcus Aurelius rests, as it has been said, on his philosophical reflections, as his "Meditations" attest. This remarkable book has come down to us, while most of the annals of the age have perished; so that even Niebuhr confesses that he knows less of the reign of Marcus Aurelius than of the early kings of Rome. Perhaps that is one reason why Gibbon begins his history with later emperors. But the "Meditations" of the good emperor survive, like the writings of Epictetus, St. Augustine, and Thomas à Kempis: one of the few immortal books, – immortal, in this case, not for artistic excellence, like the writings of Thucydides and Tacitus, but for the loftiness of thoughts alone; so precious that the saints of the Middle

Ages secretly preserved them as in accord with their own experiences. It is from these "Meditations" that we derive our best knowledge of Marcus Aurelius. They reveal the man, – and a man of sorrows, as the truly great are apt to be, when brought in contact with a world of wickedness, as were Alfred and Dante.

In these "Meditations" there is a striking resemblance to the discourses of Epictetus, which alike reveal the lofty and yet sorrowful soul, and are among the most valuable fragments which have come down from Pagan antiquity; and this is remarkable, since Epictetus was a Phrygian slave, of the lowest parentage. He belonged to the secretary and companion of Nero, whose name was Epaphroditus, and who treated this poor Phrygian with great cruelty. And yet, what is very singular, the master caused the slave to be indoctrinated in the Stoical philosophy, on account of a rare intelligence which commanded respect. He was finally manumitted, but lived all his life in the deepest poverty, to which he attached no more importance than Socrates did at Athens. In his miserable cottage he had no other furniture than a straw pallet and an iron lamp, which last somebody stole. His sole remark on the loss of the only property he possessed was, that when the thief came again he would be disappointed to find only an earthen lamp instead of an iron one. This earthen lamp was subsequently purchased by a hero-worshipper for three thousand drachmas ($150). Epictetus, much as he despised riches and display and luxury and hypocrisy and pedantry and all phariseeism, living in the depths of poverty, was yet admired by eminent men, among whom was the Emperor Hadrian himself; and he found a disciple in Arrian, who was to him what Xenophon was to Socrates, committing his precious thoughts to writing; and these thoughts were to antiquity what the "Imitation of Christ" was to the Middle Ages, – accepted by Christians as well as by pagans, and even to-day regarded as one of the most beautiful treatises on morals ever composed by man. The great peculiarity of the "Manual" and the "Discourses" is the elevation of the soul over external evils, the duty of resignation to whatever God sends, and the obligation to do right because it is right. Epictetus did not go into the dreary dialectics of the schools, but, like Socrates, confined himself to practical life, – to the practice of virtue as the greatest good, – and valued the joys of true intellectual independence. To him his mind was his fortune, and he desired no better. We do not find in the stoicism of the Phrygian slave the devout and lofty spiritualism of Plato, – thirsting for God and immortality; it may be doubted whether he believed in immortality at all: but he did recognize what is most noble in human life, – the subservience of the passions to reason, the power of endurance, patience, charity, and disinterested action. He did recognize the necessity of divine aid in the struggles of life, the glory of friendship, the tenderness of compassion, the power of sympathy. His philosophy was human, and it was cheerful; since he did not believe in misfortune, and exalted gentleness and philanthropy. Above everything, he sought inward approval, not the praises of the world, – that happiness which lies within one's self, in the absence of all ignoble fears, in contentment, in that peace of the mind which can face poverty, disease, exile, and death.

Such were the lofty views which, embodied in the discourses of Epictetus, fell into the hands of Marcus Aurelius in the progress of his education, and exercised such a great influence on his whole subsequent life. The slave became the teacher of the emperor, – which it is impossible to conceive of unless their souls were in harmony. As a Stoic, the emperor would not be less on his throne than the slave in his cottage. The trappings and pomps of imperial state became indifferent to him, since they were external, and were of small moment compared with that high spiritual life which he desired to lead. If poverty and pain were nothing to Epictetus, so grandeur and power and luxury should be nothing to him, – both alike being merely outward things, like the clothes which cover a man. And the fewer the impediments in the march after happiness and truth the better. Does a really great and preoccupied man care what he wears? "A shocking bad hat" was perhaps as indifferent to Gladstone as a dirty old cloak was to Socrates. I suppose if a man is known to be brainless, it is necessary for him to wear a disguise, – even as instinct prompts a frivolous and empty woman to put on jewels. But who expects a person recognized as a philosopher to use a mental crutch or wear a moral mask? Who expects an old man, compelling attention by his wisdom, to dress like a dandy? It is out of place; it is not even artistic, – it is ridiculous. That only is an evil which shackles the soul. Aurelius aspired to its complete emancipation. Not for the joys of a future heaven did he long, but for the realities and certitudes of earth, – the placidity and harmony and peace of his soul, so long as it was doomed to the trials and temptations of the world, and a world, too, which he did not despise, but which he sought to benefit.

So, what was contentment in the slave became philanthropy in the emperor. He would be a benefactor, not by building baths and theatres, but by promoting peace, prosperity, and virtue. He would endure cheerfully the fatigue of winter campaigns upon the frozen Danube, if the Empire could be saved from violence. To extend its boundaries, like Julius, he cared nothing; but to preserve what he had was a supreme duty. His watchword was duty, – to himself, his country, and God. He lived only for the happiness of his subjects. Benevolence became the law of his life. Self-abnegation destroyed self-indulgence. For what was he placed by Providence in the highest position in the world, except to benefit the world? The happiness of one hundred and twenty millions was greater than the joys of any individual existence. And what were any pleasures which ended in vanity to the sublime placidity of an emancipated soul? Stoicism, if it did not soar to God and immortality, yet aspired to the freedom and triumph of what is most precious in man. And it equally despised, with haughty scorn, those things which corrupted and degraded this higher nature, – the glorious dignity of unfettered intellect. The accidents of earth were nothing in his eyes, – neither the purple of kings nor the rags of poverty. It was the soul, in its transcendent dignity, which alone was to be preserved and purified.

This was the exalted realism which appears in the "Meditations" of Marcus Aurelius, and which he had learned from the inspirations of a slave. Yet such was the inborn, almost supernatural, loftiness of Aurelius, that, had he been the slave and Epictetus the emperor, the same moral wisdom would have shone in the teachings and life of each; for they both were God's witnesses of truth in an age of wickedness and shame. It was He who chose them both, and sent them out as teachers of righteousness, – the one from the humblest cottage, the other from the most magnificent palace of the capital of the world. In station they were immeasurably apart; in aim and similarity of ideas they were kindred spirits, – one of the phenomena of the moral history of our race; for the slave, in his physical degradation, had all the freedom and grandeur of an aspiring soul, and the emperor, on his lofty throne, had all the humility and simplicity of a peasant in the lowliest state of poverty and suffering. Surely circumstances had nothing to do with this marvelous exhibition. It was either the mind and soul triumphant over and superior to all outward circumstances, or it was God imparting an extraordinary moral power.

I believe it was the inscrutable design of the Supreme Governor of the universe to show, perhaps, what lessons of moral wisdom could be taught by men under the most diverse influences and under the greatest contrasts of rank and power, and also to what heights the souls of both slave and king could rise, with His aid, in the most corrupt period of human history. Noah, Abraham, and Moses did not stand more isolated amidst universal wickedness than did the Phrygian slave and the imperial master of the world. And as the piety of Noah could not save the antediluvian empires, as the faith of Abraham could not convert idolatrous nations, as the wisdom of Moses could not prevent the sensualism of emancipated slaves, so the lofty philosophy of Aurelius could not save the Empire which he ruled. And yet the piety of Noah, the faith of Abraham, the wisdom of Moses, and the stoicism of Aurelius have proved alike a spiritual power, – the precious salt which was to preserve humanity from the putrefaction of almost universal selfishness and vice, until the new revelation should arouse the human soul to a more serious contemplation of its immortal destiny.

The imperial "Meditations" are without art or arrangement, – a sort of diary, valuable solely for their precious thoughts; not lofty soarings in philosophical and religious contemplation, which tax the brain to comprehend, like the thoughts of Pascal, but plain maxims for the daily intercourse of life, showing great purity of character and extraordinary natural piety, blended with pithy moral wisdom and a strong sense of duty. "Men exist for each other: teach them or bear with them," said he. "Benevolence is invincible, if it be not an affected smile." "When thou risest in the morning unwillingly, say, 'I am rising to the work of a human being; why, then, should I be dissatisfied if I am going to do the things for which I was brought into the world?'" "Since it is possible that thou mayest depart from this life this very moment, regulate every act and thought accordingly

(... for death hangs over thee whilst thou livest), while it is in thy power to be good." "What has become of all great and famous men, and all they desired and loved? They are smoke and ashes, and a tale." "If thou findest in human life anything better than justice, temperance, fortitude, turn to it with all thy soul; but if thou findest anything else smaller (and of no value) than this, give place to nothing else." "Men seek retreats for themselves, – houses in the country, seashores, and mountains; but it is always in thy power to retire within thyself, for nowhere does a man retire with more quiet or freedom than into his own soul." Think of such sayings, written down in his diary on the evenings of the very days of battle with the barbarians on the Danube or in Hungarian marshes! Think of a man, O ye Napoleons, ye conquerors, who can thus muse and meditate in his silent tent, and by the light of his solitary lamp, after a day of carnage and of victory! Think of such a man, – not master of a little barbaric island or a half-established throne in a country no bigger than a small province, but the supreme sovereign of a vast empire, at the time of its greatest splendor and prosperity, with no mortal power to keep his will in check, – nothing but the voice within him; nothing but the sense of duty; nothing but the desire of promoting the happiness of others: and this man a Pagan!

But the state of that Empire, with all its prosperity, needed such a man to arise. If anything or anybody could save it, it was that succession of good emperors of whom Marcus Aurelius was the last, in the latter part of the second century. Let us glance, in closing, at the real condition of the Empire at that time. I take leave of the man, – this "laurelled hero and crowned philosopher," stretching out his hands to the God he but dimly saw, and yet enunciating moral truths which for wisdom have been surpassed only by the sacred writers of the Bible, to whom the Almighty gave his special inspiration. I turn reluctantly from him to the Empire he governed.

Gibbon says, in his immortal History, "If a man were called to fix the period in the history of the world during which the condition of the human race was most happy and prosperous, he would, without hesitation, name that which elapsed from the death of Domitian to the accession of Commodus."

This is the view that Gibbon takes of the prosperity of the old Roman world under such princes as the Antonines. Niebuhr, however, a greater critic, though not so great an artist, takes a different view; and both are great authorities. If Gibbon meant simply that this period was the happiest and most prosperous during the imperial reigns, he may not have been far from the truth, according to his standpoint of what human happiness consists in, – that external prosperity which was the blessing of the Old Testament, and which Macaulay exalts as proudly as Gibbon before him. There *was* this external prosperity, so far as we know, and we know but little aside from monuments and medals. Even Tacitus shrank from writing contemporaneous history, and the period he could have painted is to us dark, mysterious, and unknown. Still, it is generally supposed and conceded that the Empire at this time was outwardly splendid and prosperous. Certainly there was a period of peace, when no wars troubled the State but those which were distant, – on the very confines of the Empire, and that with rude barbarians, no more formidable in the eyes of the luxurious citizens of the capital than a revolt of the Sepoys to the eyes of the citizens of London, or Indian raids among the Rocky Mountains to the eyes of the people of New York. And there was the reign of law and order, a most grateful thing to those who had read of the conspiracy of Catiline and the tumults of Clodius, two hundred and fifty years before. And there was doubtless a magnificent material civilization which promised to be eternal, and of which every Roman was proud. There was a centralization of power in the Eternal City such as had never been seen before and has never been seen since, – a solid Empire so large that the Mediterranean, which it enclosed, was a mere central lake, around the vast circuit of whose shores were temples and palaces and villas of unspeakable beauty, and where a busy population pursued unmolested its various trades. There was commerce on every river which empties itself into this vast basin; there were manufactures in every town, and there were agricultural skill and abundance in every province. The plains of Egypt and Mesopotamia rejoiced in the richest harvests of wheat; the hills of Syria and Gaul, and Spain and Italy, were covered with grape-vines and olives. Italy boasted of fifty kinds of wine, and Gaul produced the same vegetables that are known at the present day. All kinds of fruit were plenty and luscious in every province. There were game-preserves and fish-ponds and groves. There were magnificent roads between all the great cities, – an uninterrupted highway, mostly paved, from York to Jerusalem. The productions of the East were consumed in the West, for ships whitened the sea, bearing their precious gems, and ivory, and spices, and perfumes, and silken fabrics, and carpets, and costly vessels of gold and silver, and variegated marbles; and all the provinces of an empire which extended fifteen hundred miles from north to south and three thousand from east to west were dotted with cities, some of which almost rivalled the imperial capital in size and magnificence. The little island of Rhodes contained twenty-three thousand statues, and Antioch had a street four miles in length, with double colonnades throughout its whole extent. The temple of Ephesus covered as much ground as does the cathedral of Cologne, and the library of Alexandria numbered seven hundred thousand volumes. Rome, the proud metropolis, had a diameter of eleven miles, and was forty-five miles in circuit, with a population, according to Lipsius, larger than modern London. It had seventeen thousand palaces, thirty theatres, nine thousand baths, and eleven amphitheatres, – one of which could seat eighty-seven thousand spectators. The gilding of the roof of the capitol cost fifteen millions of our money. The palace of Nero was more extensive than Versailles. The mausoleum of Hadrian became the most formidable fortress of Mediaeval times. And then, what gold and silver vessels ornamented every palace, what pictures and statues enriched every room, what costly and gilded and carved furniture was the admiration of every guest, what rich dresses decorated the women who supped at gorgeous tables of solid silver, whose very sandals were ornamented with precious stones, and whose necks were hung with priceless pearls and rubies and diamonds! Paulina wore a pearl which, it is said, cost two hundred and fifty thousand dollars of our money. All the masterpieces of antiquity were collected in this centre of luxury and pride, – all those arts which made Greece immortal, and which we can only copy. What vast structures, ornamented with pillars and marble statues, were crowded together near the Forum and Capitoline Hill! The museums of Italy contain to-day twenty thousand specimens of ancient sculpture, which no modern artist could improve. More than a million of dollars were paid for a single picture for the imperial bed-chamber, – for painting was carried to as great perfection as sculpture.

Such were the arts of the Pagan city, such the material civilization in all the cities; and these cities were guarded by soldiers who were trained to the utmost perfection of military discipline, and presided over by governors as elegant, as polished, and as intelligent as the courtiers of Louis XIV. The genius for war was only equaled by genius for government. How well administered were all the provinces! The Romans spread their laws, their language, and their institutions everywhere without serious opposition. They were great civilizers, as the English have been. "Law" became as great an idea as "glory;" and so perfect was the mechanism of government that the happiness of the people was scarcely affected by the character of the emperors. Jurisprudence, the indigenous science of the Romans, is still studied and adopted for its political wisdom.

Such was the civilization of the Roman world in the time of Marcus Aurelius, – that external grandeur, that outward prosperity, to which Gibbon points with such admiration and pride, and to which he ascribed the highest happiness which the world has ever enjoyed. Far different, probably, would have been the verdict of the good and contemplative emperor who then ruled the civilized world, when he saw the luxury, the pride, the sensuality, the selfishness, the irreligion, the worldliness, which marked all classes; producing vices too horrible to be even named, and undermining the moral health, and secretly and surely preparing the way for approaching violence and ruin.

What, then, is the reverse of the picture which Gibbon admired? What established facts have we as an offset to these gilded material glories? What should be the true judgment of mankind as to this lauded period?

The historian speaks of peace, and the prosperity which naturally flowed from it in the uninterrupted pursuit of the ordinary occupations of life. This is indisputable. There was the increase of wealth, the enjoyment of security, the absence of fears, and the reign of law. Life and property were guarded. A man could travel from one part of the Empire to the other without fear of robbers or assassins. All these things are great blessings. Materially we have no higher civilization. But with peace and prosperity were idleness, luxury, gambling, dissipation, extravagance, and looseness of morals of which we have no conception, and which no subsequent age of the world has seen. It was the age of most scandalous monopolies, and disproportionate fortunes, and abandonment to the pleasures of sense. Any Roman governor could make a fortune in a year; and his fortune was spent in banquets and fêtes and races and costly wines, and enormous retinues of slaves. The theatres, the chariot races, the gladiatorial shows, the circus, and the sports of the amphitheatre were then at their height. The central spring of society was money, since it purchased everything which Epicureanism valued. No dignitary was respected for his office, – only for the salary or gains which his office brought. All professions which were not lucrative gradually fell into disrepute; and provided they were lucrative, it was of no consequence whether or not they were infamous. Dancers, cooks, and play-actors received the highest consideration, since their earnings were large. Scholars, poets, and philosophers – what few there were – pined in attics. Epictetus lived in a miserable cottage with only a straw pallet and a single lamp. Women had no education, and were disgracefully profligate; even the wife of Marcus Aurelius (the daughter of Antoninus Pius) was one of the most abandoned women of the age, notwithstanding all the influence of their teachings and example. Slavery was so great an institution that half of the population were slaves. There were sixty millions of them in the Empire, and they were generally treated with brutal cruelty. The master of Epictetus, himself a scholar and philosopher, broke wantonly the leg of his illustrious slave to see how well he could bear pain. There were no public charities. The poor and miserable and sick were left to perish unheeded and unrelieved. Even the free citizens were fed at the public expense, not as a charity, but to prevent revolts. About two thousand people owned the whole civilized world, and their fortunes were spent in demoralizing it. What if their palaces were grand, and their villas beautiful, and their dresses magnificent, and their furniture costly, if their lives were spent in ignoble and enervating pleasures, as is generally admitted. There was a low religious life, almost no religion at all, and what there was degrading by its superstition. Everywhere were seen the rites of magical incantations, the pretended virtue of amulets and charms, soothsayers laughing at their own predictions, – nowhere the worship of the *one God* who created the heaven and the earth, nor even a genuine worship of the Pagan deities, but a general spirit of cynicism and atheism. What does St. Paul say of the Romans when he was a prisoner in the precincts of the imperial palace, and at a time of no greater demoralization? We talk of the glories of jurisprudence; but what was the practical operation of laws when such a harmless man as Paul could be brought to trial, and perhaps execution! What shall we say of the boasted justice, when judgments were rendered on technical points, and generally in favor of those who had the longest purses; so that it was not only expensive to go to law, but so expensive that it was ruinous? What could be hoped of laws, however good, when they were made the channels of extortion, when the occupation of the Bench itself was the great instrument by which powerful men protected their monopolies? We speak of the glories of art; but art was prostituted to please the lower tastes and inflame the passions. The most costly pictures were hung up in the baths, and were disgracefully indecent. Even literature was directed to the flattery of tyrants and rich men. There was no manly protest from literary men against the increasing vices of society, – not even from the philosophers. Philosophy continually declined, like literature and art. Nothing strikes us more forcibly than the absence of genius in the second century. There was no reward for genius except when it flattered and pandered to what was demoralizing. Who dared to utter manly protests in the Senate? Who discussed the principles of government? Who would venture to utter anything displeasing to the imperial masters of the world? In this age of boundless prosperity, where were the great poets, where the historians, where the writers on political economy, where the moralists? For one hundred years there were scarcely ten eminent men in any department of literature whose writings have come down to us. There was the most marked decay in all branches of knowledge, except in that knowledge which could be utilized for making money. The imperial régime cast a dismal shadow over all the efforts of independent genius, on all lofty aspirations, on all individual freedom. Architects, painters, and sculptors there were in abundance, and they were employed and well paid; but where were poets, scholars, sages? – where were politicians even? The great and honored men were the tools of emperors, –

the prefects of their guards, the generals of their armies, the architects of their palaces, the purveyors of their banquets. If the emperor happened to be a good administrator of this complicated despotism, he was sustained, like Tiberius, whatever his character. If he was weak or frivolous, he was removed by assassination. It was a government of absolute physical forces, and it is most marvelous that such a man as Marcus Aurelius could have been its representative. And what could he have done with his philosophical inquiries had he not also been a great general and a practical administrator, – a man of business as well as a man of thought?

But I cannot enumerate the evils which coexisted with all the boasted prosperity of the Empire, and which were preparing the way for ruin, – evils so disgraceful and universal that Christianity made no impression at all on society at large, and did not modify a law or remove a single object of scandal. Do you call that state of society prosperous and happy when half of the population was in base bondage to cruel masters; when women generally were degraded and slighted; when money was the object of universal idolatry; when the only pleasures were in banquets and races and other demoralizing sports; when no value was placed upon the soul, and infinite value on the body; when there was no charity, no compassion, no tenderness; when no poor man could go to law; when no genius was encouraged unless for utilitarian ends; when genius was not even appreciated or understood, still less rewarded; when no man dared to lift up his voice against any crying evil, especially of a political character; when the whole civilized world was fettered, deceived, and mocked, and made to contribute to the power, pleasure, and pride of a single man and the minions upon whom he smiled? Is all this to be overlooked in our estimate of human happiness? Is there nothing to be considered but external glories which appeal to the senses alone? Shall our eyes be diverted from the operation of moral law and the inevitable consequences of its violation? Shall we blind ourselves to the future condition of our families and our country in our estimate of happiness? Shall we ignore, in the dazzling life of a few favored extortioners, monopolists, and successful gamblers all that Christianity points out as the hope and solace and glory of mankind? Not thus would we estimate human felicity. Not thus would Marcus Aurelius, as he cast his sad and prophetic eye down the vistas of succeeding reigns, and saw the future miseries and wars and violence which were the natural result of egotism and vice, have given his austere judgment on the happiness of his Empire. In all his sweetness and serenity, he penetrated the veil which the eye of the worldly Gibbon could not pierce. *He* declares that "those things which are most valued are empty, rotten, and trifling," – these are his very words; and that the real *life* of the people, even in the days of Trajan, had ceased to exist, – that everything truly precious was lost in the senseless grasp after what can give no true happiness or permanent prosperity.

AUTHORITIES

Aurelius, Marcus, "Meditations."

Farrar, *Seekers after God*

Lord, *Old Roman World*

Montesquieu, *Considerations on the Causes of the Greatness of the Romans and their Decline*

Renan, *Life of Marcus Aurelius*

Sismondi, *Fall of the Roman Empire*

Smith, *Dictionary*

Tillemont, *History of the Emperors*

Chapter 4

CONSTANTINE THE GREAT: CHRISTIANITY ENTHRONED

A.D. 272-337

One of the links in the history of civilization is the reign of Constantine, not unworthily called the Great, since it would be difficult to find a greater than he among the Roman emperors, after Julius Caesar, while his labors were by far more beneficent. A new era began with his illustrious reign, – the triumph of Christianity as the established religion of the crumbling Empire. Under his enlightened protection the Church, persecuted from the time of Nero, and never fashionable or popular, or even powerful as an institution, arose triumphant, defiant, almost militant, with new passions and interests; ambitious, full of enthusiasm, and with unbounded hope, – a great spiritual power, whose authority even princes and nobles were at last unable to withstand. No longer did the Christians live in catacombs and hiding-places; no longer did they sing their mournful songs over the bleeding and burning bodies of the saints, but arose in the majesty of a new and irresistible power, – temporal as well as spiritual, – breathing vengeance on ancient foes, grasping great dignities, seizing the revenues of princes, and proclaiming the sovereignty of their invisible King. In defence of their own doctrines they became fierce, arrogant, dogmatic, contentious, – not with sword in one hand and crucifix in the other, like the warlike popes and bishops of mediaeval Europe, but with intense theological hatreds, and austere contempt of those luxuries and pleasures which had demoralized society.

The last great act of Diocletian – one of the ablest and most warlike of the emperors – was an unrelenting and desperate persecution of the Christians, whose religion had been steadily gaining ground for two centuries, in spite of martyrdoms and anathemas; and this was so severe and universal that it seemed to be successful. But he had no sooner retired from the government of the world (A.D. 305) than the faith he supposed he had suppressed forever sprung up with new force, and defied any future attempt to crush it.

Figure 7. Persecution of Christians in the Roman Arena. *After the painting by G. Mantegazza.*

The vitality of the new religion had been preserved in ages of unparalleled vices by two things especially, – by martyrdom and by austerities; the one a noble attestation of faith in an age of unbelief, and the other a lofty, almost stoical, disdain of those pleasures which centre in the body.

The martyrs cheerfully and heroically endured physical sufferings in view of the glorious crown of which they were assured in the future world. They lived in the firm conviction of immortality, and that eternal happiness was connected indissolubly with their courage, intrepidity, and patience in bearing testimony to the divine character and mission of Him who had shed his blood for the remission of sins. No sufferings were of any account in comparison with those of Him who died for them. Filled with transports of love for the divine Redeemer, who rescued them from the despair of Paganism, and bound with ties of supreme allegiance to Him as the Conqueror and Saviour of the world, they were ready to meet death in any form for his sake. They had become, by professing Him as their Lord and Sovereign, soldiers of the Cross, ready to endure any sacrifices for his sacred cause.

Thus enthusiasm was kindled in a despairing and unbelieving world. And probably the world never saw, in any age, such devotion and zeal for an invisible power. It was animated by the hope of a glorious immortality, of which Christianity alone, of all ancient religions, inspired a firm conviction. In this future existence were victory and blessedness everlasting, – not to be had unless one was faithful unto death. This sublime faith – this glorious assurance of future happiness, this devotion to an unseen King – made a strong impression on those who witnessed the physical torments which the sufferers bore with unspeakable triumph. There must be, they thought, something in a religion which could take away the sting of death and rob the grave of its victory. The noble attestation of faith in Jesus did perhaps more than any theological teachings towards the conversion of men to Christianity. And persecution and isolation bound the Christians together in bonds of love and harmony, and kept them from the temptations of life There was a sort of moral Freemasonry among the despised and neglected followers of Christ, such as has not been seen before or since. They were *in* the world but not *of* the world. They were the precious salt to preserve what was worth preserving in a rapidly dissolving Empire. They formed a new power, which would be triumphant amid the universal destruction of old institutions; for the soul would be saved, and Christianity taught that the soul was everything, – that nothing could be given in exchange for it.

The other influence which seemed to preserve the early Christians from the overwhelming materialism of the times was the asceticism which so early became prevalent. It had not been taught by Jesus, but seemed to arise from the necessities of the times. It was a fierce protest against the luxuries of an enervated age. The passion for dress and ornament, and the indulgence of the appetites and other pleasures which pampered the body, and which were universal, were a hindrance to the enjoyment of that spiritual life which Christianity unfolded. As the soul was immortal and the body was mortal, that which was an impediment to the welfare of what was most precious was early denounced. In order to preserve the soul from the pollution of material pleasures, a strenuous protest was made. Hence that defiance of the pleasures of sense which gave loftiness and independence of character soon became a recognized and cardinal virtue. The Christian stood aloof from the banquets and luxuries which undermined the virtues on which the strength of man is based. The characteristic vices of the Pagan world were unchastity and fondness for the pleasures of the table. To these were added the lesser vices of display and ornaments in dress. From these the Christian fled as fatal enemies to his spiritual elevation. I do not believe it was the ascetic ideas imported from India, such as marked the Brahmins, nor the visionary ideas of the Sufis and the Buddhists, and of other Oriental religionists, which gave the impulse to monastic life and led to the austerities of the Church in the second and third centuries, so much as the practical evils with which everyone was conversant, and which were plainly antagonistic to the doctrine that the life is more than meat. The triumph of the mind over the body excited an admiration scarcely less marked than the voluntary sacrifice of life to a sacred cause. Asceticism, repulsive in many of its aspects, and even unnatural and inhuman, drew a cordon around the Christians, and separated them from the sensualities of ordinary life. It was a reproof as well as a protest. It attacked Epicureanism in its most vulnerable point. "How hardly shall they who have riches enter into the kingdom of God?" Hence the voluntary poverty, the giving away of inherited wealth to the poor, the extreme simplicity of living, and even retirement from the habitations of men, which marked the more earnest of the new believers. Hence celibacy, and avoidance of the society of women, – all to resist most dangerous temptation. Hence the vows of poverty and chastity which early entered monastic life, – a life favorable to ascetic virtues. These were indeed perverted. Everything good is perverted in this world. Self-expiations, flagellations, sheepskin cloaks, root dinners, repulsive austerities, followed. But these grew out of the noble desire to keep unspotted from the world. And unless this desire had been encouraged by the leaders of the Church, the Christian would soon have been contaminated with the vices of Paganism, especially such as were fashionable, – as is deplorably the case in our modern times, when it is so difficult to draw the line between those who do not and those who do openly profess the Christian faith. It is quite probable that Christianity would not have triumphed over Paganism, had not Christianity made so strong a protest against those vices and fashions which were peculiar to an Epicurean age and an Epicurean philosophy.

It was at this period, when Christianity was a great spiritual power, that Constantine arose. He was born at Naissus, in Dacia, A.D. 274, his father being a soldier of fortune, and his mother the daughter of an innkeeper. He was eighteen when his father, Constantius, was promoted by the Emperor Diocletian to the dignity of Caesar, – a sort of lieutenant-emperor, – and early distinguished himself in the Egyptian and Persian wars. He was thirty-one when he joined his father in Britain, whom he succeeded, soon after, in the imperial dignity. Like Theodosius, he was tall, and majestic in manners; gracious, affable, and accessible, like Julius; prudent, cautious, reticent, like Fabius; insensible to the allurements of pleasure, and incredibly active and bold, like Hannibal, Charlemagne, and Napoleon; a politic man, disposed to ally himself with the rising party. The first few years of his reign, which began in A.D. 306, were devoted to the establishment of his power in Britain, where the flower of the Western army was concentrated, – foreseeing a desperate contest with the five rivals who shared between them the Empire which Diocletian had divided; which division, though possibly a necessity in those turbulent times, would yet seem to have been an unwise thing, since it led to civil wars and rivalries, and struggles for supremacy. It is a mistake to divide a great empire, unless mechanism is worn out, and a central power is impossible. The tendency of modern civilization is to a union of States, when their language and interests and institutions are identical. Yet Diocletian was wearied and oppressed by the burdens of State, and retired disgusted, dividing the Empire into two parts, the Eastern and Western. But there were subdivisions in consequence, and civil wars; and had the policy of Diocletian been continued, the Empire might have been subdivided, like Charlemagne's, until central power would have been destroyed, as in the Middle Ages. But Constantine aimed at a general union of the East and West once again, partly from the desire of centralization, and partly from ambition. The military career of Constantine for about seventeen years was directed to the establishment of his power in Britain, to the reunion of the Empire, and the subjugation of his colleagues, – a long series of disastrous civil wars. These wars are without poetic interest, – in this respect unlike the wars between Caesar and Pompey, and that between Octavius and Antony. The wars of Caesar inaugurated the imperial régime when the Empire was young and in full vigor, and when military discipline was carried to perfection; those of Constantine were in the latter days of the Empire, when it was impossible to reanimate it, and all things were tending rapidly to dissolution, – an exceedingly gloomy period, when there were neither statesmen nor philosophers nor poets nor men of genius, of historic fame, outside the Church. Therefore I shall not dwell on these uninteresting wars, brought about by the ambition of six different emperors, all of whom were aiming for undivided sovereignty. There were in the West Maximian, the old colleague of Diocletian, who had resigned with him, but who had reassumed the purple; his son, Maxentius, elevated by the Roman Senate and the Praetorian Guard, – a dissolute and imbecile young man, who reigned over Italy; and Constantine, who possessed Gaul and Britain. In the East were Galerius, who had married the daughter of Diocletian, and who was a general of considerable ability; Licinius, who had the province of Illyricum; and Maximin, who reigned over Syria and Egypt.

The first of these emperors who was disposed of was Maximian, the father of Maxentius and father-in-law of Constantine. He was regarded as a usurper, and on the capture of Marseilles, he under pressure of Constantine committed suicide by strangulation, A.D. 310. Galerius did not long survive, being afflicted with a loathsome disease, the result of intemperance and gluttony, and died in his palace in Nicomedia, in Bithynia, the capital of the Eastern provinces. The next emperor who fell was Maxentius, after a desperate struggle in Italy with Constantine, – whose passage over the Alps, and successive victories at Susa (at the foot of Mont Cenis, on the plains of Turin), at Verona, and Saxa Rubra, nine miles from Rome, from which Maxentius fled, only to perish in the Tiber, remind us of the campaigns of Hannibal and Napoleon. The triumphal arch which the victor erected at Rome to commemorate his victories still remains as a monument of the decline of Art in the fourth century. As a result of the conquest over Maxentius, the Praetorian guards were finally abolished, which gave a fatal blow to the Senate, and left the capital disarmed and exposed to future insults and dangers.

The next emperor who disappeared from the field was Maximin, who had embarked in a civil war with Licinius. He died at Tarsus, after an unsuccessful contest, A.D. 313; and there were left only Licinius and Constantine, – the former of whom reigned in the East and the latter in the West. Scarcely a year elapsed before these two emperors embarked in a bloody contest for the sovereignty of the world. Licinius was beaten, but was allowed the possession of Thrace, Asia Minor, Syria, and Egypt. A hollow reconciliation was made between them, which lasted eight years, during which Constantine was engaged in the defence of his empire from the hostile attacks of the Goths in Illyricum. He gained great victories over these barbarians, and chased them beyond the Danube. He then turned against Licinius, and the bloody battle of Adrianople, A.D. 323, when three hundred thousand combatants were engaged, followed by a still more bloody one on the heights of Chrysopolis, A.D. 324, made Constantine supreme master of the Empire thirty-seven years after Diocletian had divided his power with Maximian.

The great events of his reign as sole emperor, with enormous prestige as a general, second only to that of Julius Caesar, were the foundation of Constantinople and the establishment of Christianity as the religion of the Empire.

The ancient Byzantium, which Constantine selected as the new capital of his Empire, had been no inconsiderable city for nearly one thousand years, being founded only ninety-seven years after Rome itself. Yet, notwithstanding its magnificent site, – equally favorable for commerce and dominion, – its advantages were not appreciated until the genius of Constantine selected it as the one place in his vast dominions which combined a central position and capacities for defence against invaders. It was also a healthy locality, being exposed to no malarial poisons, like the "Eternal City." It was delightfully situated, on the confines of Europe and Asia, between the Euxine and the Mediterranean, on a narrow peninsula washed by the Sea of Marmora and the beautiful harbor called the Golden Horn, inaccessible from Asia except by water, while it could be made impregnable on the west. The narrow waters of the Hellespont and the Bosporus, the natural gates of the city, could be easily defended against hostile fleets both from the Euxine and the Mediterranean, leaving the Propontis (the deep, well-harbored body of water lying between the two straits, in modern times called the Sea of Marmora) with an inexhaustible supply of fish, and its shores lined with vineyards and gardens. Doubtless this city is more favored by nature for commerce, for safety, and for dominion, than any other spot on the face of the earth; and we cannot wonder that Russia should cast greedy eyes upon it as one of the centres of its rapidly increasing Empire. This beautiful site soon rivalled the old capital of the Empire in riches and population, for Constantine promised great privileges to those who would settle in it; and he ransacked and despoiled the cities of Italy, Greece, and Asia Minor of what was most precious in Art to make his new capital attractive, and to ornament his new palaces, churches, and theatres. In this Grecian city he surrounded himself with Asiatic pomp and ceremonies. He assumed the titles of Eastern monarchs. His palace was served and guarded with a legion of functionaries that made access to his person difficult. He created a new nobility, and made infinite gradations of rank, perpetuated by the feudal monarchs of Europe. He gave pompous names to his officers, both civil and military, using expressions still in vogue in European courts, like "Your Excellency," "Your Highness," and "Your Majesty," – names which the emperors who had reigned at Rome had uniformly disdained. He cut himself loose from all the traditions of the past, especially all relics of republicanism. He divided the civil government of the Empire into thirteen great dioceses, and these he subdivided into one hundred and sixteen provinces. He separated the civil from the military functions of governors. He installed eunuchs in his palace, to wait upon his person and perform menial offices. He made his chamberlain one of the highest officers of State. He guarded his person by bodies of cavalry and infantry. He clothed himself in imposing robes; elaborately arranged his hair; wore a costly diadem; ornamented his person with gems and pearls, with collars and bracelets. He lived, in short, more like a Heliogabalus than a Trajan or an Aurelian. All traces of popular liberty were effaced. All dignities and honors and offices emanated from him. The Caesars had been absolute monarchs, but disguised their power. Constantine made an ostentatious display of his. Moreover he increased the burden of taxation throughout the Empire. The last fourteen years of his reign was a period of apparent prosperity, but the internal strength of the Empire and the character of the emperor sadly degenerated. He became effeminate, and committed crimes which sullied his fame. He executed his oldest son on mere suspicion of crime, and on a charge of infidelity even put to death the wife with whom he had lived for twenty years, and who was the mother of future emperors.

But if he had great faults he had also great virtues. No emperor since Augustus had a more enlightened mind, and no one ever reigned at Rome who, in one important respect, did so much for the cause of civilization. Constantine is most lauded as the friend and promoter of Christianity. It is by his service to the Church that he has won the name of the first Christian emperor. His efforts in behalf of the Church throw into the shade all the glory he won as a general and as a statesman. The real interest of his reign centres in his Christian legislation, and in those theological controversies in which he interfered. With Constantine began the enthronement of Christianity, and for one thousand years what is most vital in European history is connected with Christian institutions and doctrines.

It was when he was marching against Maxentius that his conversion to Christianity took place, A.D. 312, when he was thirty-eight, in the sixth year of his reign. Up to this period he was a zealous Pagan, and made magnificent offerings to the gods of his ancestors, and erected splendid temples, especially in honor of Apollo. The turn of his mind was religious, or, as we are taught by modern science to say, superstitious. He believed in omens, dreams, visions, and supernatural influences.

Now it was in a very critical period of his campaign against his Pagan rival, on the eve of an important battle, as he was approaching Rome for the first time, filled with awe of its greatness and its recollections, that he saw – or fancied he saw – a little after noon, just above the sun which he worshipped, a bright Cross, with this inscription, [Greek: En touto nika] – "In this conquer;" and in the following night, when sleep had overtaken him, he dreamed that Christ appeared to him, and enjoined him to make a banner in the shape of the celestial sign which he had seen. Such is the legend, unhesitatingly received for centuries, yet which modern critics are not disposed to accept as a miracle, although attested by Eusebius, and confirmed by the emperor himself on oath. Whether some supernatural sign really appeared or not, or whether some natural phenomenon appeared in the heavens in the form of an illuminated Cross, it is not worthwhile to discuss. We know this, however, that if the greatest religious revolution of antiquity was worthy to be announced by special signs and wonders, it was when a Roman emperor of extraordinary force of character declared his intention to acknowledge and serve the God of the persecuted Christians. The miracle rests on the authority of a single bishop, as sacredly attested by the emperor, in whom he saw no fault; but the fact of the conversion remains as one of the most signal triumphs of Christianity, and the conversion itself was the most noted and important in its results since that of Saul of Tarsus. It may have been from conviction, and it may have been from policy. It may have been merely that he saw, in the vigorous vitality of the Christian principle of devotion to a single Person, a healthier force for the unification of his great empire than in the disintegrating vices of Paganism. But, whatever his motive, his action stirred up the enthusiasm of a body of men which gave the victory of the Milvian Bridge. All that was vital in the Empire was found among the Christians, – already a powerful and rising party, that persecution could not put down. Constantine became the head and leader of this party, whose watchword ever since has been "Conquer," until all powers and principalities and institutions are brought under the influence of the gospel. So far as we know, no one has ever doubted the sincerity of Constantine. Whatever were his faults, especially that of gluttony, which he was never able to overcome, he was ever afterwards strict and fervent in his devotions. He employed his evenings in the study of the Scriptures, as Marcus Aurelius meditated on the verities of a spiritual life after the fatigues and dangers of the day. He was not so good a man as was the pious Antoninus, who would, had *he* been converted to Christianity, have given to it a purer and loftier legislation. It may be doubted whether Aurelius would have made popes of bishops, or would have invested metaphysical distinctions in theology with so great an authority. But the magnificent patronage which Constantine gave to the clergy was followed by greater and more enlightened sovereigns than he, – by Theodosius, by Charlemagne, and by Alfred; while the dogmas which were defended by Athanasius with such transcendent ability at the council where the emperor presided in person, formed an anchor to the faith in the long and dreary period when barbarism filled Europe with desolation and fear.

Constantine, as a Roman emperor, exercised the supreme right of legislation, – the highest prerogative of men in power. So that his acts as legislator naturally claim our first notice. His edicts were laws which could not be gainsaid or resisted. They were like the laws of the Medes and Persians, except that they could be repealed or modified.

One of the first things he did after his conversion was to issue an edict of toleration, which secured the Christians from any further persecution, – an act of immeasurable benefit to humanity, yet what any man would naturally have done in his circumstances. If he could have inaugurated the reign of toleration for all religious opinions, he would have been a still greater benefactor. But it was something to free a persecuted body of believers who had been obliged to hide or suffer for two hundred years. By the edict of Milan, A.D. 313, he secured the revenues as well as the privileges of the Church, and restored to the Christians the lands and houses of which they had been stripped by the persecution of Diocletian. Eight years later he allowed persons to bequeath property to Christian institutions and churches. He assigned in every city an allowance of corn in behalf of charities to the poor. He confirmed the clergy in the right of being tried in their own courts and by their peers, when accused of crime, – a great privilege in the fourth century, but a great abuse in the fourteenth. The arbitration of bishops had the force of positive law, and judges were instructed to execute the episcopal decrees. He transferred to the churches the privilege of sanctuary granted to those fleeing from justice in the Mosaic legislation. He ordained that Sunday should be set apart for religious observances in all the towns and cities of the Empire. He abolished crucifixion as a punishment. He prohibited gladiatorial games. He discouraged slavery, infanticide, and easy divorces. He allowed the people to choose their own ministers, nor did he interfere in the election of bishops. He exempted the clergy from all services to the State, from all personal taxes, and all municipal duties. He seems to have stood in awe of bishops, and to have treated them with great veneration and respect, giving to them lands and privileges, enriching their churches with ornaments, and securing to the clergy an ample support. So prosperous was the Church under his beneficence, that the average individual income of the eighteen hundred bishops of the Empire has been estimated by Gibbon at three thousand dollars a year, when money was much more valuable than it is in our times.

In addition to his munificent patronage of the clergy, Constantine was himself deeply interested in all theological affairs and discussions. He convened and presided over the celebrated Council of Nicaea, or Nice, as it is usually called, composed of three hundred and eighteen bishops, and of two thousand and forty-eight ecclesiastics of lesser note, listening to their debates and following their suggestions. The Christian world never saw a more imposing spectacle than this great council, which was convened to settle the creed of the Church. It met in a spacious basilica, where the emperor, arrayed in his purple and silk robes, with a diadem of precious jewels on his head, and a voice of gentleness and softness, and an air of supreme majesty, exhorted the assembled theologians to unity and concord.

The vital question discussed by this magnificent and august assembly was metaphysical as well as religious; yet it was the question of the age, on which everybody talked, in public and in private, and which was deemed of far greater importance than any war or any affair of State. The interest in this subject seems strange to many, in an age when positive science and material interests have so largely crowded out theological discussions. But the doctrine of the Trinity was as vital and important in the eyes of the divines of the fourth century as that of Justification by Faith was to the Germans when they assembled in the great hall of the Electoral palace of Leipsic to hear Luther and Dr. Eck advocate their separate sides.

In the time of Constantine everything pertaining to Christianity and the affairs of the Church became invested with supreme importance. All other subjects and interests were secondary, certainly among the Christians themselves. As redemption is the central point of Christianity, public preaching and teaching had been directed chiefly, at first, to the passion, death, and resurrection of the Saviour of the world. Then came discussions and controversies, naturally, about the person of Christ and his relation to the Godhead. Among the early followers of our Lord there had been no pride of reason and a very simple creed. Least of all did they seek to explain the mysteries of their faith by metaphysical reasoning. Their doctrines were not brought to the test of philosophy. It was enough for these simple and usually unimportant and unlettered people to accept generally accredited facts. It was enough that Christ had suffered and died for them, in his boundless love, and that their souls would be saved in consequence. And as to doctrines, all they sought to know was what our Lord and his apostles said. Hence there was among them no system of theology, as we understand it, beyond the Apostles' Creed. But in the early part of the second century Justin Martyr, a converted philosopher, devoted much labor to a metaphysical development of the doctrine drawn from the expressions of the Apostle John in reference to the Logos, or Word, as identical with the Son.

In the third century the whole Church was agitated by the questions which grew out of the relations between the Father and the Son. From the person of Christ – so dear to the Church – the discussion naturally passed to the Trinity. Then arose the great Alexandrian school of theology, which attempted to explain and harmonize the revealed truths of the Bible by Grecian dialectics. Hence interminable disputes among divines and scholars, as to whether the Father and the Logos were one; whether the Son was created or uncreated; whether or not he was subordinate to the Father;

whether the Father, Son, and Holy Ghost were distinct, or one in essence. Origen, Clement, and Dionysius were the most famous of the doctors who discussed these points. All classes of Christians were soon attracted by them. They formed the favorite subjects of conversation, as well as of public teaching. Zeal in discussion created acrimony and partisan animosity. Things were lost sight of, and words alone prevailed. Sects and parties arose. The sublime efforts of such men as Justin and Clement to soar to a knowledge of God were perverted to vain disputations in reference to the relations between the three persons of the Godhead.

Alexandria was the centre of these theological agitations, being then, perhaps, the most intellectual city in the Empire. It was filled with Greek philosophers and scholars and artists, and had the largest library in the world. It had the most famous school of theology, the learned and acute professors of which claimed to make theology a science. Philosophy became wedded to theology, and brought the aid of reason to explain the subjects of faith.

Among the noted theologians of this Christian capital was a presbyter who preached in the principal church. His name was Arius, and he was the most popular preacher of the city. He was a tall, spare man, handsome, eloquent, with a musical voice and earnest manner. He was the idol of fashionable women and cultivated men. He was also a poet, like Abélard, and popularized his speculations on the Trinity. He was as reproachless in morals as Dr. Channing or Theodore Parker; ascetic in habits and dress; bold, acute, and plausible; but he shocked the orthodox party by such sayings as these: "God was not always Father; once he was not Father; afterwards he became Father." He affirmed, in substance, that the Son was created by the Father, and hence was inferior in power and dignity. He did not deny the Trinity, any more than Abélard did in after times; but his doctrines, pushed out to their logical sequence, were a virtual denial of the divinity of Christ. If he were created, he was a creature, and, of course, not God. A created being cannot be the Supreme Creator. He may be commissioned as a divine and inspired teacher, but he cannot be God himself. Now his bishop, Alexander, maintained that the Son (Logos, or Word) is eternally of the same essence as the Father, uncreated, and therefore equal with the Father. Seeing the foundation of the faith, as generally accepted, undermined, he caused

Arius to be deposed by a synod of bishops. But the daring presbyter was not silenced, and obtained powerful and numerous adherents. Men of influence – like Eusebius the historian – tried to compromise the difficulties for the sake of unity; and some looked on the discussion as a war of words, which did not affect salvation. In time the bitterness of the dispute became a scandal. It was deemed disgraceful for Christians to persecute each other for dogmas which could not be settled except by authority, and in the discussion of which metaphysics so strongly entered. Alexander thought otherwise. He regarded the speculations of Arius as heretical, as derogating from the supreme allegiance which was due to Christ. He thought that the very foundations of Christianity were being undermined.

No one was more disturbed by these theological controversies than the Emperor himself. He was a soldier, and not a metaphysician; and, as Emperor, he was Pontifex Maximus, – head of the Church. He hated these contentions between good and learned men. He felt that they compromised the interests of the Church universal, of which he was the protector. Therefore he despatched Hosius, Bishop of Cordova, in Spain, – in whom he had great confidence, who was in fact his ecclesiastical adviser, – to both Alexander and Arius, to bring about a reconciliation. As well reconcile Luther with Dr. Eck, or Pascal with the Jesuits! The divisions widened. The party animosities increased. The Church was rent in twain. Metaphysical divinity destroyed Christian union and charity. So Constantine summoned the first general council in Church history to settle the disputed points, and restore harmony and unity. It convened at Nicaea, or Nice, in Asia Minor, not far from Constantinople.

Arius, as the author of all the troubles, was of course present at the council. As a presbyter he could speak, but not vote. He was sixty years of age, and in the height of his power and fame, and he was able in debate.

But there was one man in the assembly on whom all eyes were soon riveted as the greatest theologian and logician that had arisen in the Church since the apostolic age. He was archdeacon to the bishop of Alexandria, – a lean, attenuated man, small in stature, with fiery eye, haughty air, and impetuous eloquence. His name was Athanasius, – neither Greek nor Roman, but a Coptic African. He was bitterly opposed to Arius and his

doctrines. No one could withstand his fervor and his logic. He was like
Bernard at the council of Soissons. He was not a cold, dry, unimpassioned
impersonation of mere intellect, like Thomas Aquinas or Calvin, but more
like St. Augustine, – another African, warm, religious, profound, with
human passions, but lofty soul. He also had that intellectual pride and
dogmatism which afterward marked Bossuet. For two months he appealed
to the assembly, and presented the consequences of the new heresy. With his
slight figure, his commanding intellectual force, his conservative tendencies,
his clearness of statement, his logical exactness and fascinating
persuasiveness, he was to churchmen what Alexander Hamilton was to
statesmen. He gave a constitution to the Church, and became a theological
authority scarcely less than Augustine in the next generation, or Lainez at
the Council of Trent.

And the result of the deliberations of that famous council led by
Athanasius, – although both Hosius and Eusebius of Caesarea had more
prelatic authority and dignity than he, – was the Nicene Creed. Who can
estimate the influence of those formulated doctrines? They have been
accepted for fifteen hundred years as the standard of the orthodox faith, in
both Catholic and Protestant churches, – not universally accepted, for
Arianism still has its advocates, under new names, and probably will have
so long as the received doctrines of Christianity are subjected to the test of
reason. Outward unity was, however, restored to the Church, both by prelatic
and imperial authority, although learned and intellectual men continued to
speculate and to doubt. The human mind cannot be chained. But it was a
great thing to establish a creed which the Christian world could accept in the
rude and ignorant ages which succeeded the destruction of the old
civilization. That creed was the anchor of religious faith in the Middle Ages.
It is still retained in the liturgies of Christendom.

It is not my province to criticise the Nicene Creed, which is virtually the
old Apostles' Creed, with the addition of the Trinity, as defined by
Athanasius. The subject is too complicated and metaphysical. It is allied with
questions concerning which men have always differed and ever will differ.
Although the Alexandrian divines invoked the aid of reason, it is a matter
which reason cannot settle. It is a matter to be received, if received at all, as

a mystery which is insoluble. It belongs to the realm of faith and authority. And the realms of faith and reason are eternally distinct. As metaphysics cannot solve material phenomena, so reason cannot explain subjects which do not appeal to consciousness. Bacon was a great benefactor when he separated the world of physical Nature from the world of Mind; and Pascal was equally a profound philosopher when he showed that faith could not take cognizance of science, nor science of faith. The blending of distinct realms has ever been attended with scepticism. "Canst thou by searching find out God?" What He has revealed for our acceptance should not be confounded with truths to be settled by inquiry. It is a legitimate yet underrated department of Christian inquiry to establish the authenticity and meaning of texts of Scripture from which deductions are made. If the premises are wrong, confusion and error are the result. We must be sure of the premises on which theological dogmas are based. If as much time and genius and learning had been expended in unravelling the meaning of Scripture declarations as have been spent in theological deductions and metaphysical distinctions, we should have had a more universally accepted faith. Happily, in our day, the aspirations and ambitions of exact scholarship are more and more directed to the elucidation of the sacred Scriptures of Christianity. Exegesis and philosophy alike appeal to the intellect; but the one can be so aided by learning that the truth can be reached, while the other pushes the inquirer into an unfathomable sea of difficulties. All moral truths are so bounded and involved with other moral truths that they seem to qualify the meaning of each other. Almost any assumed truth in religion, when pushed to its utmost logical sequence, appears to involve absurdities. The "divine justice" of theologians ends, by severe logical sequences, in apparent injustice, and "divine mercy" in the sweeping away of all retribution.

It may not unreasonably be asked, has not theology attempted too much? Has it solved the truths for the solution of which it borrowed the aid of reason, and has it not often made a religion which is based on deductions and metaphysical distinctions as imperative as a religion based on simple declarations? Has it not appealed to the head, when it should have appealed to the heart and conscience; and thus has not religion often been cold and dry and polemical, when it should have been warm, fervent, and simple? Such seem to have been some of the effects of the Trinitarian controversy between Athanasius and Arius, and their respective followers even to our own times. A belief in the unity of God, as distinguished from polytheism, has been made no more imperative than a belief in the supposed relations between the Father and the Son. The real mission of Christ, to save souls, with all the glorious peace which salvation procures, has often been lost sight of in the covenant supposed to have been made between the Father and the Son. Nothing could exceed the acrimony of the Nicene Fathers in their opposition to those who could not accept their deductions. And the more subtile the distinctions the more violent were the disputes; until at last religious persecution marked the conduct of Christians towards each other, – as fierce almost as the persecutions they had suffered from the Pagans. And so furious was the strife between those theological disputants, estimable in other respects as were their characters, that even the Emperor Constantine at last lost all patience and banished Athanasius himself to a Gaulish city, after he had promoted him to the great See of Alexandria as a reward for his services to the Church at the Council of Nice. To Constantine the great episcopal theologian was simply "turbulent," "haughty," "intractable."

With the establishment of the doctrine of the Trinity by the Council of Nice, the interest in the reign of Constantine ceases, although he lived twelve years after it. His great work as a Christian emperor was to unite the Church with the State. He did not elevate the Church above the State; that was the work of the Mediaeval Popes. But he gave external dignity to the clergy, of whom he was as great a patron as Charlemagne. He himself was a sort of imperial Pope, attending to things spiritual as well as to things temporal. His generosity to the Church made him an object of universal admiration to prelates and abbots and ecclesiastical writers. In this munificent patronage he doubtless secularized the Church, and gave to the clergy privileges they afterwards abused, especially in the ecclesiastical courts. But when the condition of the Teutonic races in barbaric times is considered, his policy may have proved beneficent. Most historians consider that the elevation of the clergy to an equality with barons promoted order and law, especially in the absence of central governments. If Constantine made a mistake in enriching and exalting the clergy, it was endorsed by Charlemagne and Alfred.

After a prosperous and brilliant reign of thirty-one years, the emperor died in the year 337, in the suburbs of Nicomedia, which Diocletian had selected as the capital of the East. In great pomp, and amid expressions of universal grief, his body was transferred to the city he had built and called by his name; it was adorned with every symbol of grandeur and power, deposited on a golden bed, and buried in a consecrated church, which was made the sepulchre of the Greek emperors until the city was taken by the Turks. The sacred rite of baptism by which Constantine was united with the visible Church, strange to say, was not administered until within a few days before his death.

No emperor has received more praises than Constantine. He was fortunate in his biographers, who saw nothing to condemn in a prince who made Christianity the established religion of the Empire. If not the greatest, he was one of the greatest, of all the absolute monarchs who controlled the destinies of over one hundred millions of subjects. If not the best of the emperors, he was one of the best, as sovereigns are judged. I do not see in his character any extraordinary magnanimity or elevation of sentiment, or gentleness, or warmth of affection. He had great faults and great virtues, as strong men are apt to have. If he was addicted to the pleasures of the table, he was chaste and continent in his marital relations. He had no mistresses, like Julius Caesar and Louis XIV He had a great reverence for the ordinances of the Christian religion. His life, in the main, was as decorous as it was useful. He was a very successful man, but he was also a very ambitious man; and an ambitious man is apt to be unscrupulous and cruel. Though he had to deal with bigots, he was not himself fanatical. He was tolerant and enlightened. His most striking characteristic was policy. He was one of the most politic sovereigns that ever lived, – like Henry IV of France, forecasting the future, as well as balancing the present. He could not have decreed such a massacre as that of Thessalonica, or have revoked such an edict as that of Nantes. Nor could he have stooped to such a penance as Ambrose inflicted on Theodosius, or given his conscience to a Father Le Tellier. He tried to do right, not because it was right, like Marcus Aurelius, but because it was wise and expedient; he was a Christian, because he saw that Christianity was a better religion than Paganism, not because he craved a lofty religious life; he was a theologian, after the pattern of Queen Elizabeth, because theological inquiries and disputations were the fashion of the day; but when theologians became rampant and arrogant he put them down, and dictated what they should believe. He was comparatively indifferent to slaughter, else he would not have spent seventeen years of his life in civil war, in order to be himself supreme. He cared little for the traditions of the Empire, else he would not have transferred his capital to the banks of the Bosporus. He was more like Peter the Great than like Napoleon I.; yet he was a better man than either, and bestowed more benefits on the world than both together, and is to be classed among the greatest benefactors that ever sat upon the throne.

AUTHORITIES

The following are original authorities of the life of Constantine:

Arius; Athanasius; Bishop of Caesarea, his friend and admirer;
     Eusebius
Gibbon; Hosius, of Cordova
Milman; Neander (especially his German Church histories)
Socrates
Sozomen; Stanley
Theodoret
TillemontZosimus
Cardinal Newman, *History of the Arians*

Chapter 5

PAULA: WOMAN AS FRIEND

A.D. 347-404

The subject of this lecture is Paula, an illustrious Roman lady of rank and wealth, whose remarkable friendship for Saint Jerome, in the latter part of the fourth century, has made her historical. If to her we do not date the first great change in the social relations of man with woman, yet she is the most memorable example that I can find of that exalted sentiment which Christianity called out in the intercourse of the sexes, and which has done more for the elevation of society than any other sentiment except that of religion itself.

Female friendship, however, must ever have adorned and cheered the world; it naturally springs from the depths of a woman's soul. However dark and dismal society may have been under the withering influences of Paganism, it is probable that glorious instances could be chronicled of the devotion of woman to man and of man to woman, which was not intensified by the passion of love. Nevertheless, the condition of women in the Pagan world, even with all the influences of civilization, was unfavorable to that sentiment which is such a charm in social life.

The Pagan woman belonged to her husband or her father rather than to herself. As more fully shown in the discussion of Cleopatra, she was universally regarded as inferior to man, and made to be his slave. She was miserably educated; she was secluded from intercourse with strangers; she was shut up in her home; she was given in marriage without her consent; she was guarded by female slaves; she was valued chiefly as a domestic servant, or as an animal to prevent the extinction of families; she was seldom honored; she was doomed to household drudgeries as if she were capable of nothing higher; in short, her lot was hard, because it was unequal, humiliating, and sometimes degrading, making her to be either timorous, frivolous, or artful. Her amusements were trivial, her taste vitiated, her education neglected, her rights violated, her aspirations scorned. The poets represented her as capricious, fickle, and false. She rose only to fall; she lived only to die. She was a victim, a toy, or a slave. Bedizened or burdened, she was either an object of degrading admiration or of cold neglect.

The Jewish women seem to have been more favored and honored than women were in Greece or Rome, even in the highest periods of their civilization. But in Jewish history woman was the coy maiden, or the vigilant housekeeper, or the ambitious mother, or the intriguing wife, or the obedient daughter, or the patriotic song-stress, rather than the sympathetic friend. Though we admire the beautiful Rachel, or the heroic Deborah, or the virtuous Abigail, or the affectionate Ruth, or the fortunate Esther, or the brave Judith, or the generous Shunamite, we do not find in the Rachels and Esthers the hallowed ministrations of the Marys, the Marthas and the Phoebes, until Christianity had developed the virtues of the heart and kindled the loftier sentiments of the soul. Then woman became not merely the gentle nurse and the prudent housewife and the disinterested lover, but a *friend*, an angel of consolation, the equal of man in character, and his superior in the virtues of the heart and soul. It was not till then that she was seen to have those qualities which extort veneration, and call out the deepest sympathy, whenever life is divested of its demoralizing egotisms. The original beatitudes of the Garden of Eden returned, and man awoke from the deep sleep of four thousand years, to discover, with Adam, that woman was a partner for whom he should resign all the other attachments of life; and she became his star of worship and his guardian angel amid the entanglements of sin and cares of toil.

I would not assert that there were not noble exceptions to the frivolities and slaveries to which women were generally doomed in Pagan Greece and Rome. Paganism records the fascinations of famous women who could allure the greatest statesmen and the wisest moralists to their charmed circle of admirers, – of women who united high intellectual culture with physical beauty. It tells us of Artemisia, who erected to her husband a mausoleum which was one of the wonders of the world; of Telesilla, the poetess, who saved Argos by her courage; of Hipparchia, who married a deformed and ugly cynic, in order that she might make attainments in learning and philosophy; of Phantasia, who wrote a poem on the Trojan war, which Homer himself did not disdain to utilize; of Sappho, who invented a new measure in lyric poetry, and who was so highly esteemed that her countrymen stamped their money with her image; of Volumnia, screening Rome from the vengeance of her angry son; of Servilia, parting with her jewels to secure her father's liberty; of Sulpicia, who fled from the luxuries of Rome to be a partner of the exile of her husband; of Hortensia, pleading for justice before the triumvirs in the market-place; of Octavia, protecting the children of her rival Cleopatra; of Lucretia, destroying herself rather than survive the dishonor of her house; of Cornelia, inciting her sons, the Gracchi, to deeds of patriotism; and many other illustrious women. We read of courage, fortitude, patriotism, conjugal and parental love; but how seldom do we read of those who were capable of an exalted friendship for men, without provoking scandal or exciting rude suspicion? Who among the poets paint friendship without love; who among them extol women, unless they couple with their praises of mental and moral qualities a mention of the delights of sensual charms and of the joys of wine and banquets? Poets represent the sentiments of an age or people; and the poets of Greece and Rome have almost libelled humanity itself by their bitter sarcasms, showing how degraded the condition of woman was under Pagan influences.

Now, I select Paula, to show that friendship – the noblest sentiment in woman – was not common until Christianity had greatly modified the opinions and habits of society; and to illustrate how indissolubly connected this noble sentiment is with the highest triumphs of an emancipating religion. Paula was a highly favored as well as a highly gifted woman. She was a descendant of the Scipios and the Gracchi, and was born A.D. 347, at Rome, ten years after the death of the Great Constantine who enthroned Christianity, but while yet the social forces of the empire were entangled in the meshes of Paganism. She was married at seventeen to Toxotius, of the still more illustrious Julian family. She lived on Mount Aventine, in great magnificence. She owned, it is said, a whole city in Italy. She was one of the richest women of antiquity, and belonged to the very highest rank of society in an aristocratic age. Until her husband died, she was not distinguished from other Roman ladies of rank, except for the splendor of her palace and the elegance of her life. It seems that she was first won to Christianity by the virtues of the celebrated Marcella, and she hastened to enroll herself, with her five daughters, as pupils of this learned woman, at the same time giving up those habits of luxury which thus far had characterized her, together with most ladies of her class. On her conversion, she distributed to the poor the quarter part of her immense income, – charity being one of the forms which religion took in the early ages of Christianity. Nor was she contented to part with the splendor of her ordinary life. She became a nurse of the miserable and the sick; and when they died she buried them at her own expense. She sought out and relieved distress wherever it was to be found.

But her piety could not escape the asceticism of the age; she lived on bread and a little oil, wasted her body with fastings, dressed like a servant, slept on a mat of straw, covered herself with haircloth, and denied herself the pleasures to which she had been accustomed; she would not even take a bath. The Catholic historians have unduly magnified these virtues; but it was the type which piety then assumed, arising in part from a too literal interpretation of the injunctions of Christ. We are more enlightened in these times, since modern Christian civilization seeks to solve the problem how far the pleasures of this world may be reconciled with the pleasures of the world to come. But the Christians of the fourth century were more austere, like the original Puritans, and made but little account of pleasures which weaned them from the contemplation of God and divine truth, and chained them to the triumphal car of a material and infidel philosophy. As the great and besetting sin of the Jews before the Captivity was idolatry, which thus was the principal subject of rebuke from the messengers of Omnipotence, –

the one thing which the Jews were warned to avoid; as hypocrisy and Pharisaism and a technical and legal piety were the greatest vices to be avoided when Christ began his teachings, – so Epicureanism in life and philosophy was the greatest evil with which the early Christians had to contend, and which the more eminent among them sought to shun, like Athanasius, Basil, and Chrysostom. The asceticism of the early Church was simply the protest against that materialism which was undermining society and preparing the way to ruin; and hence the loftiest type of piety assumed the form of deadly antagonism to the luxuries and self-indulgence which pervaded every city of the empire.

This antagonism may have been carried too far, even as the Puritan made war on many innocent pleasures; but the spectacle of a self-indulgent and pleasure-seeking Christian was abhorrent to the piety of those saints who controlled the opinions of the Christian world. The world was full of misery and poverty, and it was these evils they sought to relieve. The leaders of Pagan society were abandoned to gains and pleasures, which the Christians would fain rebuke by a lofty self-denial, – even as Stoicism, the noblest remonstrance of the Pagan intellect, had its greatest example in an illustrious Roman emperor, who vainly sought to stem the vices which he saw were preparing the way for the conquests of the barbarians. The historian who does not take cognizance of the great necessities of nations, and of the remedies with which good men seek to meet these necessities, is neither philosophical nor just; and instead of railing at the saints, – so justly venerated and powerful, – because they were austere and ascetic, he should remember that only an indifference to the pleasures and luxuries which were the fatal evils of their day could make a powerful impression even on the masses, and make Christianity stand out in bold contrast with the fashionable, perverse, and false doctrines which Paganism indorsed. And I venture to predict, that if the increasing and unblushing materialism of our times shall at last call for such scathing rebukes as the Jewish prophets launched against the sin of idolatry, or such as Christ himself employed when he exposed the hollowness of the piety of the men who took the lead in religious instruction in his day, then the loftiest characters – those whose example is most revered – will again disdain and shun a style of life which seriously conflicts with the triumphs of a spiritual Christianity.

Paula was an ascetic Roman matron on her conversion, or else her conversion would then have seemed nominal. But her nature was not austere. She was a woman of great humanity, and distinguished for those generous traits which have endeared Augustine to the heart of the world. Her hospitalities were boundless; her palace was the resort of all who were famous, when they visited the great capital of the empire. Nor did her asceticism extinguish the natural affections of her heart. When one of her daughters died, her grief was as immoderate as that of Bernard on the loss of his brother. The woman was never lost in the saint. Another interesting circumstance was her enjoyment of cultivated society, and even of those literary treasures which imperishable art had bequeathed. She spoke the Greek language as an English or Russian nobleman speaks French, as a theological student understands German. Her companions were gifted and learned women. Intimately associated with her in Christian labors was Marcella, – a lady who refused the hand of the reigning Consul, and yet, in spite of her duties as a leader of Christian benevolence, so learned that she could explain intricate passages of the Scriptures; versed equally in Greek and Hebrew; and so revered, that, when Rome was taken by the Goths, her splendid palace on Mount Aventine was left unmolested by the barbaric spoliators. Paula was also the friend and companion of Albina and Marcellina, sisters of the great Ambrose, whose father was governor of Gaul. Felicita, Principia, and Feliciana also belonged to her circle, – all of noble birth and great possessions. Her own daughter, Blessella, was married to a descendant of Camillus; and even the illustrious Fabiola, whose life is so charmingly portrayed by Cardinal Wiseman, was also a member of this chosen circle.

It was when Rome was the field of her charities and the scene of her virtues, when she equally blazed as a queen of society and a saint of the most self-sacrificing duties, that Paula fell under the influence of Saint Jerome, at that time secretary of Pope Damasus, – the most austere and the most learned man of Christian antiquity, the great oracle of the Latin Church, sharing with

Augustine the reverence bestowed by succeeding ages, whose translation of the Scriptures into Latin has made him an immortal benefactor.

Figure 8. St. Jerome in His Cell. *After the painting by J.L. Gérôme.*

Nor was Jerome a plebeian; he was a man of rank and fortune, – like the more famous of the Fathers, – but gave away his possessions to the poor, as did so many others of his day. Nothing had been spared on his education by his wealthy Illyrian parents. At eighteen he was sent to Rome to complete his studies. He became deeply imbued with classic literature, and was more interested in the great authors of Greece and Rome than in the material glories of the empire. He lived in their ideas so completely, that in after times his acquaintance with even the writings of Cicero was a matter of self-reproach. Disgusted, however, with the pomps and vanities around him, he sought peace in the consolations of Christianity. His ardent nature impelled him to embrace the ascetic doctrines which were so highly esteemed and venerated; he buried himself in the catacombs, and lived like a monk. Then his inquiring nature compelled him to travel for knowledge, and he visited whatever was interesting in Italy, Greece, and Asia Minor, and especially Palestine, finally fixing upon Chalcis, on the confines of Syria, as his abode. There he gave himself up to contemplation and study, and to the writing of letters to all parts of Christendom. These letters and his learned treatises, and especially the fame of his sanctity, excited so much interest that Pope Damasus summoned him back to Rome to become his counsellor and secretary. More austere than Bossuet or Fénelon at the court of Louis XIV., he was as accomplished, and even more learned than they. They were courtiers; he was a spiritual dictator, ruling, not like Dunstan, by an appeal to superstitious fears, but by learning and sanctity. In his coarse garments he maintained his equality with princes and nobles. To the great he appeared proud and repulsive. To the poor he was affable, gentle, and sympathetic; they thought him as humble as the rich thought him arrogant.

Such a man – so learned and pious, so courtly in his manners, so eloquent in his teachings, so independent and fearless in his spirit, so brilliant in conversation, although tinged with bitterness and sarcasm – became a favorite in those high circles where rank was adorned by piety and culture. The spiritual director became a friend, and his friendship was especially valued by Paula and her illustrious circle. Among those brilliant and religious women he was at home, for by birth and education he was their equal. At the house of Paula he was like Whitefield at the Countess of Huntingdon's, or Michael Angelo in the palace of Vittoria Colonna, – a friend, a teacher, and an oracle.

So, in the midst of a chosen and favored circle did Jerome live, with the bishops and the doctors who equally sought the exalted privilege of its courtesies and its kindness. And the friendship, based on sympathy with Christian labors, became strengthened every day by mutual appreciation, and by that frank and genial intercourse which can exist only with cultivated and honest people. Those high-born ladies listened to his teachings with enthusiasm, entered into all his schemes, and gave him most generous co-operation; not because his literary successes had been blazed throughout the world, but because, like them, he concealed under his coarse garments and his austere habits an ardent, earnest, eloquent soul, with intense longings after truth, and with noble aspirations to extend that religion which was the only hope of the decaying empire. Like them, he had a boundless contempt for empty and passing pleasures, for all the plaudits of the devotees to fashion; and he appreciated their trials and temptations, and pointed out, with more than fraternal tenderness, those insidious enemies that came in the disguise of angels of light. Only a man of his intuitions could have understood the disinterested generosity of those noble women, and the passionless serenity with which they contemplated the demons they had by grace exorcised; and it was only they, with their more delicate organization and their innate insight, who could have entered upon his sorrows, and penetrated the secrets he did not seek to reveal. He gave to them his choicest hours, explained to them the mysteries, revealed his own experiences, animated their hopes, removed their stumbling-blocks, encouraged them in missions of charity, ignored their mistakes, gloried in their sacrifices, and held out to them the promised joys of the endless future. In return, they consoled him in disappointment, shared his resentments, exulted in his triumphs, soothed him in his toils, administered to his wants, guarded his infirmities, relieved him from irksome details, and inspired him to exalted labors by increasing his self-respect. Not with empty flatteries, nor idle dalliances, nor frivolous arts did they mutually encourage and assist each other. Sincerity and truthfulness were the first conditions of their holy intercourse, – "the communion of saints," in which they believed, the sympathies of earth purified by the aspirations of heaven; and neither he nor they were ashamed to feel that such a friendship was more precious than rubies, being sanctioned by apostles and martyrs; nay, without which a Bethany would have been as dreary as the stalls and tables of money-changers in the precincts of the Temple.

A mere worldly life could not have produced such a friendship, for it would have been ostentatious, or prodigal, or vain; allied with sumptuous banquets, with intellectual tournaments, with selfish aims, with foolish presents, with emotions which degenerate into passions *Ennui*, disappointment, burdensome obligation, ultimate disgust, are the result of what is based on the finite and the worldly, allied with the gifts which come from a selfish heart, with the urbanities which are equally showered on the evil and on the good, with the graces which sometimes conceal the poison of asps. How unsatisfactory and mournful the friendship between Voltaire and Frederic the Great, with all their brilliant qualities and mutual flatteries! How unmeaning would have been a friendship between Chesterfield and Dr.

Johnson, even had the latter stooped to all the arts of sycophancy! The world can only inspire its votaries with its own idolatries. Whatever is born of vanity will end in vanity. "Even in laughter the heart is sorrowful, and the end of that mirth is heaviness." But when we seek in friends that which can perpetually refresh and never satiate, – the counsel which maketh wise, the voice of truth and not the voice of flattery; that which will instruct and never degrade, the influences which banish envy and mistrust, – then there is a precious life in it which survives all change. In the atmosphere of admiration, respect, and sympathy suspicion dies, and base desires pass away for lack of their accustomed nourishment; we see defects through the glass of our own charity, with eyes of love and pity, while all that is beautiful is rendered radiant; a halo surrounds the mortal form, like the glory which mediaeval artists aspired to paint in the faces of Madonnas; and adoration succeeds to sympathy, since the excellences we admire are akin to the perfections we adore. "The occult elements" and "latent affinities," of which material pursuits never take cognizance, are "influences as potent in adding a charm to labor or repose as dew or air, in the natural world, in giving a tint to flowers or sap to vegetation."

In that charmed circle, in which it would be difficult to say whether Jerome or Paula presided, the aesthetic mission of woman was seen fully, – perhaps for the first time, – which is never recognized when love of admiration, or intellectual hardihood, or frivolous employments, or usurped prerogatives blunt original sensibilities and sap the elements of inward life. Sentiment proved its superiority over all the claims of intellect, – as when Flora Macdonald effected the escape of Charles Stuart after the fatal battle of Culloden, or when Mary poured the spikenard on Jesus' head, and wiped his feet with the hairs of her head. The glory of the mind yielded to the superior radiance of an admiring soul, and equals stood out in each other's eyes as gifted superiors whom it was no sin to venerate. Radiant in the innocence of conscious virtue, capable of appreciating any flights of genius, holding their riches of no account except to feed the hungry and clothe the naked, these friends lived only to repair the evils which unbridled sin inflicted on mankind, – glorious examples of the support which our frail nature needs, the sun and joy of social life, perpetual benedictions, the sweet rest of a harassed soul.

Strange it is that such a friendship was found in the most corrupt, conventional, luxurious city of the empire. It is not in cities that friendships are supposed to thrive. People in great towns are too preoccupied, too busy, too distracted to shine in those amenities which require peace and rest and leisure. Bacon quotes the Latin adage, *Magna civitas, magna solitudo*. It is in cities where real solitude dwells, since friends are scattered, "and crowds are not company, and faces are only as a gallery of pictures, and talk but a tinkling cymbal, where there is no love."

The history of Jerome and Paula suggests another reflection, – that the friendship which would have immortalized them, had they not other and higher claims to the remembrance and gratitude of mankind, rarely exists except with equals. There must be sympathy in the outward relations of life, as we are constituted, in order for men and women to understand each other. Friendship is not philanthropy: it is a refined and subtile sentiment which binds hearts together in similar labors and experiences. It must be confessed it is exclusive, esoteric, – a sort of moral freemasonry. Jerome, and the great bishops, and the illustrious ladies to whom I allude, all belonged to the same social ranks. They spent their leisure hours together, read the same books, and kindled at the same sentiments. In their charmed circle they unbent; indulged, perchance, in ironical sallies on the follies they alike despised. They freed their minds, as Cicero did to Atticus; they said things to each other which they might have hesitated to say in public, or among fools and dunces. I can conceive that those austere people were sometimes even merry and jocose. The ignorant would not have understood their learned allusions; the narrow-minded might have been shocked at the treatment of their shibboleths; the vulgar would have repelled them by coarseness; the sensual would have disgusted them by their lower tastes.

There can be no true harmony among friends when their sensibilities are shocked, or their views are discrepant. How could Jerome or Paula have discoursed with enthusiasm of the fascinations of Eastern travel to those who had no desire to see the sacred places; or of the charms of Grecian literature to those who could talk only in Latin; or of the corrupting music of the poets to people of perverted taste; or of the sublimity of the Hebrew prophets to those who despised the Jews; or of the luxury of charity to those who had no superfluities; or of the beatitudes of the passive virtues to soldiers; or of the mysteries of faith to speculating rationalists; or of the greatness of the infinite to those who lived in passing events? A Jewish prophet must have seemed a rhapsodist to Athenian critics, and a Grecian philosopher a conceited cynic to a converted fisherman of Galilee, – even as a boastful Darwinite would be repulsive to a believer in the active interference of the moral Governor of the universe. Even Luther might not have admired Michael Angelo, any more than the great artist did the courtiers of Julius II.; and John Knox might have denounced Lord Bacon as a Gallio for advocating moderate measures of reform. The courtly Bossuet would not probably have sympathized with Baxter, even when both discoursed on the eternal gulf between reason and faith. Jesus – the wandering, weary Man of Sorrows – loved Mary and Martha and Lazarus; but Jesus, in the hour of supreme grief, allowed the most spiritual and intellectual of his disciples to lean on his bosom. It was the son of a king whom David cherished with a love surpassing the love of woman. It was to Plato that Socrates communicated his moral wisdom; it was with cultivated youth that Augustine surrounded himself in the gardens of Como; Caesar walked with Antony, and Cassius with Brutus; it was to Madame de Maintenon that Fénelon poured out the riches of his intellect, and the lofty Saint Cyran opened to Mère Angelique the sorrows of his soul. We associate Aspasia with Pericles; Cicero with Atticus; Héloïse with Abélard; Hildebrand with the Countess Matilda; Michael Angelo with Vittoria Colonna; Cardinal de Retz with the Duchess de Longueville; Dr. Johnson with Hannah More.

Those who have no friends delight most in the plaudits of a plebeian crowd. A philosopher who associates with the vulgar is neither an oracle nor a guide. A rich man's son who fraternizes with hostlers will not long grace a party of ladies and gentlemen. A politician who shakes hands with the rabble will lose as much in influence as he gains in power. In spite of envy, poets cling to poets and artists to artists. Genius, like a magnet, draws only congenial natures to itself. Had a well-bred and titled fool been admitted into the Turk's-Head Club, he might have been the butt of good-natured irony;

but he would have been endured, since gentlemen must live with gentlemen and scholars with scholars, and the rivalries which alienate are not so destructive as the grossness which repels. More genial were the festivities of a feudal castle than any banquet between Jews and Samaritans. Had not Mrs. Thrale been a woman of intellect and sensibility, the hospitalities she extended to Johnson would have been as irksome as the dinners given to Robert Hall by his plebeian parishioners; and had not Mrs. Unwin been as refined as she was sympathetic, she would never have soothed the morbid melancholy of Cowper, while the attentions of a fussy, fidgety, talkative, busy wife of a London shopkeeper would have driven him absolutely mad, even if her disposition had been as kind as that of Dorcas, and her piety as warm as that of Phoebe. Paula was to Jerome what Arbella Johnson was to John Winthrop, because their tastes, their habits, their associations, and their studies were the same, – they were equals in rank, in culture, and perhaps in intellect.

But I would not give the impression that congenial tastes and habits and associations formed the basis of the holy friendship between Paula and Jerome. The fountain and life of it was that love which radiated from the Cross, – an absorbing desire to extend the religion which saves the world. Without this foundation, their friendship might have been transient, subject to caprice and circumstances, – like the gay intercourse between the wits who assembled at the Hôtel de Rambouillet, or the sentimental affinities which bind together young men at college or young girls at school, when their vows of undying attachment are so often forgotten in the hard struggles or empty vanities of subsequent life. Circumstances and affinities produced those friendships, and circumstances or time dissolved them, – like the merry meetings of Prince Hal and Falstaff; like the companionship of curious or *ennuied* travelers on the heights of Righi or in the galleries of Florence. The cord which binds together the selfish and the worldly in the quest for pleasure, in the search for gain, in the toil for honors, at a bacchanalian feast, in a Presidential canvass, on a journey to Niagara, – is a rope of sand; a truth which the experienced know, yet which is so bitter to learn. It is profound philosophy, as well as religious experience, which confirms this solemn truth. The soul can repose only on the certitudes of heaven; those who are joined together by the gospel feel alike the misery of the fall and the glory of the restoration. The impressive earnestness which overpowers the mind when eternal and momentous truths are the subjects of discourse binds people together with a force of sympathy which cannot be produced by the sublimity of a mountain or the beauty of a picture. And this enables them to bear each other's burdens, and hide each other's faults, and soothe each other's resentments; to praise without hypocrisy, rebuke without malice, rejoice without envy, and assist without ostentation. This divine sympathy alone can break up selfishness, vanity, and pride. It produces sincerity, truthfulness, disinterestedness, – without which any friendship will die. It is not the remembrance of pleasure which keeps alive a friendship, but the perception of virtues. How can that live which is based on corruption or a falsehood? Anything sensual in friendship passes away, and leaves a residuum of self-reproach, or undermines esteem. That which preserves undying beauty and sacred harmony and celestial glory is wholly based on the spiritual in man, on moral excellence, on the joys of an emancipated soul. It is not easy, in the giddy hours of temptation or folly, to keep this truth in mind, but it can be demonstrated by the experience of every struggling character. The soul that seeks the infinite and imperishable can be firmly knit only to those who live in the realm of adoration, – the adoration of beauty, or truth, or love; and unless a man or woman *does* prefer the infinite to the finite, the permanent to the transient, the true to the false, the incorruptible to the corruptible there is not even the capacity of friendship, unless a low view be taken of it to advance our interests, or enjoy passing pleasures which finally end in bitter disappointments and deep disgusts.

Moreover, there must be in lofty friendship not only congenial tastes, and an aspiration after the imperishable and true, but some common end which both parties strive to secure, and which they love better than they love themselves. Without this common end, friendship might wear itself out, or expend itself in things unworthy of an exalted purpose. Neither brilliant conversation, nor mutual courtesies, nor active sympathies will make social intercourse a perpetual charm. We tire of everything, at times, except the felicities of a pure and fervid love. But even husband and wife might tire without the common guardianship of children, or kindred zeal in some practical aims which both alike seek to secure; for they are helpmates as well as companions. Much more is it necessary for those who are not tied together in connubial bonds to have some common purpose in education, in philanthropy, in art, in religion. Such was pre-eminently the case with Paula and Jerome. They were equally devoted to a cause which was greater than themselves.

And this was the extension of monastic life, which in their day was the object of boundless veneration, – the darling scheme of the Church, indorsed by the authority of sainted doctors and martyrs, and resplendent in the glories of self-sacrifice and religious contemplation. At that time its subtile contradictions were not perceived, nor its practical evils developed. It was not a withered and cunning hag, but a chaste and enthusiastic virgin, rejoicing in poverty and self-denial, jubilant with songs of adoration, seeking the solution of mysteries, wrapt in celestial reveries, yet going forth from dreary cells to feed the hungry and clothe the naked, and still more, to give spiritual consolations to the poor and miserable. It was a great scheme of philanthropy, as well as a haven of rest. It was always sombre in its attire, ascetic in its habits, intolerant in its dogmas, secluded in its life, narrow in its views, and repulsive in its austerities; but its leaders and dignitaries did not then conceal under their coarse raiments either ambition, or avarice, or gluttony. They did not live in stately abbeys, nor ride on mules with gilded bridles, nor entertain people of rank and fashion, nor hunt heretics with fire and sword, nor dictate to princes in affairs of state, nor fill the world with spies, nor extort from wives the secrets of their husbands, nor peddle indulgences for sin, nor undermine morality by a specious casuistry, nor incite to massacres, insurrections, and wars. This complicated system of despotism, this Protean diversified institution of beggars and tyrants, this strange contradiction of glory in debasement and debasement in glory (type of the greatness and littleness of man), was not then matured, but was resplendent with virtues which extort esteem, – chastity, poverty, and obedience, devotion to the miserable, a lofty faith which spurned the finite, an unbounded charity amid the wreck of the dissolving world. As I have before said, it was a protest which perhaps the age demanded. The vow of poverty was a rebuke to that venal and grasping spirit which made riches the end of life; the vow of chastity was the resolution to escape that degrading sensuality which was one of the greatest evils of the times; and the vow of obedience was the recognition of authority amid the disintegrations of society. The monks would show that a cell could be the blessed retreat of learning and philosophy, and that even in a desert the soul could rise triumphant above the privations of the body, to the contemplation of immortal interests.

For this exalted life, as it seemed to the saints of the fourth century, – seclusion from a wicked world, leisure for study and repose, and a state favorable to Christian perfection, – both Paula and Jerome panted: he, that he might be more free to translate the Scriptures and write his commentaries, and to commune with God; she, to minister to his wants, stimulate his labors, enjoy the beatific visions, and set a proud example of the happiness to be enjoyed amid barren rocks or scorching sands. At Rome, Jerome was interrupted, diverted, disgusted. What was a Vanity Fair, a Babel of jargons, a school for scandals, a mart of lies, an arena of passions, an atmosphere of poisons, such as that city was, in spite of wonders of art and trophies of victory and contributions of genius, to a man who loved the certitudes of heaven, and sought to escape from the entangling influences which were a hindrance to his studies and his friendships? And what was Rome to an emancipated woman, who scorned luxuries and demoralizing pleasure, and who was perpetually shocked by the degradation of her sex even amid intoxicating social triumphs, by their devotion to frivolous pleasures, love of dress and ornament, elaborate hair-dressings, idle gossipings, dangerous dalliances, inglorious pursuits, silly trifles, emptiness, vanity, and sin? "But in the country," writes Jerome, "it is true our bread will be coarse, our drink water, and our vegetables we must raise with our own hands; but sleep will not snatch us from agreeable discourse, nor satiety from the pleasures of study. In the summer the shade of the trees will give us shelter, and in the autumn the falling leaves a place of repose. The fields will be painted with flowers, and amid the warbling of birds we will more cheerfully chant our songs of praise."

So, filled with such desires, and possessing such simplicity of tastes, – an enigma, I grant, to an age like ours, as indeed it may have been to his, –

Jerome bade adieu to the honors and luxuries and excitements of the great city (without which even a Cicero languished), and embarked at Ostia, A.D. 385, for those regions consecrated by the sufferings of Christ. Two years afterwards, Paula, with her daughter, joined him at Antioch, and with a numerous party of friends made an extensive tour in the East, previous to a final settlement in Bethlehem. They were everywhere received with the honors usually bestowed on princes and conquerors. At Cyprus, Sidon, Ptolemais, Caesarea, and Jerusalem these distinguished travelers were entertained by Christian bishops, and crowds pressed forward to receive their benediction. The Proconsul of Palestine prepared his palace for their reception, and the rulers of every great city besought the honor of a visit. But they did not tarry until they reached the Holy Sepulchre, until they had kissed the stone which covered the remains of the Saviour of the world. Then they continued their journey, ascending the heights of Hebron, visiting the house of Mary and Martha, passing through Samaria, sailing on the Lake Tiberias, crossing the brook Cedron, and ascending the Mount of Transfiguration. Nor did they rest with a visit to the sacred places hallowed by associations with kings and prophets and patriarchs. They journeyed into Egypt, and, by the route taken by Joseph and Mary in their flight, entered the sacred schools of Alexandria, visited the cells of Nitria, and stood beside the ruins of the temples of the Pharaohs.

A whole year was thus consumed by this illustrious party, – learning more than they could in ten years from books, since every monument and relic was explained to them by the most learned men on earth. Finally they returned to Bethlehem, the spot which Jerome had selected for his final resting-place, and there Paula built a convent near to the cell of her friend, which she caused to be excavated from the solid rock. It was there that he performed his mighty literary labors, and it was there that his happiest days were spent. Paula was near, to supply *his* simple wants, and give, with other pious recluses, all the society he required. He lived in a cave, it is true, but in a way afterwards imitated by the penitent heroes of the Fronde in the vale of Chevreuse; and it was not disagreeable to a man sickened with the world, absorbed in literary labors, and whose solitude was relieved by visits from accomplished women and illustrious bishops and scholars. Fabiola, with a splendid train, came from Rome to listen to his wisdom. Not only did he translate the Bible and write commentaries, but he resumed his pious and learned correspondence with devout scholars throughout the Christian world. Nor was he too busy to find time to superintend the studies of Paula in Greek and Hebrew, and read to her his most precious compositions; while she, on her part, controlled a convent, entertained travelers from all parts of the world, and diffused a boundless charity, – for it does not seem that she had parted with the means of benefiting both the poor and the rich.

Nor was this life at Bethlehem without its charms. That beautiful and fertile town, – as it then seems to have been, – shaded with sycamores and olives, luxurious with grapes and figs, abounding in wells of the purest water, enriched with the splendid church that Helena had built, and consecrated by so many associations, from David to the destruction of Jerusalem, was no dull retreat, and presented far more attractions than did the vale of Port Royal, where Saint Cyran and Arnauld discoursed with the Mère Angelique on the greatness and misery of man; or the sunny slopes of Cluny, where Peter the Venerable sheltered and consoled the persecuted Abélard. No man can be dull when his faculties are stimulated to their utmost stretch, if he does live in a cell; but many a man is bored and *ennuied* in a palace, when he abandons himself to luxury and frivolities. It is not to animals, but to angels, that the higher life is given.

Nor during those eighteen years which Paula passed in Bethlehem, or the previous sixteen years at Rome, did ever a scandal rise or a base suspicion exist in reference to the friendship which has made her immortal. There was nothing in it of that Platonic sentimentality which marked the mediaeval courts of love; nor was it like the chivalrous idolatry of flesh and blood bestowed on queens of beauty at a tournament or tilt; nor was it poetic adoration kindled by the contemplation of ideal excellence, such as Dante saw in his lamented and departed Beatrice; nor was it mere intellectual admiration which bright and enthusiastic women sometimes feel for those who dazzle their brains, or who enjoy a great *éclat*; still less was it that impassioned ardor, that wild infatuation, that tempestuous frenzy, that dire unrest, that mad conflict between sense and reason, that sad forgetfulness sometimes of fame and duty, that reckless defiance of the future, that selfish, exacting, ungovernable, transient impulse which ignores God and law and punishment, treading happiness and heaven beneath the feet, – such as doomed the greatest genius of the Middle Ages to agonies more bitter than scorpions' stings, and shame that made the light of heaven a burden; to futile expiations and undying ignominies. No, it was none of these things, – not even the consecrated endearments of a plighted troth, the sweet rest of trust and hope, in the bliss of which we defy poverty, neglect, and hardship; it was not even this, the highest bliss of earth, but a sentiment perhaps more rare and scarcely less exalted, – that which the apostle recognized in the holy salutation, and which the Gospel chronicles as the highest grace of those who believed in Jesus, the blessed balm of Bethany, the courageous vigilance which watched beside the tomb.

But the time came – as it always must – for the sundering of all earthly ties; austerities and labors accomplished too soon their work. Even saints are not exempted from the penalty of violated physical laws. Pascal died at thirty-seven. Paula lingered to her fifty-seventh year, worn out with cares and vigils. Her death was as serene as her life was lofty; repeating, as she passed away, the aspirations of the prophet-king for his eternal home. Not ecstasies, but a serene tranquility, marked her closing hours. Raising her finger to her lip, she impressed upon it the sign of the cross, and yielded up her spirit without a groan. And the icy hand of death neither changed the freshness of her countenance nor robbed it of its celestial loveliness; it seemed as if she were in a trance, listening to the music of angelic hosts, and glowing with their boundless love. The Bishop of Jerusalem and the neighboring clergy stood around her bed, and Jerome closed her eyes. For three days numerous choirs of virgins alternated in Greek, Latin, and Syriac their mournful but triumphant chants. Six bishops bore her body to the grave, followed by the clergy of the surrounding country. Jerome wrote her epitaph in Latin, but was too much unnerved to preach her funeral sermon. Inhabitants from all parts of Palestine came to her funeral: the poor showed the garments which they had received from her charity; while the whole multitude, by their sighs and tears, evinced that they had lost a nursing mother. The Church received the sad intelligence of her death with profound grief, and has ever since cherished her memory, and erected shrines and monuments to her honor. In that wonderful painting of Saint Jerome by Domenichino, – perhaps the greatest ornament of the Vatican, next to that miracle of art, the "Transfiguration" of Raphael, – the saint is represented in repulsive aspects as his soul was leaving his body, ministered unto by the faithful Paula. But Jerome survived his friend for fifteen years, at Bethlehem, still engrossed with those astonishing labors which made him one of the greatest benefactors of the Church, yet austere and bitter, revealing in his sarcastic letters how much he needed the soothing influences of that sister of mercy whom God had removed to the choir of angels, and to whom the Middle Ages looked as an intercessor, like Mary herself, with the Father of all, for the pardon of sin.

But I need not linger on Paula's deeds of fame. We see in her life, pre-eminently, that noble sentiment which was the first development in woman's progress from the time that Christianity snatched her from the pollution of Paganism. She is made capable of friendship for man without sullying her soul, or giving occasion for reproach. Rare and difficult as this sentiment is, yet her example has proved both its possibility and its radiance. It is the choicest flower which a man finds in the path of his earthly pilgrimage. The coarse-minded interpreter of a woman's soul may pronounce that rash or dangerous in the intercourse of life which seeks to cheer and assist her male associates by an endearing sympathy; but who that has had any great literary or artistic success cannot trace it, in part, to the appreciation and encouragement of those cultivated women who were proud to be his friends? Who that has written poetry that future ages will sing; who that has sculptured a marble that seems to live; who that has declared the saving truths of an unfashionable religion, – has not been stimulated to labor and duty by women with whom he lived in esoteric intimacy, with mutual admiration and respect?

Whatever the heights to which woman is destined to rise, and however exalted the spheres she may learn to fill, she must remember that it was friendship which first distinguished her from Pagan women, and which will ever constitute one of her most peerless charms. Long and dreary has been her progress from the obscurity to which even the Middle Ages doomed her, with all the boasted admiration of chivalry, to her present free and exalted state. She is now recognized to be the equal of man in her intellectual gifts, and is sought out everywhere as teacher and as writer. She may become whatever she pleases, – actress, singer, painter, novelist, poet, or queen of society, sharing with man the great prizes bestowed on genius and learning. But her nature cannot be half developed, her capacities cannot be known, even to herself, until she has learned to mingle with man in the free interchange of those sentiments which keep the soul alive, and which stimulate the noblest powers. Then only does she realize her aesthetic mission. Then only can she rise in the dignity of a guardian angel, an educator of the heart, a dispenser of the blessings by which she would atone for the evil originally brought upon mankind. Now, to administer this antidote to evil, by which labor is made sweet, and pain assuaged, and courage fortified, and truth made beautiful, and duty sacred, – this is the true mission and destiny of woman. She made a great advance from the pollutions and slaveries of the ancient world when she proved herself, like Paula, capable of a pure and lofty friendship, without becoming entangled in the snares and labyrinths of an earthly love; but she will make a still greater advance when our cynical world shall comprehend that it is not for the gratification of passing vanity, or foolish pleasure, or matrimonial ends that she extends her hand of generous courtesy to man, but that he may be aided by the strength she gives in weakness, encouraged by the smiles she bestows in sympathy, and enlightened by the wisdom she has gained by inspiration.

AUTHORITIES

Butler, *Lives of the Saints*
Cave, *Lives of the Fathers*
Dolci, *De Rebus Gestis Hieronymi* [*The Achievements of Jerome*]
Epistles of Saint Jerome
Gibbon, *Decline and Fall*
Neander, *Church History*.
Tillemont, *Ecclesiastical History*

Chapter 6

CHRYSOSTOM: SACRED ELOQUENCE

A.D. 347-407

The first great moral force, after martyrdom, which aroused the degenerate people of the old Roman world from the torpor and egotism and sensuality which were preparing the way for violence and ruin, was the Christian pulpit. Sacred eloquence, then, as impersonated in Chrysostom, "the golden-mouthed," will be the subject of this Lecture, for it was by the "foolishness of preaching" that a new spiritual influence went forth to save a dying world. Chrysostom was not, indeed, the first great preacher of the new doctrines which were destined to win such mighty triumphs, but he was the most distinguished of the pulpit orators of the early Church. Yet even he is buried in his magnificent cause. Who can estimate the influence of the pulpit for fifteen hundred years in the various countries of Christendom? Who can grasp the range of its subjects and the dignity of its appeals? In ages even of ignorance and superstition it has been eloquent with themes of redemption and of a glorious immortality.

Eloquence has ever been admired and honored among all nations, especially among the Greeks. It was the handmaid of music and poetry when the divinity of mind was adored – perhaps with Pagan instincts, but still adored – as a birthright of genius, upon which no material estimate could be placed, since it came from the Gods, like physical beauty, and could neither be bought nor acquired. Long before Christianity declared its inspiring themes and brought peace and hope to oppressed millions, eloquence was a mighty power. But then it was secular and mundane; it pertained to the political and social aspects of States; it belonged to the Forum or the Senate; it was employed to save culprits, to kindle patriotic devotion, or to stimulate the sentiments of freedom and public virtue. Eloquence certainly did not belong to the priest. It was his province to propitiate the Deity with sacrifices, to surround himself with mysteries, to inspire awe by dazzling rites and emblems, to work on the imagination by symbols, splendid dresses, smoking incense, slaughtered beasts, grand temples. He was a man to conjure, not to fascinate; to kindle superstitious fears, not to inspire by thoughts which burn. The gift of tongues was reserved for rhetoricians, politicians, lawyers, and Sophists.

Now Christianity at once seized and appropriated the arts of eloquence as a means of spreading divine truth. Christianity ever has made use of all the arts and gifts and inventions of men to carry out the concealed purposes of the Deity. It was not intended that Christianity should always work by miracles, but also by appeals to the reason and conscience of mankind, and through the truths which had been supernaturally declared, – the required means to accomplish an end. Therefore, she enriched and dignified an art already admired and honored. She carried away in triumph the brightest ornament of the Pagan schools and placed it in the hands of her chosen ministers. So that the Christian pulpit soon began to rival the Forum in an eloquence which may be called artistic, – a natural power of moving men, allied with learning and culture and experience. Young men of family and fortune at last, like Gregory Nazianzen and Basil, prepared themselves in celebrated schools; for eloquence, though a gift, is impotent without study. See the labors of the most accomplished of the orators of Pagan antiquity. It was not enough for an ancient Greek to have natural gifts; he must train himself by the severest culture, mastering all knowledge, and learning how he could best adapt himself to those he designed to move. So when the gospel was left to do its own work on people's hearts, after supernatural influence is supposed to have been withdrawn, the Christian preachers, especially in the Grecian cities, found it expedient to avail themselves of that culture which the Greeks ever valued, even in degenerate times. Indeed, when has Christianity rejected learning and refinement? Paul, the most successful of the apostles, was also the most accomplished, – even as Moses, the most gifted man among the ancient Jews, was also the most learned. It is a great mistake to suppose that those venerated Fathers, who swayed by their learning and eloquence the Christian world, were merely saints. They were the intellectual giants of their day, living in courts, and associating with the wise, the mighty, and the noble. And nearly all of them were great preachers: Cyprian, Athanasius, Augustine, Ambrose, and even Leo, if they yielded to Origen and Jerome in learning, were yet very polished, cultivated men, accustomed to all the refinements which grace and dignify society.

But the eloquence of these bishops and orators was rendered potent by vastly grander themes than those which had been dwelt upon by Pericles, or Demosthenes, or Cicero, and enlarged by an amazing depth of new subjects, transcending in dignity all and everything on which the ancient orators had discoursed or discussed. The bishop, while he baptized believers, and administered the symbolic bread and wine, also taught the people, explained to them the mysteries, enforced upon them their duties, appealed to their intellects and hearts and consciences, consoled them in their afflictions, stimulated their hopes, aroused their fears, and kindled their devotions. He plunged fearlessly into every subject which had a bearing on religious life. While he stood before them clad in the robes of priestly office, holding in his hands the consecrated elements which told of their redemption, and offering up to God before the altar prayers in their behalf, he also ascended the pulpit to speak of life and death in all their sublime relations. "There was nothing touching," says Talfourd, "in the instability of fortune, in the fragility of loveliness, in the mutability of mortal friendship, or the decay of systems, nor in the fall of States and empires, which he did not present, to give humiliating ideas of worldly grandeur. Nor was there anything heroic in sacrifice, or grand in conflict, or sublime in danger, – nothing in the loftiness of the soul's aspirations, nothing of the glorious promises of everlasting life, – which he did not dwell upon to stimulate the transported crowds who hung upon his lips. It was his duty and his privilege," continues this eloquent and Christian lawyer, "to dwell on the older history of the world, on the beautiful simplicities of patriarchal life, on the stern and marvelous story of the Hebrews, on the glorious visions of the prophets, on the songs of the inspired melodists, on the countless beauties of the Scriptures, on the character and teachings and mission of the Saviour. It was his to trace the Spirit of the boundless and the eternal, faintly breathing in every part of the mystic circle of superstition, – unquenched even amidst the most barbarous rites of savage tribes, and in the cold and beautiful shapes of Grecian mould."

How different this eloquence from that of the expiring nations! Their eloquence is sad, sounding like the tocsin of departed glories, protesting earnestly – but without effect – against those corruptions which it was too late to heal. How touching the eloquence of Demosthenes, pointing out the dangers of the State, and appealing to liberty, when liberty had fled. In vain his impassioned appeals to men insensible to elevated sentiments. He sang the death-song of departed greatness without the possibility of a new creation. He spoke to audiences cultivated indeed, but divided, enervated, embittered, infatuated, incapable of self-sacrifice, among whom liberty was a mere tradition and patriotism a dream; and he spoke in vain. Nor could Cicero – still more accomplished, if not so impassioned – kindle among the degenerate Romans the ancient spirit which had fled when demagogues began their reign. How mournful was the eloquence of this great patriot, this experienced statesman, this wise philosopher, who, in spite of all his weaknesses, was admired and honored by all who spoke the Latin tongue. But had he spoken with the tongue of an archangel it would have been all the same, on any worldly or political subject. The old sentiments had died out. Faith was extinguished amid universal scepticism and indifference. He had no material to work on. The birthright of ancient heroes had been sold for a mess of pottage, and this he knew; and therefore with his last philippics he bowed his venerable head, and prepared himself for the sword of the executioner, which he accepted as an inevitable necessity.

These great orators appealed to traditions, to sentiments which had passed away, to glories which could not possibly return; and they spoke in vain. All they could do was to utter their manly and noble protests, and die, with the dispiriting and hopeless feeling that the seeds of ruin, planted in a soil of corruption, would soon bear their wretched fruits, – even violence and destruction.

But the orators who preached a new religion of regenerating forces were more cheerful. They knew that these forces would save the world, whatever the depth of ignominy, wretchedness, and despair. Their eloquence was never sad and hopeless, but triumphant, jubilant, overpowering. It kindled the fires of an intense enthusiasm. It kindled an enthusiasm not based on the conquest of the earth, but on the conquests of the soul, on the never-fading glories of immortality, on the ever-increasing power of the kingdom of Christ. The new orators did not preach liberty, or the glories of material life, or the majesty of man, or even patriotism, but Salvation, – the future destinies of the soul. A new arena of eloquence was entered; a new class of orators arose, who discoursed on subjects of transcending comfort to the poor and miserable. They made political slavery of no account in comparison with the eternal redemption and happiness promised in the future state. The old institutions could not be saved: perhaps the orators did not care to save them; they were not worth saving; they were rotten to the core. But new institutions should arise upon their ruins; creation should succeed destruction; melodious birth-songs should be heard above the despairing death-songs. There should be a new heaven and a new earth, in which should dwell righteousness; and the Prince of Peace – Prophet, Priest, and King – should reign therein forever and ever.

Of the great preachers who appeared in thousands of pulpits in the fourth century, – after Christianity was seated on the throne of the Roman world, and before it had sunk into the eclipse which barbaric spoliations and papal usurpations, and general ignorance, madness, and violence produced, – there was one at Antioch (the seat of the old Greco-Asiatic civilization, alike refined, voluptuous, and intellectual) who was making a mighty stir and creating a mighty fame. This was Chrysostom, whose name has been a synonym of eloquence for more than fifteen hundred years. His father, named Secundus, was a man of high military rank; his mother, Anthusa, was a woman of rare Christian graces, – as endeared to the Church as Monica, the sainted mother of Augustine; or Nonna, the mother of Gregory

Nazianzen. And it is a pleasing fact to record, that most of the great Fathers received the first impulse to their memorable careers from the influence of pious mothers; thereby showing the true destiny and glory of women, as the guardians and instructors of their children, more eager for their salvation than ambitious of worldly distinction. Buried in the blessed sanctities and certitudes of home, – if this can be called a burial, – those Christian women could forego the dangerous fascination of society and the vanity of being enrolled among its leaders. Anthusa so fortified the faith of her yet unconverted son by her wise and affectionate counsels, that she did not fear to intrust him to the teachings of Libanius, the Pagan rhetorician, deeming an accomplished education as great an ornament to a Christian gentleman as were the good principles she had instilled a support in dangerous temptation. Her son John – for that was his baptismal and only name – was trained in all the learning of the schools, and, like so many of the illustrious of our world, made in his youth a wonderful proficiency. He was precocious, like Cicero, like Abélard, like Pascal, like Pitt, like Macaulay, and Stuart Mill; and like them he panted for distinction and fame. The most common path to greatness for high-born youth, then as now, was the profession of the law. But the practice of this honorable profession did not, unfortunately, at least in Antioch, correspond with its theory. Chrysostom (as we will call him, though he did not receive this appellation until some centuries after his death) was soon disgusted and disappointed with the ordinary avocations of the Forum, – its low standard of virtue, and its diversion of what is ennobling in the pure fountains of natural justice into the turbid and polluted channels of deceit, chicanery, and fraud; its abandonment to usurious calculations and tricks of learned and legalized jugglery, by which the end of law itself was baffled and its advocates alone enriched. But what else could be expected of lawyers in those days and in that wicked city, or even in any city of the whole Empire, when justice was practically a marketable commodity; when one half of the whole population were slaves; when the circus and the theatre were as necessary as the bath; when only the rich and fortunate were held in honor; when provincial governments were sold to the highest bidder; when effeminate favorites were the grand chamberlains of emperors; when fanatical mobs rendered all order a mockery; when the greed for money was the master passion of the people; when utility was the watchword of philosophy, and material gains the end and object of education; when public misfortunes were treated with the levity of atheistic science; when private sorrows, miseries, and sufferings had no retreat and no shelter; when conjugal infelicities were scarcely a reproach; when divorces were granted on the most frivolous pretexts; when men became monks from despair of finding women of virtue for wives; and when everything indicated a rapid approach of some grand catastrophe which should mingle, in indiscriminate ruin, the masters and the slaves of a corrupt and prostrate world?

Such was society, and such the signs of the times, when Chrysostom began the practice of the law at Antioch, – perhaps the wickedest city of the whole Empire. His eyes speedily were opened. He could not sleep, for grief and disgust; he could not embark on a profession which then, at least, added to the evils it professed to cure; he began to tremble for his higher interests; he abandoned the Forum forever; he fled as from a city of destruction; he sought solitude, meditation, and prayer, and joined those monks who lived in cells, beyond the precincts of the doomed city. The ardent, the enthusiastic, the cultivated, the conscientious, the lofty Chrysostom fraternized with the visionary inhabitants of the desert, speculated with them on the mystic theogonies of the East, discoursed with them on the origin of evil, studied with them the Christian mysteries, fasted with them, prayed with them, slept like them on a bed of straw, denied himself his accustomed luxuries, abandoning himself to alternate transports of grief and sublime enthusiasm, now contending with the demons who sought his destruction; then soaring to comprehend the Man-God, – the Word made flesh, the incarnation of the divine Logos, – and the still more subtle questions pertaining to the nature and distinctions of the Trinity.

Such were the forms and modes of his conversion, – somewhat different from the experience of Augustine or of Luther, yet not less real and permanent. Those days were the happiest of his life. He had leisure and he had enthusiasm. He desired neither riches nor honors, but the peace of a forgiven soul He was a monk without losing his humanity; a philosopher without losing his taste for the Bible; a Christian without repudiating the learning of the schools. But the influence of early education, his practical yet speculative intellect, his inextinguishable sympathies, his desire for usefulness, and possibly an unsubdued ambition to exert a greater influence would not allow him wholly to bury himself. He made long visits to the friends and habitations he had left, in order to stimulate their faith, relieve their necessities, and encourage them in works of benevolence; leading a life of alternate study and active philanthropy, – learning from the accomplished Diodorus the historical mode of interpreting the Scriptures, and from the profound Theodorus the systems of ancient philosophy. Thus did he train himself for his future labors, and lay the foundation for his future greatness. It was thus he accumulated those intellectual treasures which he afterwards lavished at the imperial court.

But his health at last gave way; and who can wonder? Who can long thrive amid exhausting studies on root dinners and ascetic severities? He was obliged to leave his cave, where he had dwelt six blessed years; and the bishop of Antioch, who knew his merits, pressed him into the active service of the Church, and ordained him deacon, – for the hierarchy of the Church was then established, whatever may have been the original distinctions of the clergy. With these we have nothing to do. But it does not appear that he preached as yet to the people, but performed like other deacons the humble office of reader, leaving to priests and bishops the higher duties of a public teacher. It was impossible, however, for a man of his piety and his gifts, his melodious voice, his extensive learning, and his impressive manners long to remain in a subordinate post. He was accordingly ordained a presbyter, A.D. 381, by Bishop Flavian, in the spacious basilica of Antioch, and the active labors of his life began at the age of thirty-four.

Many were the priests associated with him in that great central metropolitan church; "but upon him was laid the duty of especially preaching to the people, – the most important function recognized by the early Church. He generally preached twice in the week, on Saturday and Sunday mornings, often at break of day, in consequence of the heat of the sun. And such was his popularity and unrivalled power, that the bishop, it is said, often allowed him to finish what he had himself begun. His listeners would crowd around his pulpit, and even interrupt his teachings by their applause. They were unwearied, though they stood generally beyond an hour. His elocution, his gestures, and his matter were alike enchanting." Like Bernard, his very voice would melt to tears. It was music singing divine philosophy; it was harmony clothing the richest moral wisdom with the most glowing style. Never, since the palmy days of Greece, had her astonishing language been wielded by such a master. He was an artist, if sacred eloquence does not disdain that word. The people were electrified by the invectives of an Athenian orator, and moved by the exhortations of a Christian apostle. In majesty and solemnity the ascetic preacher was a Jewish prophet delivering to kings the unwelcome messages of divine Omnipotence. In grace of manner and elegance of language he was the persuasive advocate of the ancient Forum; in earnestness and unction he has been rivalled only by Savonarola; in dignity and learning he may remind us of Bossuet; in his simplicity and orthodoxy he was the worthy successor of him who preached at the day of Pentecost. He realized the perfection which sacred eloquence attained, but to which Pagan art has vainly aspired, – a charm and a wonder to both learned and unlearned, – the precursor of the Bourdaloues and Lacordaires of the Roman Catholic Church, but especially the model for "all preachers who set above all worldly wisdom those divine revelations which alone can save the world."

Everything combined to make Chrysostom the pride and the glory of the ancient Church, – the doctrines which he did not hesitate to proclaim to unwilling ears, and the matchless manner in which he enforced them, – perhaps the most remarkable preacher, on the whole, that ever swayed an audience; uniting all things, – voice, language, figure, passion, learning, taste, art, piety, occasion, motive, prestige, and material to work upon. He left to posterity more than a thousand sermons, and the printed edition of all his works numbers twelve folio volumes. Much as we are inclined to underrate the genius and learning of other days in this our age of more advanced utilities, of progressive and ever-developing civilization, – when Sabbath-school children know more than sages knew two thousand years ago, and socialistic philanthropists and scientific *savans* could put to blush Moses and Solomon and David, to say nothing of Paul and Peter, and other reputed oracles of the ancient world, inasmuch as they were so weak and credulous as to believe in miracles, and a special Providence, and a personal

God, – yet we find in the sermons of Chrysostom, preached even to voluptuous Syrians, no commonplace exhortations, such as we sometimes hear addressed to the thinkers of this generation, when poverty of thought is hidden in pretty expressions, and the waters of life are measured out in tiny gill cups, and even then diluted by weak platitudes to suit the taste of the languid and bedizened and frivolous slaves of society, whose only intellectual struggle is to reconcile the pleasures of material and sensual life with the joys and glories of the world to come. He dwelt, boldly and earnestly, and with masculine power, on the majesty of God and the comparative littleness of man, on moral accountability to Him, on human degeneracy, on the mysterious power of evil, by force of which good people in this dispensation are in a small minority, on the certainty of future retribution; yet also on the never-fading glories of immortality which Christ has brought to light by his sufferings and death, his glorious resurrection and ascension, and the promised influences of the Holy Spirit. These truths, so solemn and so grand, he preached, not with tricks of rhetoric, but simply and urgently, as an ambassador of Heaven to lost and guilty man. And can you wonder at the effect? When preachers throw themselves on the cardinal truths of Christianity, and preach with earnestness as if they believed them, they carry the people with them, producing a lasting impression, and growing broader and more dignified every day. When they seek novelties, and appeal purely to the intellect, or attempt to be philosophical or learned, they fail, whatever their talents. It is the divine truth which saves, not genius and learning, – especially the masses, and even the learned and rich, when their eyes are opened to the delusions of life.

For twelve years Chrysostom preached at Antioch, the oracle and the friend of all classes whether high or low, rich or poor, so that he became a great moral force, and his fame extended to all parts of the Empire. Senators and generals and governors came to hear his eloquence. And when, to his vast gifts, he added the graces and virtues of the humblest of his flock, – parting with a splendid patrimony to feed the hungry and clothe the naked, utterly despising riches except as a means of usefulness, living most abstemiously, shunning the society of idolaters, indefatigable in labor, accessible to those who needed spiritual consolation, healing dissensions, calming mobs, befriending the persecuted, rebuking sin in high places; a man acquainted with grief in the midst of intoxicating intellectual triumphs, – reverence and love were added to admiration, and no limits could be fixed to the moral influence he exerted.

There are few incidents in his troubled age more impressive than when this great preacher sheltered Antioch from the vengeance of Theodosius. That thoughtless and turbulent city had been disgraced by an outrageous insult to the emperor. A mob, a very common thing in that age, had rebelled against the majesty of the law, and murdered the officers of the Government. The anger of Theodosius knew no bounds, but was fortunately averted by the entreaties of the bishop, and the emperor abstained from inflicting on the guilty city the punishment he afterwards sent upon Thessalonica for a less crime. Moreover the repentance of the people was open and profound. Chrysostom had moved and melted them. It was the season of Lent. Every day the vast church was crowded. The shops were closed; the Forum was deserted; the theatre was shut; the entire day was consumed with public prayers; all pleasures were forsaken; fear and anguish sat on every countenance, as in a Mediaeval city after an excommunication. Chrysostom improved the occasion; and perhaps the most remarkable Lenten sermons ever preached, subdued the fierce spirits of the city, and Antioch was saved. It was certainly a sublime spectacle to see a simple priest, unclothed even with episcopal functions, surrounded for weeks by the entire population of a great city, ready to obey his word, and looking to him alone as their deliverer from temporal calamities, as well as their guide in fleeing from the wrath to come.

And here we have a noted example of the power as well as the dignity of the pulpit, – a power which never passed away even in ages of superstition, never disdained by abbots or prelates or popes in the plenitude of their secular magnificence (as we know from the sermons of Gregory and Bernard); a sacred force even in the hands of monks, as when Savonarola ruled the city of Florence, and Bourdaloue awed the court of France; but a still greater force among the Reformers, like Luther and Knox and Latimer, yea in all the crises and changes of both the Catholic and Protestant churches; and not to be disdained even in our utilitarian times, when from more than two hundred thousand pulpits in various countries of Christendom, every Sunday, there go forth voices, weak or strong, from gifted or from shallow men, urging upon the people their duties, and presenting to them the hopes of the life to come. Oh, what a power is this! How few realize its greatness, as a whole! What a power it is, even in its weaker forms, when the clergy abdicate their prerogatives and turn themselves into lecturers, or bury themselves in liturgies! But when they preach without egotism or vanity, scorning sensationalism and vulgarity and cant, and falling back on the great truths which save the world, then sacredness is added to dignity. And especially when the preacher is fearless and earnest, declaring most momentous truths, and to people who respond in their hearts to those truths, who are filled with the same enthusiasm as he is himself, and who catch eagerly his words of life, and follow his directions as if he were indeed a messenger of Jehovah, – then I know of no moral power which can be compared with the pulpit. Worldly men talk of the power of the press, and it is indeed an influence not to be disdained, – it is a great leaven; but the teachings of its writers, when not superficial, are contradictory, and are often mere echoes of public sentiment in reference to mere passing movements and fashions and politics and spoils. But the declarations of the clergy, for the most part, are all in unison, in all the various churches – Catholic and Protestant, Episcopalian, Presbyterian, Methodist and Baptist – which accept God Almighty as the moral governor of the universe, the great master of our destinies, whose eternal voice speaketh to the conscience of mankind. And hence their teachings, if they are true to their calling, have reference to interests and duties and aspirations and hopes as far removed in importance from mere temporal matters as the heaven is higher than the earth. Oh, what high treason to the deity whom the preacher invokes, what stupidity, what frivolity, what insincerity, what incapacity of realizing what is truly great, when he descends from the lofty themes of salvation and moral accountability, to dwell on the platitudes of aesthetic culture, the beauties and glories of Nature, or the wonders of a material civilization, and then with not half the force of those books and periodicals which are scattered in every hamlet of civilized Europe and America!

Now it was to the glory of Chrysostom that he felt the dignity of his calling and aspired to nothing higher, satisfied with his great vocation, – a vocation which can never be measured by the lustre of a church or the wealth of a congregation. Gregory Nazianzen, whether preaching in his paternal village or in the cathedral of Constantinople, was equally the creator of those opinion-makers who settle the verdicts of men. Augustine, in a little African town, wielded ten times the influence of a bishop of Rome, and his sermons to the people of the town of Hippo furnished a thesaurus of divinity to the clergy for a thousand years.

Nevertheless, Antioch was not great enough to hold such a preacher as Chrysostom. He was summoned by imperial authority to the capital of the Eastern Empire. One of the ministers of Arcadius, the son of the great Theodosius, had heard him preach, and greatly admired his eloquence, and perhaps craved the excitement of his discourses, – as the people of Rome hankered after the eloquence of Cicero when he was sent into exile. Chrysostom reluctantly resigned his post in a provincial city to become the Patriarch of Constantinople. It was a great change in his outward dignity. His situation as the highest prelate of the East was rarely conferred except on the favorites of emperors, as the episcopal sees of Mediaeval Europe were rarely given to men but of noble birth. Yet being forced, as it were, to accept what he did not seek or perhaps desire, he resolved to be true to himself and his master. Scarcely was he consecrated by Theophilus of Alexandria before he launched out his indignant invectives against the patron who had elevated him, the court which admired him, and the imperial family which sustained him. Still the preacher, when raised to the government of the Eastern church, regarding his sphere in the pulpit as the loftiest which mortal genius could fill. He feared no one, and he spared no one. None could rob a man who had parted with a princely fortune for the sake of Christ; none could bribe a man who had no favors to ask, and who could live on a crust of bread; none could silence a man who felt himself to be the minister of divine Omnipotence, and who scattered before his altar the dust of worldly grandeur.

It seems that Chrysostom regarded his first duty, even as the Metropolitan of the East, to preach the gospel. He subordinated the bishop to the preacher. True, he was the almoner of his church and the director of its revenues; but he felt that the church of Christ had a higher vocation for a bishop to fill than to be a good business man. Amid all the distractions of his great office he preached as often and as fervently as he did at Antioch. Though possessed of enormous revenues, he curtailed the expenses of his household, and surrounded himself with the pious and the learned. He lived retired within his palace; he dined alone on simple food, and always at home. The great were displeased that he would not honor with his presence their sumptuous banquets; but rich dinners did not agree with his weak digestion, and perhaps he valued too highly his precious time to waste himself, body and soul, for the enjoyment of even admiring courtiers. His power was not at the dinner-table but in the pulpit, and he feared to weaken the effects of his discourses by the exhibition of weaknesses which nearly every man displays amid the excitements of social intercourse.

Perhaps, however, Chrysostom was too ascetic. Christ dined with publicans and sinners; and a man must unbend somewhere, or he loses the elasticity of his mind, and becomes a formula or a mechanism. The convivial enjoyments of Luther enabled him to bear his burden. Had Thomas à Becket shown the same humanity as archbishop that he did as chancellor, he might not have quarreled with his royal master. So Chrysostom might have retained his favor with the court and his see until he died, had he been less austere and censorious. Yet we should remember that the asceticism which is so repulsive to us, and with reason, and which marked the illustrious saints of the fourth century, was simply the protest against the almost universal materialism of the day, – that dreadful moral blight which was undermining society. As luxury and extravagance and material pleasures were the prominent evils of the old Roman world in its decline, it was natural that the protest against these evils should assume the greatest outward antagonism. Luxury and a worldly life were deemed utterly inconsistent with a preacher of righteousness, and were disdained with haughty scorn by the prophets of the Lord, as they were by Elijah and Elisha in the days of Ahab. "What went ye out in the wilderness to see?" said our Lord, with disdainful irony, – "a man clothed in soft raiment? They that wear soft clothing are in king's houses," – as much as to say, my prophets, my ministers, rejoice not in such things.

So Chrysostom could never forget that he was a minister of Christ, and was willing to forego the trappings and pleasures of material life sooner than abdicate his position as a spiritual dictator. The secular historians of our day would call him arrogant, like the courtiers of Arcadius, who detested his plain speaking and his austere piety; but the poor and unimportant thought him as humble as the rich and great thought him proud. Moreover, he was a foe to idleness, and sent away from court to their distant sees a host of bishops who wished to bask in the sunshine of court favor, or revel in the excitements of a great city; and they became his enemies. He deposed others for simony, and they became still more hostile. Others again complained that he was inhospitable, since he would not give up his time to everybody, even while he scattered his revenues to the poor. And still others entertained towards him the passion of envy, – that which gives rancor to the *odium theologicum*, that fatal passion which caused Daniel to be cast into the lions' den, and Haman to plot the ruin of Mordecai; a passion which turns beautiful women into serpents, and learned theologians into fiends. So that even Chrysostom was assailed with danger. Even he was not too high to fall.

The first to turn against the archbishop was the Lord High Chamberlain, – Eutropius, – the minister who had brought him to Constantinople. This vulgar-minded man expected to find in the preacher he had elevated a flatterer and a tool. He was as much deceived as was Henry II when he made Thomas à Becket archbishop of Canterbury. The rigid and fearless metropolitan, instead of telling stories at his table and winking at his infamies, openly rebuked his extortions and exposed his robberies. The disappointed minister of Arcadius then bent his energies to compass the ruin of the prelate; but, before he could effect his purpose, he was himself disgraced at court. The army in revolt had demanded his head, and Eutropius fled to the metropolitan church of Saint Sophia. Chrysostom seized the occasion to impress his hearers with the instability of human greatness, and preached a sort of funeral oration for the man before he was dead. As the fallen and wretched minister of the emperor lay crouching in an agony of shame and fear beneath the table of the altar, the preacher burst out: "Oh, vanity of vanities, where is now the glory of this man? Where the splendor of the light which surrounded him; where the jubilee of the multitude which applauded him; where the friends who worshipped his power; where the incense offered to his image? All gone! It was a dream: it has fled like a shadow; it has burst like a bubble! Oh, vanity of vanity of vanities! Write it on all walls and garments and streets and houses: write it on your consciences. Let everyone cry aloud to his neighbor, Behold, all is vanity! And thou, O wretched man," turning to the fallen chamberlain, "did I not say unto thee that money is a thankless servant? Said I not that wealth is a most treacherous friend? The theatre, on which thou hast bestowed honor, has betrayed thee; the race-course, after devouring thy gains, has sharpened the sword of those whom thou hast labored to amuse. But our sanctuary, which thou hast so often assailed, now opens her bosom to receive thee, and covers thee with her wings."

But even the sacred cathedral did not protect him. He was dragged out and slain.

A more relentless foe now appeared against the prelate, – no less a personage than Theophilus, the very bishop who had consecrated him. Jealousy was the cause, and heresy the pretext, – that most convenient cry of theologians, often indeed just, as when Bernard accused Abélard, and Calvin complained of Servetus; but oftener, the most effectual way of bringing ruin on a hated man, as when the partisans of Alexander VI. brought Savonarola to the tribunal of the Inquisition. It seems that Theophilus had driven out of Egypt a body of monks because they would not assent to the condemnation of Origen's writings; and the poor men, not knowing where to go, fled to Constantinople and implored the protection of the Patriarch. He compassionately gave them shelter, and permission to say their prayers in one of his churches. Therefore he was a heretic, like them, – a follower of Origen.

Under common circumstances such an accusation would have been treated with contempt. But, unfortunately, Chrysostom had alienated other bishops also. Yet their hostility would not have been heeded had not the empress herself, the beautiful and the artful Eudoxia, sided against him. This proud, ambitious, pleasure-seeking, malignant princess – in passion a Jezebel, in policy a Catherine de Medici, in personal fascination a Mary Queen of Scots – hated the archbishop, as Mary hated John Knox, because he had ventured to reprove her levities and follies; and through her influence (and how great is the influence of a beautiful woman on an irresponsible monarch!) the emperor, a weak man, allowed Theophilus to summon and preside over a council for the trial of Chrysostom. It assembled at a place called the Oaks, in the suburbs of Chalcedon, and was composed entirely of the enemies of the Patriarch. Nothing, however, was said about his heresy: that charge was ridiculous. But he was accused of slandering the clergy – he had called them corrupt; of having neglected the duties of hospitality, for he dined generally alone; of having used expressions unbecoming of the house of God, for he was severe and sarcastic; of having encroached on the jurisdiction of foreign bishops in having shielded a few excommunicated monks; and of being guilty of high treason, since he had preached against the sins of the empress. On these charges, which he disdained to answer, and before a council which he deemed illegal, he was condemned; and the emperor accepted the sentence, and sent him into exile.

But the people of Constantinople would not let him go. They drove away his enemies from the city; they raised a sedition and a seasonable earthquake, as Gibbon might call it, and having excited superstitious fears, the empress caused him to be recalled. His return, of course, was a triumph.

The people spread their garments in his way, and conducted him in pomp to his archiepiscopal throne. Sixty bishops assembled and annulled the sentence of the Council of the Oaks. He was now more popular and powerful than before. But not more prudent. For a silver statue of the empress having been erected so near to the cathedral that the games instituted to its honor disturbed the services of the church, the bishop in great indignation ascended the pulpit, and declaimed against female vices. The empress at this was furious, and threatened another council. Chrysostom, still undaunted, then delivered that celebrated sermon, commencing thus: "Again Herodias raves; again she dances; again she demands the head of John in a basin." This defiance, which was regarded as an insult, closed the career of Chrysostom in the capital of the Empire. Both the emperor and empress determined to silence him. A new council was convened, and the Patriarch was accused of violating the canons of the Church. It seems he ventured to preach before he was formally restored, and for this technical offence he was again deposed.

No second earthquake or popular sedition saved him. He had sailed too long against the stream. What genius and what fame can protect a man who mocks or defies the powers that be, whether kings or people? If Socrates could not be endured at Athens, if Cicero was banished from Rome, how could this unarmed priest expect immunity from the possessors of absolute power whom he had offended? It is the fate of prophets to be stoned. The bold expounders of unpalatable truth ever have been martyrs, in some form or other.

Figure 9. St. Chrysostom Condemns the Vices of the Empress Eudoxia. *After the painting by Jean Paul Laurens.*

But Chrysostom met his fate with fortitude, and the only favor which he asked was to reside in Cyzicus, near Nicomedia. This was refused, and the place of his exile was fixed at Cucusus, – a remote and desolate city amid the ridges of Mount Taurus; a distance of seventy days' journey, which he was compelled to make in the heat of summer.

But he lived to reach this dreary resting-place, and immediately devoted himself to the charms of literary composition and letters to his friends. No murmurs escaped him. He did not languish, as Cicero did in his exile, or even like Thiers in Switzerland. Banishment was not dreaded by a man who disdained the luxuries of a great capital, and who was not ambitious of power and rank. Retirement he had sought, even in his youth, and it was no martyrdom to him so long as he could study, meditate, and write.

So Chrysostom was serene, even cheerful, amid the blasts of a cold and cheerless climate. It was there he wrote those noble and interesting letters, of which two hundred and forty still remain. Indeed, his influence seemed to increase with his absence from the capital; and this his enemies beheld with the rage which Napoleon felt for Madame de Staël when he had banished her to within forty leagues of Paris. So a fresh order from the Government doomed him to a still more dreary solitude, on the utmost confines of the Roman Empire, on the coast of the Euxine, even the desert of Pityus. But his feeble body could not sustain the fatigues of this second journey. He was worn out with disease, labors, and austerities; and he died at Comono, in Pontus, – near the place where Henry Martin died, – in the sixtieth year of his age, a martyr, like greater men than he.

Nevertheless this martyrdom, and at the hands of a Christian emperor, filled the world with grief. It was only equalled in intensity by the martyrdom of Becket in after ages. The voice of envy was at last hushed; one of the greatest lights of the Church was extinguished forever. Another generation, however, transported his remains to the banks of the Bosporus, and the emperor – the second Theodosius – himself advanced to receive them as far as Chalcedon, and devoutly kneeling before his coffin, even as Henry II kneeled at the shrine of Becket, invoked the forgiveness of the departed saint for the injustice and injuries he had received. His bones were interred with extraordinary pomp in the tomb of the apostles, and were afterwards removed to Rome, and deposited, still later, beneath a marble mausoleum in a chapel of Saint Peter, where they still remain.

Such were the life and death of the greatest pulpit orator of Christian antiquity. And how can I describe his influence? His sermons, indeed, remain; but since we have given up the Fathers to the Catholics, as if they had a better right to them than we, their writings are not so well known as they ought to be, – as they will be, when we become broader in our views and more modest of our own attainments. Few of the Protestant divines, whom we so justly honor, surpassed Chrysostom in the soundness of his theology, and in the learning with which he adorned his sermons. Certainly no one of them has equalled him in his fervid, impassioned, and classic eloquence. He belongs to the Church universal. The great divines of the seventeenth century made him the subject of their admiring study. In the Middle Ages he was one of the great lights of the reviving schools. Jeremy Taylor, not less than Bossuet, acknowledged his matchless services. One of his prayers has entered into the beautiful liturgy of Cranmer. He was a Bernard, a Bourdaloue, and a Whitefield combined, speaking in the language of Pericles, and on themes which Paganism never comprehended and the Middle Ages but imperfectly discussed.

The permanent influence of such a man can only be measured by the dignity and power of the pulpit itself in all countries and in all ages. So far as pulpit eloquence is an art, its greatest master still speaketh. But greater than his art was the truth which he unfolded and adorned. It is not because he held the most cultivated audiences of his age spell-bound by his eloquence, but because he did not fear to deliver his message, and because he magnified his office, and preached to emperors and princes as if they were ordinary men, and regarded himself as the bearer of most momentous truth, and soared beyond human praises, and forgot himself in his cause, and that cause the salvation of souls, – it is for these things that I most honor him, and believe that his name will be held more and more in reverence, as Christianity becomes more and more the mighty power of the world.

AUTHORITIES

The following are original authorities: Chrysostom; Du Pin; Gibbon; Mabillon; Milman; Socrates; Sozomen; Theodoret.

Baronius, *Annals*
Epistle of Saint Jerome
Fleury, *Ecclesiastical History*

Gregory Nazianzen, *Orations*
Monard, *Life of Chrysostom*
Neander, *Church History*
Perthes, Frederic M., *Life* (translated by Professor Hovey)
Stanley, *Lectures on the Eastern Church.*
Tillemont, *Ecclesiastical History*

Chapter 7

SAINT AMBROSE: EPISCOPAL AUTHORITY

A.D. 340-397

Of the great Fathers, few are dearer to the Church than Ambrose, Archbishop of Milan, both on account of his virtues and the dignity he gave to the episcopal office.

Nearly all the great Fathers were bishops, but I select Ambrose as the representative of their order, because he was more illustrious as a prelate than as a theologian or orator, although he stood high as both. He contributed more than any man who preceded him to raise the power of bishops as one of the controlling agencies of society for more than a thousand years.

The episcopal office, aside from its spiritual aspects, had become a great worldly dignity as early as the fourth century. It gave its possessor rank, power, wealth, – a superb social position, even in the eyes of worldly men. "Make me but bishop of Rome," said a great Pagan general, "and I too would become a Christian." As archbishop of Milan, the second city of Italy, Ambrose found himself one of the highest dignitaries of the Empire.

Whence this great power of bishops? How happened it that the humble ministers of a new and persecuted religion became princes of the earth? What a change from the outward condition of Paul and Peter to that of Ambrose and Leo!

It would be unpleasant to present this subject on controversial and sectarian grounds. Let those people – and they are numerous – who believe in the divine right of bishops, enjoy their opinion; it is not for me to assail them. Let any party in the Church universal advocate the divine institution of their own form of government. But I do not believe that any particular form of government is laid down in the Bible; and yet I admit that church government is as essential and fundamental a matter as a worldly government. Government, then, must be in both Church and State. This *is* recognized in the Scriptures. No institution or State can live without it. Men are exhorted by apostles to obey it, as a Christian duty. But they do not prescribe the form, – leaving that to be settled by the circumstances of the times, the wants of nations, the exigencies of the religious world. And whatever form of government arises, and is confirmed by the wisest and best men, is to be sustained, is to be obeyed. The people of Germany recognize imperial authority: it may be the best government for them. England is practically ruled by an aristocracy, – for the House of Commons is virtually as aristocratic in sympathies as the House of Lords. In this country we have a representation of the people, chosen by the people, and ruling for the people. We think this is the best form of government for us, – just now. In Athens there was a pure democracy. Which of these forms of civil government did God appoint?

So in the Church. For four centuries the bishops controlled the infant Church. For ten centuries afterwards the Popes ruled the Christian world, and claimed a divine right. The government of the Church assumed the theocratic form. At the Reformation numerous sects arose, most of them claiming the indorsement of the Scriptures. Some of these sects became very high-church; that is, they based their organization on the supposed authority of the Bible. All these sects are sincere; but they differ, and they have a right to differ. Probably the day never will come when there will be uniformity of opinion on church government, any more than on doctrines in theology.

Now it seems to me that episcopal power arose, like all other powers, from the circumstances of society, – the wants of the age. One thing cannot be disputed, that the early bishop – or presbyter, or elder, whatever name you choose to call him – was a very humble and unimportant person in the eyes of the world. He lived in no state, in no dignity; he had no wealth, and no social position outside his flock. He preached in an upper chamber or in catacombs. Saint Paul preached at Rome with chains on his arms or legs. The apostles preached to plain people, to common people, and lived sometimes by the work of their own hands. In a century or two, although the Church was still hunted and persecuted, there were nevertheless many converts. These converts contributed from their small means to the support of the poor. At first the deacons, who seem to have been laymen, had charge of this money. Paul was too busy a man himself to serve tables. Gradually there arose the need of a superintendent, or overseer; and that is the meaning of the Greek word [Greek: *episkopos*], from which we get our term *bishop*. Soon, therefore, the superintendent or bishop of the local church had the control of the public funds, the expenditure of which he directed. This was necessary. As converts multiplied and wealth increased, it became indispensable for the clergy of a city to have a head; this officer became presiding elder, or bishop, – whose great duty, however, was to preach. In another century these bishops had become influential; and when Christianity was established by Constantine as the religion of the Empire, they added power to influence, for they disbursed great revenues and ruled a large body of inferior clergy. They were looked up to; they became honored and revered; and deserved to be, for they were good men, and some of them learned. Then they sought a warrant for their power outside the circumstances to which they were indebted for their elevation. It was easy to find it. What sect cannot find it? They strained texts of Scripture, – as that great and good man, Moses Stuart, of Andover, in his zeal for the temperance cause, strained texts to prove that the wine of Palestine did not intoxicate.

But whatever were the causes which led to the elevation and ascendency of bishops, the fact is clear enough that episcopal authority began at an early date; and that bishops were influential in the third century and powerful in the fourth, – a most fortunate thing, as I conceive, for the Church at that time. As early as the third century we read of so great a man as the martyr Cyprian declaring "that bishops had the same rights as apostles, whose successors they were." In the fourth century, such illustrious men as Eusebius of Emesa, Athanasius of Alexandria, Basil of Caesarea, Gregory of Nyssa, Martin of

Tours, Chrysostom of Constantinople, and Augustine of Hippo, and sundry other great men whose writings swayed the human mind until the Reformation, advocated equally high-church pretensions. The bishops of that day lived in a state of worldly grandeur, reduced the power of presbyters to a shadow, seated themselves on thrones, surrounded themselves with the insignia of princes, claimed the right of judging in civil matters, multiplied the offices of the Church, and controlled revenues greater than the incomes of senators and patricians. As for the bishoprics of Rome, Constantinople, Alexandria, Antioch, and Milan, they were great governments, and required men of great executive ability to rule them. Preaching gave way to the multiplied duties and cares of an exalted station. A bishop was then not often selected because he could preach well, but because he knew how to govern. Who, even in our times, would think of filling the See of London, although it is Protestant, with a man whose chief merit is in his eloquence? They want a business man for such a post. Eloquence is no objection, but executive ability is the thing most needed.

So Providence imposed great duties on the bishops of the fourth century, especially in large cities; and very able as well as good men were required for this position, equally one of honor and authority.

The See of Milan was then one of the most important in the Empire. It was the seat of imperial government. Valentinian, an able general, bore the sceptre of the West; for the Empire was then divided, – Valentinian ruling the eastern, and his brother Gratian the western, portion of it, – and, as the Goths were overrunning the civilized world and threatening Italy, Valentinian fixed his seat of government at Milan. It was a turbulent city, disgraced by mobs and religious factions. The Arian party, headed by the Empress Justina, mother of the young emperor, was exceedingly powerful. It was a critical period, and even orthodoxy was in danger of being subverted. I might dwell on the miseries of that period, immediately preceding the fall of the Empire; but all I will say is, that the See of Milan needed a very able, conscientious, and wise prelate.

Hence Ambrose was selected, not by the emperor but by the people, in whom was vested the right of election. He was then governor of that part of Italy now embraced by the archbishoprics of Milan, Turin, Genoa, Ravenna, and Bologna, – the greater part of Lombardy and Sardinia. He belonged to an illustrious Roman family. His father had been praetorian prefect of Gaul, which embraced not only Gaul, but Britain and Africa, – about a third of the Roman Empire. The seat of this great prefecture was Treves; and here Ambrose was born in the year 340. His early days were of course passed in luxury and pomp. On the death of his father he retired to Rome to complete his education, and soon outstripped his noble companions in learning and accomplishments. Such was his character and position that he was selected, at the age of thirty-four, for the government of Northern Italy. Nothing eventful marked his rule as governor, except that he was just, humane, and able. Had he continued governor, his name would not have passed down in history; he would have been forgotten like other provincial governors.

But he was destined to a higher sphere and a more exalted position than that of governor of an important province. On the death of Archbishop Auxentius, A.D. 374, the See of Milan became vacant. A great man was required for the archbishopric in that age of factions, heresies, and tumults. The whole city was thrown into the wildest excitement. The emperor wisely declined to interfere with the election. Rival parties could not agree on a candidate. A tumult arose. The governor – Ambrose – proceeded to the cathedral church, where the election was going on, to appease the tumult. His appearance produced a momentary calm, when a little child cried out, "Let Ambrose our governor be our bishop!" That cry was regarded as a voice from heaven, – as the voice of inspiration. The people caught the words, re-echoed the cry, and tumultuously shouted, "Yes! let Ambrose our governor be our bishop!"

And the governor of a great province became archbishop of Milan. This is a very significant fact. It shows the great dignity and power of the episcopal office at that time: it transcended in influence and power the governorship of a province. It also shows the enormous strides which the Church had made as one of the mighty powers of the world since Constantine, only about sixty years before, had opened to organized Christianity the possibilities of influence. It shows how much more already was thought of a bishop than of a governor.

And what is very remarkable, Ambrose had not even been baptized. He was a layman. There is no evidence that he was a Christian except in name. He had passed through no deep experience such as Augustine did, shortly after this. It was a more remarkable appointment than when Henry II made his chancellor, Becket, archbishop of Canterbury. Why was Ambrose elevated to that great ecclesiastical post? What had he done for the Church? Did he feel the responsibility of his priestly office? Did he realize that he was raised in his social position, even in the eye of an emperor? Why did he not shrink from such an office, on the grounds of unfitness?

The fact is, as proved by his subsequent administration, he was the ablest man for that post to be found in Italy. He was really the most fitting man. If ever a man was called to be a priest, he was called. He had the confidence of both the emperor and the people. Such confidence can be based only on transcendent character. He was not selected because he was learned or eloquent, but because he had administrative ability; and because he was just and virtuous.

A great outward change in his life marked his elevation, as in Becket afterwards. As soon as he was baptized, he parted with his princely fortune and scattered it among the poor, like Cyprian and Chrysostom. This was in accordance with one of the great ideas of the early Church, almost impossible to resist. Charity unbounded, allied with poverty, was the great test of practical Christianity. It was afterwards lost sight of by the Catholic Church in the Middle Ages, and never was recognized by Protestantism at all, not even in theory. Thrift has been one of the watchwords of Protestantism for three hundred years. One of the boasts of Protestantism has been its superior material prosperity. Travelers have harped on the worldly thrift of Protestant countries. The Puritans, full of the Old Testament, like the Jews, rejoiced in an outward prosperity as one of the evidences of the favor of God. The Catholics accuse the Protestants, of not only giving birth to rationalism, in their desire to extend liberality of mind, but of fostering a material life in their ambition to be outwardly prosperous. I make no comment on this fact; I only state it, for everybody knows the accusation to be true, and most people rejoice in it. One of the chief arguments I used to hear for the observance of public worship was, that it would raise the value of property and improve the temporal condition of the worshippers, – so that temporal thrift was made to be indissolubly connected with public worship. "Go to church, and you will thrive in business. Become a Sabbath-school teacher, and you will gain social position." Such arguments logically grow out from linking the kingdom of heaven with success in life, and worldly prosperity with the outward performance of religious duties, – all of which may be true, and certainly marks Protestantism, but is somewhat different from the ideas of the Church eighteen hundred years ago. But those were unenlightened times, when men said, "How hardly shall they who have riches enter into the kingdom of God."

I pass now to consider the services which Ambrose rendered to the Church, and which have given him a name in history.

One of these was the zealous conservation of the truths he received on authority. To guard the purity of the faith was one of the most important functions of a primitive bishop. The last thing the Church would tolerate in one of her overseers was a Gallio in religion. She scorned those philosophical dignitaries who would sit in the seats of Moses and Paul, and use the speculations of the Greeks to build up the orthodox faith. The last thing which a primitive bishop thought of was to advance against Goliath, not with the sling of David, but with the weapons of Pagan Grecian schools. It was incumbent on the watchman who stood on the walls of Zion, to see that no suspicious enemy entered her hallowed gates. The Church gave to him that trust, and reposed in his fidelity. Now Ambrose was not a great scholar, nor a subtle theologian. Nor was he dexterous in the use of dialectical weapons, like Athanasius, Augustine, or Thomas Aquinas. But he was sufficiently intelligent to know what the authorities declared to be orthodox. He knew that the fashionable speculations about the Trinity were not the doctrines of Paul. He knew that self-expiation was not the expiation of the cross; that the mission of Christ was something more than to set a good example; that faith was not estimation merely; that regeneration was not a mere external change of life; that the Divine government was a perpetual interference to bring good out of evil, even if it were in accordance with natural law. He knew that the boastful philosophy by which some sought to bolster up Christianity was that against which the apostles had warned the faithful. He knew that the Church was attacked in her most vital points, even in doctrines, – for "as a man thinketh, so is he."

So he fearlessly entered the lists against the heretics, most of whom were enrolled among the Manicheans, Pelagians, and Arians.

The Manicheans were not the most dangerous, but they were the most offensive. Their doctrines were too absurd to gain a lasting foothold in the West. But they made great pretensions to advanced thought, and engrafted on Christianity the speculations of the East as to the origin of evil and the nature of God. They were not only dreamy theosophists, but materialists under the disguise of spiritualism. I shall have more to say of these people in the next Lecture, on Augustine, since one of his great fights was against the Manichean heresy. So I pass them by with only a brief allusion to their opinions.

The Arians were the most powerful and numerous body of heretics, – if I may use the language of historians, – and it was against these that Ambrose chiefly contended. The great battle against them had been fought by Athanasius two generations before; but they had not been put down. Their doctrines extensively prevailed among many of the barbaric chieftains, and the empress herself was an Arian, as well as many distinguished bishops. Ambrose did not deny the great intellectual ability of Arius, nor the purity of his morals; but he saw in his doctrines the virtual denial of Christ's divinity and atonement, and a glorification of the reason, and an exaltation of the will, which rendered special divine grace unnecessary. The Arian controversy, which lasted one hundred years, and has been repeatedly revived, was not a mere dialectical display, not a war of words, but the most important controversy in which theologians ever enlisted, and the most vital in its logical deductions. Macaulay sneers at the *homoousian* and the *homoiousian*; and when viewed in a technical point of view, it may seem to many frivolous and vain. But the distinctions of the Trinity, which Arius sought to sweep away, are essential to the unity and completeness of the whole scheme of salvation, as held by the Church to have been revealed in the Scriptures; for if Christ is a mere creature of God, – a creation, and not one with Him in essence, – then his death would avail nothing for the efficacy of salvation; or, – to use the language of theologians, who have ever unfortunately blended the declarations and facts of Scripture with dialectical formularies, which are deductions made by reason and logic from accepted truths, yet not so binding as the plain truths themselves, – Christ's death would be insufficient for an infinite redemption. No propitiation of a created being could atone for the sins of all other creatures. Thus by the Arian theory the Christ of the orthodox church was blotted out, and a man was substituted, who was divine only in the matchless purity of his life and the transcendent wisdom of his utterances; so that Christ, logically, was a pattern and teacher, and not a redeemer. Now, historically, everybody knows that for three hundred years Christ was viewed and worshipped as the Son of God, – a divine, uncreated being, who assumed a mortal form to make an atonement or propitiation for the sins of the world. Hence the doctrines of Arius undermined, so far as they were received, the whole theology of the early Church, and obscured the light of faith itself. I am compelled to say this, if I speak at all of the Arians, which I do historically rather than controversially. If I eliminated theology and political theories and changes from my Lectures altogether, there would be nothing left but commonplace matter.

But Ambrose had powerful enemies to contend with in his defence of the received doctrines of the Church. The Empress Faustina was herself an Arian, and the patroness of the sect. Milan was filled with its defenders, turbulent and insolent under the shield of the court. It was the headquarters of the sect at that time. Arianism was fashionable; and the empress had caused an edict to be passed, in the name of her son Valentinian, by which liberty of conscience and worship was granted to the Arians. She also caused a bishop of her nomination and creed to challenge Ambrose to a public disputation in her palace on the points in question. Now what course did Ambrose pursue? Nothing could be fairer, apparently, than the proposal of the empress, – nothing more just than her demands. We should say that she had enlightened reason on her side, for heresy can never be exterminated by force, unless the force is overwhelming, – as in the persecution of the Huguenots by Louis XIV., or the slaughter of the Albigenses by Innocent III or the princes he incited to that cruel act. Ambrose, however, did not regard the edict as suggested by the love of toleration, but as the desire for ascendency, – as an advanced post to be taken in the conflict, – introductory to the triumph of the Arian doctrines in the West, and which the Arian emperor and his bishops intended should ultimately be the established religion of the Western nations. It was not a fight for toleration, but for ascendency. Moreover Ambrose saw in Arianism a hostile creed, – a dangerous error, subversive of what is most vital in Christianity. So he determined to make no concessions at all, to give no foothold to the enemy in a desperate fight. The least concession, he thought, would be followed by the demand for new concessions, and would be a cause of rejoicing to his enemies and of humiliation to his friends; and in accordance with the everlasting principles of all successful warfare he resolved to yield not one jot or tittle. The slightest concession was a compromise, and a compromise might lead to defeat. There could be no compromise on such a vital question as the divinity of our Lord. He might have conceded the wisdom of compromise in some quarrel about temporal matters. Had he, as governor of a province, been required to make some concession to conquering barbarians, – had he been a modern statesman devising a constitution, a matter of government, – he might have acted differently. A policy about tariffs and revenues, all resting on unsettled principles of political economy, may have been a matter of compromise, – not the fundamental principles of the Christian religion, as declared by inspiration, and which he was bound to accept as they were revealed and declared, whether they could be reconciled with his reason or not. There is great moral grandeur in the conflict of fundamental principles of religion; and there is equal grandeur in the conflict between principles and principalities, between combatants armed with spiritual weapons and combatants armed with the temporal sword, between defenceless priests and powerful emperors, between subjects and the powers that be, between men speaking in the name of God Almighty and men at the head of armies, – the former strong in the invisible power of truth; the latter resplendent with material forces.

Ambrose did not shun the conflict and the danger. Never before had a priest dared to confront an emperor, except to offer up his life as a martyr. Who could resist Caesar on his own ground? In the approaching conflict we see the precursor of the Hildebrands and the Beckets. One of the claims of Luther as a hero was his open defiance of the Pope, when no person in his condition had ever before ventured on such a step. But a Roman emperor, in his own capital, was greater than a distant Pope, especially when the defiant monk was protected by a powerful prince. Ambrose had the exalted merit of being the first to resist his emperor, not as a martyr willing to die for his cause, but as a prelate in a desperate and open fight, – as a prelate seeking to conquer. He was the first notable man to raise the standard of independent spiritual authority. Consider, for a moment, what a tremendous step that was, – how pregnant with future consequences. He was the first of all the heroes of the Church who dared to contend with the temporal powers, not as a man uttering a protest, but as an equal adversary, – as a warrior bent on victory. Therefore has his name great historical importance. I know of no man who equaled him in intrepidity, and in a far-reaching policy. I fancy him looking down the vista of the ages, and deliberately laying the foundation of an arrogant spiritual power. What an example did he set for the popes and bishops of the Middle Ages! Here was a just and equal law, as we should say, – a beneficent law of religious toleration, as it would outwardly appear, – which Ambrose, as a subject of the emperor, was required to obey. True, it was in reference to a spiritual matter, but emperors, from Caesar downwards, as Pontifex Maximus, had believed it their right and province to meddle in such matters. See what a hand Constantine had in the organization of the Church, even in the discussion of religious doctrines. He presided at the Council of Nice, where the great subject of discussion was the Trinity. But the Archbishop of Milan dares to say, virtually, to the emperor, "This law-making about our church matters is none of your concern. Christianity has abrogated your power as High Priest. In spiritual things we will not obey you. Your enactments conflict with the divine laws, – higher than yours; and we, in this matter of conscience, defy your authority. We will obey God rather than you." See in this defiance the rise of a new power, – the power of the Middle Ages, – the reign of the clergy.

In the first place, Ambrose refused to take part in a religious disputation held in the palace of his enemy, – in any palace where a monarch sat as umpire. The Church was the true place for a religious controversy, and the umpire, if such were needed, should be a priest and not a layman. The idea of temporal lords settling a disputed point of theology seemed to him preposterous. So, with blended indignation and haughtiness, he declared it was against the usages of the Church for the laity to sit as judges in theological discussions; that in all spiritual matters emperors were subordinate to bishops, not bishops to emperors. Oh, how great is the posthumous influence of original heroes! Contemplate those fiery remonstrances of Ambrose, – the first on record, – when prelates and emperors contended for the mastery, and you will see why the Archbishop of Milan is so great a favorite of the Catholic Church.

And what was the response of the empress, who ruled in the name of her son, in view of this disobedience and defiance? Chrysostom dared to reprove female vices; he did not rebel against imperial power. But Ambrose raised an issue with his sovereign. And this angry sovereign sent forth her soldiers to eject Ambrose from the city. The haughty and insolent priest should be exiled, should be imprisoned, should die. Shall he be permitted to disobey an imperial command? Where would then be the imperial authority? – a mere shadow in an age of anarchy.

Ambrose did not oppose force by force. His warfare was not carnal, but spiritual. He would not, if he could, have braved the soldiers of the Government by rallying his adherents in the streets. That would have been a mob, a sedition, a rebellion.

But he seeks the shelter of his church, and prays to Almighty God. And his friends and admirers – the people to whom he preached, to whom he is an oracle – also follow him to his sanctuary. The church is crowded with his adherents, but they are unarmed. Their trust is not in the armor of Goliath, nor even in the sling of David, but in that power which protected Daniel in the lions' den. The soldiers are armed, and they surround the spacious basilica, the form which the church then assumed. And yet though they surround the church in battle array, they dare not force the doors, – they dare not enter. Why? Because the church had become a sacred place. It was consecrated to the worship of Jehovah. The soldiers were afraid of the wrath of God more than of the wrath of Faustina or Valentinian. What do you see in this fact? You see how religious ideas had permeated the minds even of soldiers. They were not strong enough or brave enough to fight the ideas of their age. Why did not the troops of Louis XVI defend the Bastille? They were strong enough; its cannon could have demolished the whole Faubourg St. Antoine. Alas! the soldiers who defended that fortress had caught the ideas of the people. They fraternized with them, rather than with the Government; they were afraid of opposing the ideas which shook France to its centre. So the soldiers of the imperial government at Milan, converted to the ideas of Christianity, or sympathizing with them, or afraid of them, dared not assail the church to which Ambrose fled for refuge. Behold in this fact the majestic power of ideas when they reach the people.

But if the soldiers dared not attack Ambrose and his followers in a consecrated place, they might starve him out, or frighten him into a surrender. At this point appears the intrepidity of the Christian hero. Day after day, and night after night, the bishop maintained his post. The time was spent in religious exercises. The people listened to exhortation; they prayed; they sang psalms. Then was instituted, amid that long-protracted religious meeting that beautiful antiphonal chant of Ambrose, which afterwards, modified and simplified by Pope Gregory, became the great attraction of religious worship in all the cathedrals and abbeys and churches of Europe for more than one thousand years. It was true congregational singing, in which all took part; simple and religious as the songs of Methodists, both to drive away fear and ennui, and fortify the soul by inspiring melodies, – not artistic music borrowed from the opera and oratorio, and sung by four people, in a distant loft, for the amusement of the rich pew-holders of a fashionable congregation, and calculated to make it forget the truths which the preacher has declared; but more like the hymns and anthems of the son of Jesse, when sung by the whole synagogue, making the vaulted roof and lofty pillars of the Medieval church re-echo the paeans of the transported worshippers.

At last there were signs of rebellion among the soldiers. The new spiritual power was felt, even among them. They were tired of their work; they hated it, since Ambrose was the representative of ideas that claimed obedience no less than the temporal powers. The spiritual and temporal powers were, in fact, arrayed against each other, – an unarmed clergy, declaring principles, against an armed soldiery with swords and lances. What an unequal fight! Why, the very weapons of the soldier are in defence of ideas! The soldier himself is very strong in defence of universally recognized principles, like law and government, whose servant he is. In the case of Ambrose, it was the supposed law of God against the laws of man. What soldier dares to fight against Omnipotence, if he believes at all in the God to whom he is as personally responsible as he is to a ruler?

Ambrose thus remained the victor. The empress was defeated. But she was a woman, and had persistency; she had no intention of succumbing to a priest, and that priest her subject. With subtle dexterity she would change the mode of attack, not relinquish the fight. She sought to compromise. She promised to molest Ambrose no more if he would allow *one* church for the Arians. If the powerful metropolitan would concede that, he might return to his palace in safety; she would withdraw the soldiers. But this he refused. Not one church, declared he, should the detractors of our Lord possess in the city over which he presided as bishop. The Government might take his revenues, might take his life; but he would be true to his cause. With his last breath he would defend the Church, and the doctrines on which it rested.

The angry empress then renewed her attack more fiercely. She commanded the troops to seize by force one of the churches of the city for the use of the Arians; and the bishop was celebrating the sacred mysteries on Palm Sunday when news was brought to him of this outrage, – of this encroachment on the episcopal authority. The whole city was thrown into confusion. Every man armed himself; some siding with the empress, and others with the bishop. The magistrates were in despair, since they could not maintain law and order. They appealed to Ambrose to yield for the sake of peace and public order. To whom he replied, in substance, "What is that to me? My kingdom is not of this world. I will not interfere in civil matters. The responsibility of maintaining order in the streets does not rest on me, but on you. See you to that. It is only by prayer that I am strong."

Again the furious empress – baffled, not conquered – ordered the soldiers to seize the person of Ambrose in his church. But they were terror-stricken. Seize the minister at the altar of Omnipotence! It was not to be thought of. They refused to obey. They sent word to the imperial palace that they would only take possession of the church on the sole condition that the emperor (who was controlled by his mother) should abandon Arianism. How angry must have been the Court! Soldiers not only disobedient, but audaciously dictating in matters of religion! But this treason on the part of the defenders of the throne was a very serious matter. The Court now became alarmed in its turn. And this alarm was increased when the officers of the palace sided with the bishop. "I perceive," said the crestfallen and defeated monarch, and in words of bitterness, "that I am only the shadow of an emperor, to whom you dare dictate my religious belief."

Valentinian was at last aroused to a sense of his danger. He might be dragged from his throne and assassinated. He saw that his throne was undermined by a priest, who used only these simple words, "It is my duty to obey God rather than man." A rebellious mob, an indignant court, a superstitious soldiery, and angry factions compelled him to recall his guards. It was a great triumph for the archbishop. Face to face he had defeated the emperor. The temporal power had yielded to the spiritual. Six hundred years before Henry IV stooped to beg the favor and forgiveness of Hildebrand, at the fortress of Canossa, the State had conceded the supremacy of the Church in the person of the fearless Ambrose.

Not only was Ambrose an intrepid champion of the Church and the orthodox faith, but he was often sent, in critical crises, as an ambassador to the barbaric courts. Such was the force and dignity of his personal character. This is one of the first examples on record of a priest being employed by kings in the difficult art of negotiation in State matters; but it became very common in the Middle Ages for prelates and abbots to be ambassadors of princes, since they were not only the most powerful but most intelligent and learned personages of their times. They had, moreover, the most tact and the most agreeable manners.

When Maximus revolted against the feeble Gratian (emperor of the West), subdued his forces, took his life, and established himself in Gaul, Spain, and Britain, the Emperor Valentinian sent Ambrose to the barbarian's court to demand the body of his murdered brother. Arriving at Treves, the seat of the prefecture, where his father had been governor, he repaired at once to the palace of the usurper, and demanded an interview with Maximus. The lord chamberlain informed him he could only be heard before council. Led to the council chamber, the usurper arose to give him the accustomed kiss of salutation among the Teutonic kings. But Ambrose refused it, and upbraided the potentate for compelling him to appear in the council chamber. "But," replied Maximus, "on a former mission you came to this chamber." "True," replied the prelate, "but then I came to sue for peace, as a suppliant; now I come to demand, as an equal, the body of Gratian." "An equal, are you?" replied the usurper; "from whom have you received this rank?" "From God Almighty," replied the prelate, "who preserves to Valentinian the empire he has given him." On this, the angry Maximus threatened the life of the ambassador, who, rising in wrath, in his turn thus addressed him, before all his councillors: "Since you have robbed an anointed prince of his throne, at least restore his ashes to his kindred. Do *you* fear a tumult when the soldiers shall see the dead body of their murdered emperor? What have you to fear from a corpse whose death you ordered? Do you say you only destroyed your enemy? Alas! he was not *your* enemy, but you were *his*. If someone had possessed himself of your provinces, as you seized those of Gratian, would not he – instead of you – be the enemy? Can you call him an enemy who only sought to preserve what was his own? Who is the lawful sovereign, – he who seeks to keep together his legitimate provinces, or he who has succeeded in wresting them away? Oh, thou successful usurper! God himself shall smite thee. Thou shalt be delivered into the hands of Theodosius. Thou shalt lose thy kingdom and thy life." How the prelate reminds us of a Jewish prophet giving to kings unwelcome messages, – of Daniel pointing out to Belshazzar the handwriting on the wall! He was not a Priam begging the dead body of his son, or hurling impotent weapons amid the crackling ruins of Troy, but an Elijah at the court of Ahab. But this fearlessness was surpassed by the boldness of rebuke which later he dared to give to Theodosius, when this great general had defeated the Goths, and postponed for a time the ruin of the Empire, of which he became the supreme and only emperor. Theodosius was in fact one of the greatest of the emperors, and the last great man who swayed the sceptre of Trajan, his ancestor. On him the vulgar and the high-born equally gazed with admiration, – and yet he was not great enough to be free from vices, patron as he was of the Church and her institutions.

Figure 10. St. Ambrose Refuses the Emperor Theodosius Admittance to His Church. *After the painting by Gebhart Fügel.*

It seems that this illustrious emperor, in a fit of passion, ordered the slaughter of the people of Thessalonica, because they had arisen and killed some half-a-dozen of the officers of the government, in a sedition, on account of the imprisonment of a favorite circus-rider. The wrath of

Theodosius knew no bounds. He had once before forgiven the people of Antioch for a more outrageous insult to imperial authority; but he would not pardon the people of Thessalonica, and caused some seven thousand of them to be executed, – an outrageous vengeance, a crime against humanity. The severity of this punishment filled the whole Empire with consternation. Ambrose himself was so overwhelmed with grief and indignation that he retired into the country in order to avoid all intercourse with his sovereign. And there he remained, until the emperor came to himself and comprehended the enormity of his crime. But Ambrose wrote a letter to the emperor, in which he insisted on his repentance and expiation. The emperor was so touched by the fidelity and eloquence of the prelate that he came to the cathedral to offer up his customary oblations.

But the bishop, in his episcopal robes, met him at the porch and forbade his entrance. "Do not think, O Emperor, to atone for the enormity of your offence by merely presenting yourself in the church. Dream not of entering these sacred precincts with your hands stained with blood. Receive with submission the sentence of the Church." Then Theodosius attempted to justify himself by the example of David. "But," retorted the bishop, "if you imitate David in his crime, imitate David in his repentance. Insult not the Church by a double crime." So the emperor, in spite of his elevated rank and power, was obliged to return. The festival of Christmas approached, the great holiday of the Church, and then was seen one of the rarest spectacles which history records. The great emperor, now with undivided authority, penetrated with grief and shame and penitence, again approached the sacred edifice, and openly made a full confession of his sins; and not till then was he received into the communion of the Church. I think this scene is grand; worthy of a great painter, – of a painter who knows history as well as art, which so few painters do know; yet ought to know if they would produce immortal pictures. Nor do I know which to admire the more, – the penitent emperor offering public penance for his abuse of imperial authority, or the brave and conscientious prelate who dared to rebuke his sin. When has such a thing happened in modern times? Bossuet had the courage to dictate, in the royal chapel, the duties of a king, and Bourdaloue once ventured to reprove his royal hearer for an outrageous scandal. These instances of priestly boldness and fidelity are cited as remarkable. And they were remarkable, when we consider what an egotistical, haughty, exacting, voluptuous monarch Louis XIV was, – a monarch who killed Racine by an angry glance. But what bishop presumed to insist on public penance for the persecutions of the Huguenots, or the lavish expenditures and imperious tyranny of the court mistresses, who scandalized France? I read of no churchman who, in more recent times, has dared to reprove and openly rebuke a sovereign, in the style of Ambrose, except John Knox. Ambrose not merely reproved, but he punished, and brought the greatest emperor, since Constantine, to the stool of penitence.

It was by such acts, as prelate, that Ambrose won immortal fame, and set an example to future ages. His whole career is full of such deeds of intrepidity. Once he refused to offer the customary oblation of the altar until Theodosius had consented to remit an unjust fine. He battled all enemies alike, – infidels, emperors, and Pagans. It was his mission to act, rather than to talk. His greatness was in his character, like that of our Washington, who was not a man of words or genius. What a failure is a man in an exalted post without character!

But he had also other qualities which did him honor, – for which we reverence him. See his laborious life, his assiduity in the discharge of every duty, his charity, his broad humanity, soaring beyond mere conventional and technical and legal piety. See him breaking in pieces the consecrated vessels of the cathedral, and turning them into money to redeem Illyrian captives; and when reproached for this apparent desecration replying thus: "Whether is it better to preserve our gold or the souls of men? Has the Church no higher mission to fulfil than to guard the ornaments made by men's hands, while the faithful are suffering exile and bonds? Do the blessed sacraments need silver and gold, to be efficacious? What greater service to the Church can we render than charities to the unfortunate, in obedience to that eternal test, 'I was an hungered, and ye gave me meat'"? See this venerated prelate giving away his private fortune to the poor; see him refusing even to handle money, knowing the temptation to avarice or greed. What a low estimate he placed on what was so universally valued, measuring money by the standard of eternal weights! See this good bishop, always surrounded with the pious and the learned, attending to all their wants, evincing with his charities the greatest capacity of friendship. His affections went out to all the world, and his chamber was open to everybody. The companion and Mentor of emperors, the prelate charged with the most pressing duties finds time for all who seek his advice or consolation.

One of the most striking facts which attest his goodness was his generous and affectionate treatment of Saint Augustine, at that time an unconverted teacher of rhetoric. It was Ambrose who was instrumental in his conversion; and only a man of broad experience, and deep convictions, and profound knowledge, and exquisite tact, could have had influence over the greatest thinker of Christian antiquity. Augustine not only praises the private life of Ambrose, but the eloquence of his sermons; and I suppose that Augustine was a judge in such matters. "For," says Augustine, "while I opened my heart to admire how eloquently he spoke, I also felt how truly he spoke." Everybody equally admired and loved this great metropolitan, because his piety was enlightened, because he was above all religious tricks and pious frauds. He even refused money for the Church when given grudgingly, or extorted by plausible sophistries. He remitted to a poor woman a legacy which her brother had given to the Church, leaving her penniless and dependent; declaring that "if the Church is to be enriched at the expense of fraternal friendships, if family ties are to be sundered, the cause of Christ would be dishonored rather than advanced." We see here not only a broad humanity, but a profound sense of justice, – a practical piety, showing an enlightened and generous soul. He was not the man to allow a family to be starved because a conscience-stricken husband or father wished, under ghostly influences and in face of death, to make a propitiation for a life of greediness and usurious grindings, by an unjust disposition of his fortune to the Church. Possibly he had doubts whether any money would benefit the Church which was obtained by wicked arts, or had been originally gained by injustice and hard-heartedness.

Thus does Saint Ambrose come down to us from antiquity, – great in his feats of heroism, great as an executive ruler of the Church, great in deeds of benevolence, rather than as orator, theologian, or student. Yet, like Chrysostom, he preached every Sunday, and often in the week besides, and his sermons had great power on his generation. When he died in 397 he left behind him even a rich legacy of theological treatises, as well as some fervid, inspiring hymns, and an influence for the better in the modes of church music, which was the beginning of the modern development of that great element in public worship. As a defender of the faith by his pen, he may have yielded to greater geniuses than he; but as the guardian of the interests of the Church, as a stalwart giant, who prostrated the kings of the earth before him and gained the first great battles of the spiritual over the temporal power, Ambrose is worthy to be ranked among the great Fathers, and will continue to receive the praises of enlightened Christendom.

AUTHORITIES

The following are original authorities: Baronius; Milman; Theodoret; Zosimus.

Biographie Universelle [*Universal Biography*]
Butler, *Lives of the Saints*
Epistles of Ambrose
Gibbon, *Decline and Fall*
Neander, *Church Histories*
Paulinus, *Life of Ambrose*.
Tillemont, *Memoires Ecclesiastique* [*Ecclesiastical Memoirs*]

Chapter 8

SAINT AUGUSTINE: CHRISTIAN THEOLOGY

A.D. 354-430

The most intellectual of all the Fathers of the Church was doubtless Saint Augustine. He is the great oracle of the Latin Church. He directed the thinking of the Christian world for a thousand years. He was not perhaps so learned as Origen, nor so critical as Jerome; but he was broader, profounder, and more original than they, or any other of the great lights who shed the radiance of genius on the crumbling fabric of the ancient civilization. He is the sainted doctor of the Church, equally an authority with both Catholics and Protestants. His penetrating genius, his comprehensive views of all systems of ancient thought, and his marvellous powers as a systematizer of Christian doctrines place him among the immortal benefactors of mankind; while his humanity, his breadth, his charity, and his piety have endeared him to the heart of the Christian world.

Let me present, as well as I can, his history, his services, and his personal character, all of which form no small part of the inheritance bequeathed to us by the giants of the fourth and fifth centuries, – that which we call the Patristic literature, – the only literature worthy of preservation in the declining days of the old Roman world.

Augustine was born at Tagaste, or Tagastum, near Carthage, in the Numidian province of the Roman Empire, in the year 354, – a province rich, cultivated, luxurious, where the people (at least the educated classes) spoke the Latin language, and had adopted the Roman laws and institutions. They were not black, like negroes, though probably swarthy, being descended from Tyrians and Greeks, as well as Numidians. They were as civilized as the Spaniards or the Gauls or the Syrians. Carthage then rivalled Alexandria, which was a Grecian city. If Augustine was not as white as Ptolemy or Cleopatra, he was probably no darker than Athanasius.

Unlike most of the great Fathers, his parentage was humble. He owed nothing to the circumstances of wealth and rank. His father was a heathen, and lived, as Augustine tells us, in "heathenish sin." But his mother was a woman of remarkable piety and strength of mind, who devoted herself to the education of her son. Augustine never alludes to her except with veneration; and his history adds additional confirmation to the fact that nearly all the remarkable men of our world have had remarkable mothers. No woman is dearer to the Church than Monica, the sainted mother of Augustine, and chiefly in view of her intense solicitude for his spiritual interests, and her extraordinary faith in his future conversion, in spite of his youthful follies and excesses, – encouraged by that good bishop who told her "that it was impossible that the child of so many prayers could be lost."

Augustine, in his "Confessions," – that remarkable book which has lasted fifteen hundred years, and is still prized for its intensity, its candor, and its profound acquaintance with the human heart, as well as evangelical truth; not an egotistical parade of morbid sentimentalities, like the "Confessions" of Rousseau, but a mirror of Christian experience, – tells us that until he was sixteen he was obstinate, lazy, neglectful of his studies, indifferent to reproach, and abandoned to heathenish sports. He even committed petty thefts, was quarrelsome, and indulged in demoralizing pleasures. At nineteen he was sent to Carthage to be educated, where he went still further astray; was a follower of stage-players (then all but infamous), and gave himself up to unholy loves. But his intellect was inquiring, his nature genial, and his habits as studious as could be reconciled with a life of pleasure, – a sort of Alcibiades, without his wealth and rank, willing to listen to any Socrates who would stimulate his mind. With all his excesses and vanities, he was not frivolous, and seemed at an early age to be a sincere inquirer after truth. The first work which had a marked effect on him was the "Hortensius" of Cicero, – a lost book, which contained an eloquent exhortation to philosophy, or the love of wisdom. From that he turned to the Holy Scriptures, but they seemed to him then very poor, compared with the stateliness of Tully, nor could his sharp wit penetrate their meaning. Those who seemed to have the greatest influence over him were the Manicheans, – a transcendental, oracular, indefinite, illogical, pretentious set of philosophers, who claimed superior wisdom, and were not unlike (at least in spirit) those modern *savans* in the Christian commonwealth, who make a mockery of what is most sacred in Christianity while themselves propounding the most absurd theories.

The Manicheans claimed to be a Christian sect, but were Oriental in their origin and Pagan in their ideas. They derived their doctrines from Manes, or Mani, who flourished in Persia in the second half of the third century, and who engrafted some Christian doctrines on his system, which was essentially the dualism of Zoroaster and the pantheism of Buddha. He assumed two original substances, – God and Hyle, light and darkness, good and evil, – which were opposed to each other. Matter, which is neither good nor evil, was regarded as bad in itself, and identified with darkness, the prince of which overthrew the primitive man. Among the descendants of the fallen man light and darkness have struggled for supremacy, but matter, or darkness, conquered; and Christ, who was confounded with the sun, came to break the dominion. But the light of his essential being could not unite with darkness; therefore he was not born of a woman, nor did he die to rise again. Christ had thus no personal existence. As the body, being matter, was thought to be essentially evil, it was the aim of the Manicheans to set the soul free from matter; hence abstinence, and the various forms of asceticism which early entered into the pietism of the Oriental monks. That which gave the Manicheans a hold on the mind of Augustine, seeking after truth, was their arrogant claim to the solution of mysteries, especially the origin of evil, and their affectation of superior knowledge. Their watchwords were Reason, Science, Philosophy. Moreover, like the Sophists in the time of Socrates, they were assuming, specious, and rhetorical. Augustine – ardent, imaginative, credulous – was attracted by them, and he enrolled himself in their esoteric circle.

The coarser forms of sin he now abandoned, only to resign himself to the emptiness of dreamy speculations and the praises of admirers. He won prizes and laurels in the schools. For nine years he was much flattered for his philosophical attainments. I can almost see this enthusiastic youth scandalizing and shocking his mother and her friends by his bold advocacy of doctrines at war with the gospel, but which he supposed to be very philosophical. Pert and bright young men in these times often talk as he did, but do not know enough to see their own shallowness.

"Drink deep, or taste not the Pierian spring."

The mind of Augustine, however, was logical, and naturally profound; and at last he became dissatisfied with the nonsense with which plausible pretenders ensnared him. He was then what we should call a schoolmaster, or what some would call a professor, and taught rhetoric for his support, which was a lucrative and honorable calling. He became a master of words. From words he ascended to definitions, and like all true inquirers began to love the definite, the precise. He wanted a basis to stand upon. He sought certitudes, – elemental truths which sophistry could not cover up. Then the Manicheans could no longer satisfy him. He had doubts, difficulties, which no Manichean could explain, not even Dr. Faustus of Mileve, the great oracle and leader of the sect, – a subtle dialectician and brilliant orator, but without depth or earnestness, – whom he compares to a cup-bearer presenting a costly goblet, but without anything in it. And when it became clear that this high-priest of pretended wisdom was ignorant of the things in which he was supposed to excel, but which Augustine himself had already learned, his disappointment was so great that he lost faith both in the teacher and his doctrines. Thus this Faustus, "neither willing nor witting it," was the very man who loosened the net which had ensnared Augustine for so many years.

He was now thirty years of age, and had taught rhetoric in Carthage, the capital of Northern Africa, with brilliant success, for three years; but panting for new honors or for new truth, he removed to Rome, to pursue both his profession and his philosophical studies. He entered the capital of the world in the height of its material glories, but in the decline of its political importance, when Damasus occupied the episcopal throne, and Saint Jerome was explaining the Scriptures to the high-born ladies of Mount Aventine, who grouped around him, – women like Paula, Fabiola, and Marcella. Augustine knew none of these illustrious people. He lodged with a Manichean, and still frequented the meetings of the sect; convinced, indeed, that the truth was not with them, but despairing to find it elsewhere. In this state of mind he was drawn to the doctrines of the New Academy, – or, as Augustine in his "Confessions" calls them, the Academics, – whose representatives, Arcesilaus and Carneades, also made great pretensions, but denied the possibility of arriving at absolute truth, – aiming only at probability. However lofty the speculations of these philosophers, they were sceptical in their tendency. They furnished no anchor for such an earnest thinker as Augustine. They gave him no consolation. Yet his dislike of Christianity remained.

Moreover, he was disappointed with Rome. He did not find there the great men he sought, or if great men were there he could not get access to them. He found himself in a moral desert, without friends and congenial companions. He found everybody so immersed in pleasure, or gain, or frivolity, that they had no time or inclination for the quest for truth, except in those circles he despised. "Truth," they cynically said, "what *is* truth? Will truth enable us to make eligible matches with rich women? Will it give us luxurious banquets, or build palaces, or procure chariots of silver, or robes of silk, or oysters of the Lucrine lake, or Falernian wines? Let us eat and drink, for to-morrow we die." Inasmuch as the arts of rhetoric enabled men to rise at the bar or shine in fashionable circles, he had plenty of scholars; but they left his lecture-room when required to pay. At Carthage his pupils were boisterous and turbulent; at Rome they were tricky and mean. The professor was not only disappointed, – he was disgusted. He found neither truth nor money. Still, he was not wholly unknown or unsuccessful. His great abilities were seen and admired; so that when the people of Milan sent to Symmachus, the prefect of the city, to procure for them an able teacher of rhetoric, he sent Augustine, – a providential thing, since in the second capital of Italy he heard the great Ambrose preach; he found one Christian whom he respected, whom he admired, – and him he sought. And Ambrose found time to show him an episcopal kindness. At first Augustine listened as a critic, trying the eloquence of Ambrose, whether it answered the fame thereof, or flowed fuller or lower than was reported; "but of the matter I was," says Augustine, "a scornful and careless looker-on, being delighted with the sweetness of his discourse. Yet I was, though by little and little, gradually drawing nearer and nearer to truth; for though I took no pains to learn *what* he spoke, only to hear *how* he spoke, yet, together with the words which I would choose, came into my mind the things I would refuse; and while I opened my heart to admire how eloquently he spoke, I also felt how truly he spoke. And so by degrees I resolved to abandon forever the Manicheans, whose falsehoods I detested, and determined to be a catechumen of the Catholic Church."

This was the great crisis of his life. He had renounced a false philosophy; he sought truth from a Christian bishop; he put himself under Christian influences. Fortunately at this time his mother Monica, to whom he had lied and from whom he had run away, joined him; also his son Adeodatus, – the son of the woman with whom he had lived in illicit intercourse for fifteen years. But his conversion was not accomplished. He purposed marriage, sent away his concubine to Africa, and yet fell again into the mazes of another unlawful and entangling love. It was not easy to overcome the loose habits of his life. Sensuality ever robs a man of the power of will. He had a double nature, – a strong sensual body, with a lofty and inquiring soul. And awful were his conflicts, not with an unfettered imagination, like Jerome in the wilderness, but with positive sin. The evil that he would not, that he did, followed with remorse and shame; still a slave to his senses, and perhaps to his imagination, for though he had broken away from the materialism of the Manicheans, he had not abandoned philosophy. He read the books of Plato, which had a good effect, since he saw, what he had not seen before, that true realities are purely intellectual, and that God, who occupies the summit of the world of intelligence, is a pure spirit, inaccessible to the senses; so that Platonism to him, in an important sense, was the vestibule of Christianity.

Platonism, the loftiest development of pagan thought, however, did not emancipate him. He comprehended the Logos of the Athenian sage; but he did not comprehend the Word made flesh, the Word attached to the Cross. The mystery of the Incarnation offended his pride of reason.

Figure 11. St. Augustine and His Mother. *After the painting by Ary Scheffer.*

At length light beamed in upon him from another source, whose simplicity he had despised. He read Saint Paul. No longer did the apostle's style seem barbarous, as it did to Cardinal Bembo, – it was a fountain of life. He was taught two things he had not read in the books of the Platonists, –

the lost state of man, and the need of divine grace. The Incarnation appeared in a new light. Jesus Christ was revealed to him as the restorer of fallen humanity.

He was now "rationally convinced." He accepted the theology of Saint Paul; but he could not break away from his sins. And yet the awful truths he accepted filled him with anguish, and produced dreadful conflicts. The law of his members warred against the law of his mind. In agonies he cried, "Oh, wretched man that I am! Who shall deliver me from this body of death?" He shunned all intercourse. He withdrew to his garden, reclined under a fig-tree, and gave vent to bitter tears. He wrestled with the angel, and his deliverance was at hand. It was under the fig-tree of his garden that he fancied he heard a voice of boy or girl, he could not tell, chanting and often repeating, "Take up and read; take up and read." He opened the Scriptures, and his eye alighted not on the text which had converted Antony the monk, "Go and sell all that thou hast and give to the poor, and thou shalt have treasure in heaven," but on this: "Let us walk honestly, as in the day, not in rioting, drunkenness, and wantonness, but put ye on the Lord Jesus Christ, and not make provision for the flesh, to fulfil the lusts thereof." That text decided him, and broke his fetters. His conversion was accomplished. He poured forth his soul in thanksgiving and praise.

He was now in the thirty-second year of his age, and resolved to renounce his profession, – or, to use his language, "to withdraw from the marts of lip-labor and the selling of words," – and enter the service of the new master who had called him to prepare himself for a higher vocation. He retired to a country house, near Milan, which belonged to his friend Veracundus, and he was accompanied in his retreat by his mother, his brother Navigius, his son Adeodatus, Alypius his confidant, Trigentius and Licentius his scholars, and his cousins Lastidianus and Rusticus. I should like to describe those blissful and enchanting days, when without asceticism and without fanaticism, surrounded with admiring friends and relatives, he discoursed on the highest truths which can elevate the human mind. Amid the rich olive-groves and dark waving chesnuts which skirted the loveliest of Italian lakes, in sight of both Alps and Apennines, did this great master of Christian philosophy prepare himself for his future labors, and forge the weapons with which he overthrew the high-priests who assailed the integrity of the Christian faith. The hand of opulent friendship supplied his wants, as Paula ministered to Jerome in Bethlehem. Often were discussions with his pupils and friends prolonged into the night and continued until the morning. Plato and Saint Paul reappeared in the gardens of Como. Thus three more glorious years were passed in study, in retirement, and in profitable discourse, without scandal and without vanity. The proud philosopher was changed into a humble Christian, thirsting for a living union with God. The Psalms of David, next to the Epistles of Saint Paul, were his favorite study, – that pure and lofty poetry "which strips away the curtains of the skies, and approaches boldly but meekly into the presence of Him who dwells in boundless and inaccessible majesty." In the year 387, at the age of thirty-three, he received the rite of baptism from the great archbishop who was so instrumental in his conversion, and was admitted into the ranks of the visible Church, and prepared to return to Africa. But before he could embark, his beloved mother died at Ostia, feeling, with Simeon, that she could now depart in peace, having seen the salvation of the Lord, – but to the immoderate grief of Augustine who made no effort to dry his tears. It was not till the following year that he sailed for Carthage, not long tarrying there, but retiring to Tagaste, to his paternal estate, where he spent three years more in study and meditation, giving away all he possessed to religion and charity, living with his friends in a complete community of goods. It was there that some of his best works were composed. In the year 391, on a visit to Hippo, a Numidian seaport, he was forced into more active duties. Entering the church, the people clamored for his ordination; and such was his power as a pulpit orator, and so universally was he revered, that in two years after he became coadjutor bishop, and his great career began.

As a bishop he won universal admiration. Councils could do nothing without his presence. Emperors condescended to sue for his advice. He wrote letters to all parts of Christendom. He was alike saint, oracle, prelate, and preacher. He labored day and night, living simply, but without monkish austerity. At table, reading and literary conferences were preferred to secular conversation. His person was accessible. He interested himself in everybody's troubles, and visited the forlorn and miserable. He was indefatigable in reclaiming those who had strayed from the fold. He won every heart by charity, and captivated every mind with his eloquence; so that Hippo, a little African town, was no longer "least among the cities of Judah," since her prelate was consulted from the extremities of the earth, and his influence went forth throughout the crumbling Empire, to heal division and establish the faith of the wavering, – a Father of the Church universal.

Yet it is not as bishop, but as doctor, that he is immortal. It was his mission to head off the dissensions and heresies of his age, and to establish the faith of Paul even among the Germanic barbarians. He is the great theologian of the Church, and his system of divinity not only was the creed of the Middle Ages, but is still an authority in the schools, both Catholic and Protestant.

Let us, then, turn to his services as theologian and philosopher. He wrote over a thousand treatises, and on almost every subject that has interested the human mind; but his labors were chiefly confined to the prevailing and more subtle and dangerous errors of his day. Nor was it by dry dialectics that he refuted these heresies, although the most logical and acute of men, but by his profound insight into the cardinal principles of Christianity, which he discoursed upon with the most extraordinary affluence of thought and language, disdaining all sophistries and speculations. He went to the very core, – a realist of the most exalted type, permeated with the spirit of Plato, yet bowing down to Paul.

We first find him combating the opinions which had originally enthralled him, and which he understood better than any theologian who ever lived.

But I need not repeat what I have already said of the Manicheans, – those arrogant and shallow philosophers who made such high pretension to superior wisdom; men who adored the divinity of mind, and the inherent evil of matter; men who sought to emancipate the soul, which in their view needed no regeneration from all the influences of the body. That this soul, purified by asceticism, might be reunited to the great spirit of the universe from which it had originally emanated, was the hopeless aim and dream of these theosophists, – not the control of passions and appetites, which God commands, but their eradication; not the worship of a Creator who made the heaven and the earth, but a vague worship of the creation itself. They little dreamed that it is not the body (neither good nor evil in itself) which is sinful, but the perverted mind and soul, the wicked imagination of the heart, out of which proceeds that which defileth a man, and which can only be controlled and purified by Divine assistance. Augustine showed that purity was an inward virtue, not the crucifixion of the body; that its passions and appetites are made to be subservient to reason and duty; that the law of temperance is self-restraint; that the soul was not an emanation or evolution from eternal light, but a distinct creation of Almighty God, which He has the power to destroy, as well as the body itself; that nothing in the universe can live without His pleasure; that His intervention is a logical sequence of His moral government. But his most withering denunciation of the Manicheans was directed against their pride of reason, against their darkened understanding, which led them not only to believe a lie, but to glory in it, – the utter perverseness of the mind when in rebellion to divine authority, in view of which it is almost vain to argue, since truth will neither be admitted nor accepted.

There was another class of Christians who provoked the controversial genius of Augustine, and these were the Donatists. These men were not heretics, but bigots. They made the rite of baptism to depend on the character of the officiating priest; and hence they insisted on rebaptism, if the priest who had baptized proved unworthy. They seemed to forget that no clergyman ever baptized from his own authority or worthiness, but only in the name of the Father, and the Son, and the Holy Ghost. Nobody knows who baptized Paul, and he felt under certain circumstances even that he was sent not to baptize, but to preach the gospel. Lay baptism has always been held valid. Hence, such reformers as Calvin and Knox did not deem it necessary to rebaptize those who had been converted from the Roman Catholic faith; and, if I do not mistake, even Roman Catholics do not insist on rebaptizing Protestants. But the Donatists so magnified, not the rite, but the form of it, that they lost the spirit of it, and became seceders, and created a mournful division in the Church, – a schism which gave rise to bitter animosities. The churches of Africa were rent by their implacable feuds, and on so small a matter, – even as the ranks of the reformers under Luther were so soon divided by the Anabaptists. In proportion to the unimportance of the shibboleth was tenacity to it, – a mark which has ever characterized narrow and illiberal minds. It is not because a man accepts a shibboleth that he is narrow and small, but because he fights for it. As a minute critic would cast out from the fraternity of scholars him who cannot tell the difference between *ac* and *et*, so the Donatist would expel from the true fold of Christ those who accepted baptism from an unworthy priest. Augustine at first showed great moderation and patience and gentleness in dealing with these narrow-minded and fierce sectarians, who carried their animosity so far as to forbid bread to be baked for the use of the Catholics in Carthage, when they had the ascendency; but at last he became indignant, and implored the aid of secular magistrates.

Augustine's controversy with the Donatists led to two remarkable tracts, – one on the evil of suppressing heresy by the sword, and the other on the unity of the Church.

In the first he showed a spirit of toleration beyond his age; and this is more remarkable because his temper was naturally ardent and fiery. But he protested in his writings, and before councils, against violence in forcing religious convictions, and advocated a liberality worthy of John Locke.

In the second tract he advocated a principle which had a prodigious influence on the minds of his generation, and greatly contributed to establish the polity of the Roman Catholic Church. He argued the necessity of unity in government as well as unity in faith, like Cyprian before him; and this has endeared him to the Roman Catholic Church, I apprehend, even more than his glorious defence of the Pauline theology. There are some who think that all governments arise out of the circumstances and the necessities of the times, and that there are no rules laid down in the Bible for any particular form or polity, since a government which may be adapted to one age or people may not be fitted for another; – even as a monarchy would not succeed in New England any more than a democracy in China. But the most powerful sects among Protestants, as well as among the Catholics themselves, insist on the divine authority for their several forms of government, and all would have insisted, at different periods, on producing conformity with their notions. The high-church Episcopalian and the high-church Presbyterian equally insist on the divine authority for their respective institutions. The Catholics simply do the same, when they make Saint Peter the rock on which the supremacy of their Church is based. In the time of Augustine there was only one form of the visible Church, – there were no Protestants; and he naturally wished, like any bishop, to strengthen and establish its unity, – a government of bishops, of which the bishop of Rome was the acknowledged head. But he did not anticipate – and I believe he would not have indorsed – their future encroachments and their ambitious schemes for enthralling the mind of the world, to say nothing of personal aggrandizement and the usurpation of temporal authority. And yet the central power they established on the banks of the Tiber was, with all its corruptions, fitted to conserve the interests of Christendom in rude ages of barbarism and ignorance; and possibly Augustine, with his profound intuitions, and in view of the approaching desolations of the Christian world, wished to give to the clergy and to their head all the moral power and prestige possible, to awe and control the barbaric chieftains, for in his day the Empire was crumbling to pieces, and the old civilization was being trampled under foot. If there was a man in the whole Empire capable of taking comprehensive views of the necessities of society, that man was the Bishop of Hippo; so that if we do not agree with his views of church government, let us bear in mind the age in which he lived, and its peculiar dangers and necessities. And let us also remember that his idea of the unity of the Church has a spiritual as well as a temporal meaning, and in that sublime and lofty sense can never be controverted so long as *One Lord, One Faith, One Baptism* remain the common creed of Christians in all parts of the world. It was to preserve this unity that he entered so zealously into all the great controversies of the age, and fought heretics as well as schismatics.

The great work which pre-eminently called out his genius, and for which he would seem to have been raised up, was to combat the Pelagian heresy, and establish the doctrine of the necessity of Divine Grace, – even as it was the mission of Athanasius to defend the doctrine of the Trinity, and that of Luther to establish Justification by Faith. In all ages there are certain heresies, or errors, which have spread so dangerously, and been embraced so generally by the leading and fashionable classes, that they seem to require some extraordinary genius to arise in order to combat them successfully, and rescue the Church from the snares of a false philosophy. Thus Bernard was raised up to refute the rationalism and nominalism of Abélard, whose brilliant and subtile inquiries had a tendency to extinguish faith in the world, and bring all mysteries to the test of reason. The enthusiastic and inquiring young men who flocked to his lectures from all parts of Europe carried back to their homes and convents and schools insidious errors, all the more dangerous because they were mixed with truths which were universally recognized. It required such a man as Bernard to expose these sophistries and destroy their power, not so much by dialectical weapons as by appealing to those lofty truths, those profound convictions, those essential and immutable principles which consciousness reveals and divine authority confirms. It took a greater than Abélard to show the tendency of his speculations, from the logical sequence of which even he himself would have fled, and which he did reject when misfortunes had broken his heart, and disease had brought him to face the realities of the future life. So God raised up Pascal to expose the sophistries of the Jesuits and unravel that subtle casuistry which was undermining the morality of the age, and destroying the authority of Saint Augustine on some of the most vital principles which entered into the creed of the Catholic Church. Thus Jonathan Edwards, the ablest theologian which this country has seen, controverted the fashionable Arminianism of his day. Thus some great intellectual giant will certainly and in due time appear to demolish with scathing irony the theories and speculations of some of the progressive schools of our day, and present their absurdities and boastings and pretensions in such a ridiculous light that no man with any intellectual dignity will dare to belong to their fraternity, unless he impiously accepts – sometimes with ribald mockeries – the logical sequence of their doctrines.

Now it was not the Manicheans or Donatists who were the most dangerous people in the time of Augustine, – nor were their doctrines likely to be embraced by the Christian schools, especially in the West; but it was the Pelagians who in high places were assailing the Pauline theology. And they advocated principles which lay at the root of most of the subsequent controversies of the Church. They were intellectual men, generally good men, who could not be put down, and who would thrive under any opposition. Augustine did not attack the character of these men, but rendered a great service to the Church by pointing out, clearly and luminously, the antichristian character of their theories, when rigorously pushed out, by a remorseless logic, to their necessary sequence.

Whatever value may be attached to that science which is based on deductions drawn from the truths of revelation, certain it is that it was theology which most interested Christians in the time of Augustine, as in the time of Athanasius; and his controversy with the Pelagians made then a mighty stir, and is at the root of half the theological discussions from that age to ours. If we would understand the changes of human thought in the Middle Ages, if we would seek to know what is most vital in Church history, that celebrated Pelagian controversy claims our special attention.

It was at a great crisis in the Church when a British monk of extraordinary talents, persuasive eloquence, and great attainments, – a man accustomed to the use of dialectical weapons and experienced by extensive travels, ambitious, ardent, plausible, adroit, – appeared among the churches and advanced a new philosophy. His name was Pelagius; and he was accompanied by a man of still greater logical power than he himself possessed, though not so eloquent or accomplished or pleasing in manner, who was called Celestius, – two doctors of whom the schools were justly proud, and who were admired and honored by enthusiastic young men, as Abélard was in after-times.

Nothing disagreeable marked these apostles of the new philosophy, nor could the malignant voice of theological hatred and envy bring upon their lives either scandal or reproach. They had none of the infirmities which so often have dimmed the lustre of great benefactors. They were not dogmatic like Luther, nor severe like Calvin, nor intolerant like Knox. Pelagius, especially, was a most interesting man, though more of a philosopher than a Christian. Like Zeno, he exalted the human will; like Aristotle, he subjected all truth to the test of logical formularies; like Abélard, he would believe nothing which he could not explain or comprehend. Self-confident, like Servetus, he disdained the Cross. The central principle of his teachings was man's ability to practise any virtue, independently of divine grace. He made perfection a thing easy to be attained. There was no need, in his eyes, as his adversaries maintained, of supernatural aid in the work of salvation. Hence a Saviour was needless. By faith, he is represented to mean mere intellectual convictions, to be reached through the reason alone. Prayer was useful simply to stimulate a man's own will. He was further represented as repudiating miracles as contrary to reason, of abhorring divine sovereignty as fatal to the exercise of the will, of denying special providences as opposing the operation of natural laws, as rejecting native depravity and maintaining that the natural tendency of society was to rise in both virtue and knowledge, and of course rejecting the idea of a Devil tempting man to sin. "His doctrines," says one of his biographers, "were pleasing to pride, by flattering its pretension; to nature, by exaggerating its power; and to reason, by extolling its capacity." He asserted that death was not the penalty of Adam's transgression; he denied the consequences of his sin; and he denied the spiritual resurrection of man by the death of Christ, thus rejecting him as a divine Redeemer. Why should there be a divine redemption if man could save himself? He blotted out Christ from the book of life by representing him merely as a martyr suffering for the declaration of truths which were not appreciated, – like Socrates at Athens, or Savonarola at Florence. In support of all these doctrines, so different from those of Paul, he appealed, not to the apostle's authority, but to human reason, and sought the aid of Pagan philosophy, rather than the Scriptures, to arrive at truth.

Thus was Pelagius represented by his opponents, who may have exaggerated his heresies, and have pushed his doctrines to a logical sequence which he would not accept but would even repel, in the same manner as the Pelagians drew deductions from the teachings of Augustine which were exceedingly unfair, – making God the author of sin, and election to salvation to depend on the foreseen conduct of men in regard to an obedience which they had no power to perform.

But whether Pelagius did or did not hold all the doctrines of which he was accused, it is certain that the spirit of them was antagonistic to the teachings of Paul, as understood by Augustine, who felt that the very foundations of Christianity were assailed, – as Athanasius regarded the doctrines of Arius. So he came to the rescue, not of the Catholic Church, for

Pelagius belonged to it as well as he, but to the rescue of Christian theology. The doctrines of Pelagius were becoming fashionable and prevalent in many parts of the Empire. Even the Pope at one time favored them. They might spread until they should be embraced by the whole Catholic world, for Augustine believed in the vitality of error as well as in the vitality of truth, – of the natural and inevitable tendency of society towards Paganism, without the especial and restraining grace of God. He armed himself for the great conflict with the infidelity of his day, not with David's sling, but Goliath's sword. He used the same weapons as his antagonist, even the arms of reason and knowledge, and constructed an argument which was overwhelming, if Paul's Epistles were to be the accepted premises of his irresistible logic. Great as was Pelagius, Augustine was a far greater man, – broader, deeper, more learned, more logical, more eloquent, more intense. He was raised up to demolish, with the very reason he professed to disdain, the sophistries and dogmas of one of the most dangerous enemies which the Church had ever known, – to leave to posterity his logic and his conclusions when similar enemies of his faith should rise up in future ages. He furnished a thesaurus not merely to Bernard and Thomas Aquinas, but even to Calvin and Bossuet and Pascal. And it will be the marvellous lucidity of the Bishop of Hippo which shall bring back to the true faith, if it is ever brought back, that part of the Roman Catholic Church which accepts the verdict of the Council of Trent, when that famous council indorsed the opinions of Pelagius while upholding the authority of Augustine as the greatest doctor of the Church.

To a man like Augustine, with his deep experiences, – a man rescued from a seductive philosophy and a corrupt life, as he thought, by the special grace of God and in answer to his mother's prayers, – the views of Pelagius were both false and dangerous. He could find no words sufficiently intense whereby to express his gratitude for his deliverance from both sin and error. To him this Deliverer is so personal, so loving, that he pours out his confession to Him as if He were both friend and father. And he felt that all that is vital in theology must radiate from the recognition of His sovereign power in the renovation and salvation of the world. All his experiences and observations of life confirmed the authority of Scripture, – that the world, as a matter of fact, was sunk in a state of sin and misery, and could be rescued only by that divine power which converted Paul. His views of predestination, grace, and Providence all radiate from the central principle of the majesty of God and the littleness of man. All his ideas of the servitude of the will are confirmed by his personal experience of the awful fetters which sin imposes, and the impossibility of breaking away from them without direct aid from the God who ruleth the world in love. And he had an infinitely greater and deeper conviction of the reality of this divine love, which had rescued him, than Pelagius had, who felt that his salvation was the result of his own merits. The views of Augustine were infinitely more cheerful than those of his adversary respecting salvation, since they gave more hope to the miserable population of the Empire who could not claim the virtues of Pelagius, and were impotent of themselves to break away from the bondage which degraded them. There is nothing in the writings of Augustine, – not in this controversy, or any other controversy, – to show that God delights in the miseries or the penalty which are indissolubly connected with sin; on the contrary, he blesses and adores the divine hand which releases men from the constraints which sin imposes. This divine interposition is wholly based on a divine and infinite love. It is the helping hand of Omnipotence to the weak will of man, – the weak will even of Paul, when he exclaimed, "The evil that I would not, that I do." It is the unloosing, by His loving assistance, of the wings by which the emancipated soul would rise to the lofty regions of peace and contemplation.

I know very well that the doctrines which Augustine systematized from Paul involve questions which we cannot answer; for why should not an infinite and omnipotent God give to all men the saving grace that he gave to Augustine? Why should not this loving and compassionate Father break all the fetters of sin everywhere, and restore the primeval Paradise in this wicked world where Satan seems to reign? Is He not more powerful than devils? Alas! the prevalence of evil is more mysterious than the origin of evil. But this is something, – and it is well for the critic and opponent of the Augustinian theology to bear this in mind, – that Augustine was an earnest seeker after truth, even when enslaved by the fornications of Carthage; and his own free-will in persistently seeking truth, through all the mazes of

Manichean and Grecian speculation, is as manifest as the divine grace which came to his assistance. God Almighty does not break fetters until there is some desire in men to have them broken. If men *will* hug sins, they must not complain of their bondage. Augustine recognized free-will, which so many think he ignored, when his soul aspired to a higher life. When a drunkard in his agonies cries out to God, then help is near. A drowning man who calls for a rope when a rope is near stands a good chance of being rescued.

I need not detail the results of this famous controversy. Augustine, appealing to the consciousness of mankind as well as to the testimony of Paul, prevailed over Pelagius, who appealed to the pride of reason. In those dreadful times there were more men who felt the need of divine grace than there were philosophers who reveled in the speculations of the Greeks. The danger from the Pelagians was not from their organization as a sect, but their opinions as individual men. Probably there were all shades of opinion among them, from a modest and thoughtful semi-Pelagianism to the rankest infidelity. There always have been, and probably ever will be, sceptical and rationalistic people, even in the bosom of the Church.

Now had it not been for Augustine, – a profound thinker, a man of boundless influence and authority, – it is not unlikely that Pelagianism would have taken so deep a root in the mind of Christendom, especially in the hearts of princes and nobles, that it would have become the creed of the Church. Even as it was, it was never fully eradicated in the schools and in the courts and among worldly people of culture and fashion.

But the fame of Augustine does not rest on his controversies with heretics and schismatics alone. He wrote treatises on almost all subjects of vital interest to the Church. His essay on the Trinity was worthy of Athanasius, and has never been surpassed in lucidity and power. His soliloquies on a blissful life, and the order of the universe, and the immortality of the soul are pregnant with the richest thought, equal to the best treatises of Cicero or Boethius. His commentary on the Psalms is sparkling with tender effusions, in which every thought is a sentiment and every sentiment is a blazing flame of piety and love. Perhaps his greatest work was the amusement of his leisure hours for thirteen years, – a philosophical treatise called "The City of God," in which he raises and replies to all the great questions of his day; a sort of Christian poem upon our origin and end, and a final answer to Pagan theogonies, – a final sentence on all the gods of antiquity. In that marvellous book he soars above his ordinary excellence, and develops the designs of God in the history of States and empires, furnishing for Bossuet the groundwork of his universal history. Its great excellence, however, is its triumphant defence of Christianity over all other religions, – the last of the great apologies which, while settling the faith of the Christian world, demolished forever the last stronghold of a defeated Paganism. As "ancient Egypt pronounced judgments on her departed kings before proceeding to their burial, so Augustine interrogates the gods of antiquity, shows their impotence to sustain the people who worshipped them, triumphantly sings their departed greatness, and seals with his powerful hand the sepulchre into which they were consigned forever."

Besides all the treatises of Augustine, – exegetical, apologetical, dogmatical, polemical, ascetic, and autobiographical, – three hundred and sixty-three of his sermons have come down to us, and numerous letters to the great men and women of his time. Perhaps he wrote too much and too loosely, without sufficient regard to art, – like Varro, the most voluminous writer of antiquity, and to whose writings Augustine was much indebted. If Saint Augustine had written less, and with more care, his writings would now be more read and more valued. Thucydides compressed the labors of his literary life into a single volume; but that volume is immortal, is a classic, is a text-book. Yet no work of man is probably more lasting than the "Confessions" of Augustine, from the extraordinary affluence and subtilty of his thoughts, and his burning, fervid, passionate style. When books were scarce and dear, his various works were the food of the Middle Ages: and what better books ever nourished the European mind in a long period of ignorance and ignominy? So that we cannot overrate his influence in giving a direction to Christian thought. He lived in the writings of the sainted doctors of the Scholastic schools. And he was a very favored man in living to a good old age, wearing the harness of a Christian laborer and the armor of a Christian warrior until he was seventy-six. He was a bishop nearly forty years. For forty years he was the oracle of the Church, the light of doctors. His social and private life had also great charms: he lived the doctrines that he preached; he completely triumphed over the temptations which once assailed him. Everybody loved as well as revered him, so genial was his humanity, so broad his charity. He was affable, courteous, accessible, full of sympathy and kindness. He was tolerant of human infirmities in an age of angry controversy and ascetic rigors. He lived simply, but was exceedingly hospitable. He cared nothing for money, and gave away what he had. He knew the luxury of charity, having no superfluities. He was forgiving as well as tolerant; saying, it is necessary to pardon offences, not seven times, but seventy times seven. No one could remember an idle word from his lips after his conversion. His humility was as marked as his charity, ascribing all his triumphs to divine assistance. He was not a monk, but gave rules to monastic orders. He might have been a metropolitan patriarch or pope; but he was contented with being bishop of a little Numidian town. His only visits beyond the sanctuary were to the poor and miserable. As he won every heart by love, so he subdued every mind by eloquence. He died leaving no testament, because he had no property to bequeath but his immortal writings, – some ten hundred and thirty distinct productions. He died in the year 430, when his city was besieged by the Vandals, and in the arms of his faithful Alypius, then a neighboring bishop, full of visions of the ineffable beauty of that blissful state to which his renovated spirit had been for forty years constantly soaring.

"Thus ceased to flow," said a contemporary, "that river of eloquence which had watered the thirsty fields of the Church; thus passed away the glory of preachers, the master of doctors, and the light of scholars; thus fell the courageous combatant who with the sword of truth had given heresy a mortal blow; thus set this glorious sun of Christian doctrine, leaving a world in darkness and in tears."

His vacant see had no successor. "The African province, the cherished jewel of the Roman Empire, sparkled for a while in the Vandal diadem. The Greek supplanted the Vandal, and the Saracen supplanted the Greek, and the home of Augustine was blotted out from the map of Christendom." The light of the gospel was totally extinguished in Northern Africa. The acts of Rome and the doctrines of Cyprian were equally forgotten by the Mahommedan conquerors. Only in Bona, as Hippo is now called, has the memory of the great bishop been cherished, – the one solitary flower which escaped the successive desolations of Vandals and Saracens. And when Algiers was conquered by the French in 1830, the sacred relics of the saint were transferred from Pavia (where they had been deposited by the order of Charlemagne), in a coffin of lead, enclosed in a coffin of silver, and the whole secured in a sarcophagus of marble, and finally committed to the earth near the scenes which had witnessed his transcendent labors. I do not know whether any monument of marble and granite was erected to his memory; but he needs no chiseled stone, no storied urn, no marble bust, to perpetuate his fame. For nearly fifteen hundred years he has reigned as the great oracle of the Church, Catholic and Protestant, in matters of doctrine, – the precursor of Bernard, of Leibnitz, of Calvin, of Bossuet, all of whom reproduced his ideas, and acknowledged him as the fountain of their own greatness. "Whether," said one of the late martyred archbishops of Paris, "he reveals to us the foundations of an impure polytheism, so varied in its developments, yet so uniform in its elemental principles; or whether he sports with the most difficult problems of philosophy, and throws out thoughts which in after times are sufficient to give an immortality to Descartes, – we always find in this great doctor all that human genius, enlightened by the Spirit of God, can explain, and also to what a sublime height reason herself may soar when allied with faith."

AUTHORITIES

The following are original authorities: Baronius; Geisler; Gibbon; Mabillon; Mosheim; Milman; Neander; Tillemont

Butler, *Lives of the Saints*
History of M. Poujoulat
Vaughan's *Life of Thomas Aquinas*
Works of Saint Augustine (especially his "Confessions.")

Chapter 9

THEODOSIUS THE GREAT:
LATTER DAYS OF ROME

A.D. 346-395

The last of those Roman emperors whom we call great was Theodosius. After him there is no great historic name, unless it be Justinian, who reigned when Rome had fallen. With Theodosius is associated the life-and-death struggle of Rome with the Gothic barbarians, and the final collapse of Paganism as a tolerated religion. Paganism in its essence, its spirit, was not extinguished; it entered into new forms, even into the Church itself; and it still exists in Christian countries. When Bismarck was asked why he did not throw down his burdens, he is reported to have said: "Because no man can take my place. I should like to retire to my estates and raise cabbages; but I have work to do against Paganism: I live among Pagans." Neither Theodosius nor Bismarck was what we should call a saint. Both have been stained by acts which it is hard to distinguish from crimes; but both have given evidence of hatred of certain evils which undermine society. Theodosius, especially, made war and fought nobly against the two things which most imperilled the Empire, – the barbarians who had begun their ravages, and the Paganism which existed both in and outside the Church.

For which reasons he has been praised by most historians, in spite of great crimes and some vices. The worldly Gibbon admires him for the noble stand he took against external dangers, and the Fathers of the Church almost adored him for his zealous efforts in behalf of orthodoxy. An eminent scholar of the advanced school has seen nothing in him to admire, and much to blame. But he was undoubtedly a very great man, and rendered important services to his age and to civilization, although he could not arrest the fatal disease which even then had destroyed the vitality of the Empire. It was already doomed when he ascended the throne. No mortal genius, no imperial power, could have saved the crumbling Empire.

In my lecture on Marcus Aurelius I alluded to the external prosperity and internal weakness of the old Roman world during his reign. That outward prosperity continued for a century after he was dead, – that is, there were peace, thrift, art, wealth, and splendor. Men were unmolested in the pursuit of pleasure. There were no great wars with enemies beyond the limits of the Empire. There were wars of course; but these chiefly were civil wars between rival aspirants for imperial power, or to suppress rebellions, which did not alarm the people. They still sat under their own vines and fig-trees, and danced to voluptuous music, and rejoiced in the glory of their palaces. They feasted and married and were given in marriage, like the antediluvians. They never dreamed that a great catastrophe was near, that great calamities were impending.

I do not say that the people in that century were happy or contented, or even generally prosperous. How could they be happy or prosperous when monsters and tyrants sat on the throne of Augustus and Trajan? How could they be contented when there was such a vast inequality of condition, – when slaves were more numerous than freemen, – when most of the women were guarded and oppressed, – when scarcely a man felt secure of the virtue of his wife, or a wife of the fidelity of her husband, – when there was no relief from corroding sorrows but in the sports of the amphitheatre and circus, or some form of demoralizing excitement or public spectacle, – when the great mass were ground down by poverty and insult, and the few who were rich and favored were satiated with pleasure, ennuéd, and broken down by dissipation, – when there was no hope in this world or in the next, no true consolation in sickness or in misfortune, except among the Christians, who fled by thousands to desert places to escape the contaminating vices of society?

But if the people were not happy or fortunate as a general thing, they anticipated no overwhelming calamities; the outward signs of prosperity remained, – all the glories of art, all the wonders of imperial and senatorial magnificence; the people were fed and amused at the expense of the State; the colosseum was still daily crowded with its eighty-seven thousand spectators, and large hogs were still roasted whole at senatorial banquets, and wines were still drunk which had been stored one hundred years. The "dark-skinned daughters of Isis" still sported unmolested in wanton mien with the priests of Cybele in their discordant cries. The streets still were filled with the worshippers of Bacchus and Venus, with barbaric captives and their Teuton priests, with chariots and horses, with richly appareled young men, and fashionable ladies in quest of new perfumes. The various places of amusement were still thronged with giddy youth and gouty old men who would have felt insulted had any one told them that the most precious thing they had was the most neglected. Everywhere, as in the time of Trajan, were unrestricted pleasures and unrestricted trades. What cared the shopkeepers and the carpenters and the bakers whether a Commodus or a Severus reigned? They were safe. It was only great nobles who were in danger of being robbed or killed by grasping emperors. The people, on the whole, lived for one hundred years after the accession of Commodus as they did under Trajan and Marcus Aurelius. True, there had been great calamities during this hundred years. There had been terrible plagues and pestilences: in some of these as many as five thousand people died daily in Rome alone. There were tumults and revolts; there were wars and massacres; there was often the reign of monsters or idiots. Yet even as late as the reign of Aurelian, ninety years after the death of Aurelius, the Empire was thought to be eternal; nor was any triumph ever celebrated with greater pride and magnificence than his. And as the victorious emperor in his triumphal chariot marched along the Via Sacra up the Capitoline hill, with the spoils and trophies of one hundred battles, with ambassadors and captives, including Zenobia herself, fainting with the weight of jewels and golden fetters, it would seem that Rome was destined to overcome all the vicissitudes of Nature, and reign as mistress of the world forever.

But that century did not close until real dangers stared the people in the face, and so alarmed the guardians of the Empire that they no longer could retire to their secluded villas for luxurious leisure, but were forced to perpetual warfare, and with foes they had hitherto despised.

Two things marked the one hundred years before the accession of Theodosius of especial historical importance, – the successful inroads of barbarians carrying desolation and alarm to the very heart of the Empire; and the wonderful spread of the Christian religion. Persecution ended with Diocletian; and under Constantine Christianity seated herself upon his throne. During this century of barbaric spoliations and public miseries, – the desolation of provinces, the sack of cities, the ruin of works of art, the burning of palaces, all the unnumbered evils which universal war created, – the converts to Christianity increased, for Christianity alone held out hope amid despair and ruin. The public dangers were so great that only successful generals were allowed to wear the imperial purple.

The ablest men of the Empire were at last summoned to govern it. From the year 268 to 394 most of the emperors were able men, and some were great and virtuous. Perhaps the Empire was never more ably administered than was the Roman in the day of its calamities. Aurelian, Diocletian, Constantine, Theodosius, are alike immortal. They all alike fought with the same enemies, and contended with the same evils. The enemies were the Gothic barbarians; the evils were the degeneracy and vices of Roman soldiers, which universal corruption had at last produced. It was a sad hour in the old capital of the world when its blinded inhabitants were aroused from the stupendous delusion that they were invincible; when the crushing fact blazed upon them that the legions had been beaten, that province after province had been overrun, that the proudest cities had fallen, that the barbarians were advancing, – everywhere advancing, – treading beneath their feet temples, palaces, statues, libraries, priceless works of art; that there was no shelter to which they could fly; that Rome herself was doomed. In the year 378 the Emperor Valens himself was slain, almost under the walls of his capital, with two-thirds of his army, – some sixty thousand infantry and six thousand cavalry, – while the victorious Goths, gorged with spoils, advanced to take possession of the defeated and crumbling Empire. From the shores of the Bosporus to the Julian Alps nothing was seen but conflagration, murders, and depredations, and the cry of anguish went up to heaven in accents of almost universal despair.

In such a crisis a great man was imperatively needed, and a great man arose. The dismayed emperor cast his eyes over the whole extent of his dominions to find a deliverer. And he found the needed hero living quietly and in modest retirement on a farm in Spain. This man was Theodosius the Great, a young man then, – as modest as David amid the pastures, as unambitious as Cincinnatus at the plough. "The vulgar," says Gibbon, "gazed with admiration on the manly beauty of his face and the graceful majesty of his person, while in the qualities of his mind and heart intelligent observers perceived the blended excellences of Trajan and Constantine." As prudent as Fabius, as persevering as Alfred, as comprehensive as Charlemagne, as full of resources as Frederic II., no more fitting person could be found to wield the sceptre of Trajan his ancestor. No greater man than he did the Empire then contain, and Gratian was wise and fortunate in associating with himself so illustrious a man in the imperial dignity.

If Theodosius was unassuming, he was not obscure and unimportant. His father had been a successful general in Britain and Africa, and he himself had been instructed by his father in the art of war, and had served under him with distinction. As Duke of Maesia he had vanquished an army of Sarmatians, saved the province, deserved the love of his soldiers, and provoked the envy of the court. But his father having incurred the jealousy of Gratian and been unjustly executed, he was allowed to retire to his patrimonial estates near Valladolid, where he gave himself up to rural enjoyments and ennobling studies. He was not long permitted to remain in this retirement; for the public dangers demanded the service of the ablest general in the Empire, and there was no one so illustrious as he. And how lofty must have been his character, if Gratian dared to associate with himself in the government of the Empire a man whose father he had unjustly executed! He was thirty-three when he was invested with imperial purple and intrusted with the conduct of the Gothic war.

The Goths, who under Fritigern had defeated the Roman army before the walls of Adrianople, were Germanic barbarians who lived between the Rhine and the Vistula in those forests which now form the empire of Germany. They belonged to a family of nations which had the same natural characteristics, – love of independence, passion for war, veneration for women, and religious tendency of mind. They were brave, persevering, bold, hardy, and virtuous, for barbarians. They cast their eyes on the Roman provinces in the time of Marius, and were defeated by him under the name of Teutons. They had recovered strength when Caesar conquered the Gauls. They were very formidable in the time of Marcus Aurelius, and had formed a general union for the invasion of the Roman world. But a barrier had been made against their incursions by those good and warlike emperors who preceded Commodus, so that the Romans had peace for one hundred years. These barbarians went under different names, which I will not enumerate, – different tribes of the same Germanic family, whose remote ancestors lived in Central Asia and were kindred to the Medes and Persians. Like the early inhabitants of Greece and Italy, they were of the Aryan race. All the members of this great family, in their early history, had the same virtues and vices. They worshipped the forces of Nature, recognizing behind these a supreme and superintending deity, whose wrath they sought to deprecate by sacrifices. They set a great value on personal independence, and hence had great individuality of character. They delighted in the pleasures of the chase. They were generally temperate and chaste. They were superstitious, social, and quarrelsome, bent on conquest, and migrated from country to country with a view of improving their fortunes.

The Goths were the first of these barbarians who signally triumphed over the Roman arms. "Starting from their home in the Scandinavian Peninsula, they pressed upon the Slavic population of the Vistula, and by rapid conquests established themselves in southern and eastern Germany. Here they divided. The Visi or West Goths advanced to the Danube." In the reign of Decius (249-251) they crossed the river and ravaged the Roman territory. In 269 they imposed a tribute on the Emperor Gratian, and seem to have been settled in Dacia. After this they made several successful raids, – invading Bythinia, entering the Propontis, and advancing as far as Athens and Corinth, even to the coasts of Asia Minor; destroying in their ravages the Temple of Diana at Ephesus, with its one hundred and twenty-seven marble columns.

Figure 12. Invasion of the Goths into the Roman Empire. *After the painting by O. Fritsche.*

These calamities happened in the middle of the third century, during the reign of the frivolous Gallienus, who received the news with his accustomed indifference. While the Goths were burning the Grecian cities, this royal cook and gardener was soliciting a place in the Areopagus of Athens.

In the reign of Claudius the barbarians united under the Gothic standard, and in six thousand vessels prepared again to ravage the world. Against three hundred and twenty thousand of these Goths Claudius advanced, and defeated them at Naissus in Dalmatia. Fifty thousand were slain, and three Gothic women fell to the share of every soldier. On the return of spring nothing of that mighty host was seen. Aurelian – who succeeded Claudius, and whose father had been a peasant of Sirmium – put an end to the Gothic war, and the Empire again breathed; but only for a time, for the barbarians continually advanced, although they were continually beaten by the warlike emperors who succeeded Gallienus. In the middle of the third century they were firmly settled in Dacia, by permission of Valerian. One hundred years after, pressed by Huns, they asked for lands south of the Danube, which request was granted by Valens; but they were rudely treated by the Roman officials, especially their women, and treachery was added to their other wrongs. Filled with indignation, they made a combination and swept everything before them, – plundering cities, and sparing neither age nor sex. These ravages continued for a year. Valens, aroused, advanced against them, and was slain in the memorable battle on the plains of Adrianople, 9th of August, 378, – the most disastrous since the battle of Cannae, and from which the Empire never recovered.

To save the crumbling world, Theodosius was now made associate emperor. And in that great crisis prudence was more necessary than valor. No Roman army at that time could contend openly in the field, face to face, with the conquering hordes who assembled under the standard of Fritigern, – the first historic name among the Visigoths. Theodosius "fixed his headquarters at Thessalonica, from whence he could watch the irregular actions of the barbarians and direct the movements of his lieutenants." He strengthened his defences and fortifications, from which his soldiers made frequent sallies, – as Alfred did against the Danes, – and accustomed themselves to the warfare of their most dangerous enemies. He pursued the same policy that Fabius did after the battle of Cannae, to whose wisdom the Romans perhaps were more indebted for their ultimate success than to the brilliant exploits of Scipio. The death of Fritigern, the great predecessor of Alaric, relieved Theodosius from many anxieties; for it was followed by the dissension and discord of the barbarians themselves, by improvidence and disorderly movements; and when the Goths were once more united under Athanaric, Theodosius succeeded in making an honorable treaty with him, and in entertaining him with princely hospitalities in his capital, whose glories alike astonished and bewildered him. Temperance was not one of the virtues of Gothic kings under strong temptation, and Athanaric, yielding to the force of banquets and imperial seductions, soon after died. The politic emperor gave his late guest a magnificent funeral, and erected to his memory a stately monument; which won the favor of the Goths, and for a time converted them to allies. In four years the entire capitulation of the Visigoths was effected.

Theodosius then turned his attention to the Ostro or East Goths, who advanced, with other barbarians, to the banks of the lower Danube, on the Thracian frontier. Allured to cross the river in the night, the barbarians found a triple line of Roman war-vessels chained to each other in the middle of the river, which offered an effectual resistance to their six thousand canoes, and they perished with their king.

Having gradually vanquished the most dangerous enemies of the Empire, Theodosius has been censured for allowing them to settle in the provinces they had desolated, and still more for incorporating fifty thousand of their warriors in the imperial armies, since they were secret enemies, and would burst through their limits whenever an opportunity offered. But they were really too formidable to be driven back beyond the frontiers of the crumbling Empire. Theodosius could only procure a period of peace; and this was not to be secured save by adroit flatteries. The day was past for the extermination of the Goths by Roman soldiers, who had already thrown away their defensive armor; nor was it possible that they would amalgamate with the people of the Empire, as the Celtic barbarians had done in Spain and Gaul after the victories of Caesar. Though the kingly power was taken away from them and they fought bravely under the imperial standards, it was evident from their insolence and their contempt of the effeminate masters that the day was not distant when they would be the conquerors of the Empire. It does not speak well for an empire that it is held together by the virtues and abilities of a single man. Nor could the fate of the Roman empire be doubtful when barbarians were allowed to settle in its provinces; for after the death of Valens the Goths never abandoned the Roman territory. They took possession of Thrace, as Saxons and Danes took possession of England.

After the conciliation of the Goths, – for we cannot call it the conquest, – Theodosius was obliged to turn his attention to the affairs of the Western Empire; for he ruled only the Eastern provinces. It would seem that Gratian, who had called him to his assistance to preserve the East from the barbarians, was now in trouble in the West. He had not fulfilled the great expectation that had been formed of him. He degraded himself in the eyes of the Romans by his absorbing passion for the pleasures of the chase; while public affairs imperatively demanded his attention. He received a body of Alans into the military and domestic service of the palace. He was indolent and pleasure-seeking, but was awakened from his inglorious sports by a revolt in Britain. Maximus, a native of Spain and governor of the island, had been proclaimed emperor by his soldiers. He invaded Gaul with a large fleet and army, followed by the youth of Britain, and was received with acclamations by the armies of that province. Gratian, then residing in Paris, fled to Lyons, deserted by his troops, and was assassinated by the orders of Maximus. The usurper was now acknowledged by the Western provinces as emperor, and was too powerful to be resisted at that time by Theodosius, who accepted his ambassadors, and made a treaty with the usurper by which he was permitted to reign over Britain, Gaul, and Spain, provided that the other Western provinces, including Wales, should accept and acknowledge Valentinian, the brother of the murdered Gratian, who was however a mere boy, and was ruled by his mother Justina, an Arian, – that celebrated woman who quarreled with Ambrose, archbishop of Milan. Valentinian was even more feeble than Gratian, and Maximus, not contented with the sovereignty of the three most important provinces of the Empire, resolved to reign over the entire West. Theodosius, who had dissembled his anger and waited for opportunity, now advanced to the relief of Valentinian, who had been obliged to fly from Milan, – the seat of his power. But in two months Theodosius subdued his rival, who fled to Italy, only, however, to be dragged from the throne and executed.

Having terminated the civil war, and after a short residence in Milan, Theodosius made his triumphal entry into the ancient capital of the world. He was now the absolute and undisputed master of the East and the West, as Constantine had been, whom he resembled in his military genius and executive ability; but he gave to Valentinian (a youth of twenty, murdered a few months after) the provinces of Italy and Illyria, and intrusted Gaul to the care of Arbogastes, – a gallant soldier among the Franks, who, like Maximus, aspired to reign. But power was dearer to the valiant Frank than a name; and he made his creature, the rhetorician Eugenius, the nominal emperor of the West. Hence another civil war; but this more serious than the last, and for which Theodosius was obliged to make two years' preparation. The contest was desperate. Victory at one time seemed even to be on the side of Arbogastes: Theodosius was obliged to retire to the hills on the confines of Italy, apparently subdued, when, in the utmost extremity of danger, a desertion of troops from the army of the triumphant barbarian again gave him the advantage, and the bloody and desperate battle on the banks of the Frigidus re-established Theodosius as the supreme ruler of the world. Both Arbogastes and Eugenius were slain, and the East and West were once more and for the last time united. The division of the Empire under Diocletian had not proved a wise policy, but was perhaps necessary; since only a Hercules could have borne the burdens of undivided sovereignty in an age of turbulence, treason, revolts, and anarchies. It was probably much easier for Tiberius or Trajan to rule the whole world than for one of the later emperors to rule a province. Alfred had a harder task than Charlemagne, and Queen Elizabeth than Queen Victoria.

I have dwelt very briefly on those contests in which the great Theodosius was obliged to fight for his crown and for the Empire. For a time he had delivered the citizens from the fear of the Goths, and had re-established the imperial sovereignty over the various provinces. But only for a time. The external dangers reappeared at his death. He only averted impending ruin; he only propped up a crumbling Empire. No human genius could have long prevented the fall. Hence his struggles with barbarians and with rebels have no deep interest to us. We associate with his reign something more important than these outward conflicts. Civilization at large owes him a great debt for labors in another field, for which he is most truly immortal, – for which his name is treasured by the Church, – for which he was one of the great benefactors.

These labors were directed to the improvement of jurisprudence, and the final extinction of Paganism as a tolerated religion. He gave to the Church and to Christianity a new prestige. He rooted out, so far as genius and authority can, those heresies which were rapidly assimilating the new religion to the old. He was the friend and patron of those great ecclesiastics whose names are consecrated. The great Ambrose was his special friend, in whose arms he expired. Augustine, Martin of Tours, Jerome, Gregory

Nazianzen, Basil, Chrysostom, Damasus, were all contemporaries, or nearly so. In his day the Church was really seated on the high-places of the earth. A bishop was a greater man than a senator; he exercised more influence and had more dignity than a general. He was ambassador, courtier, and statesman, as well as prelate. Theodosius handed over to the Church the government of mankind. To him we date that ecclesiastical government which was perfected by Charlemagne, and which was dominant in the Middle Ages. Anarchy and misery spread over the world; but the new barbaric forces were obedient to the officers of the Church. The Church looms up in the days of Theodosius as the great power of the world.

Theodosius is lauded as a Christian prince even more than Constantine, and as much as Alfred. He was what is called orthodox, and intensely so. He saw in Arianism a heresy fatal to the Church. "It is our pleasure," said he, "that all nations should steadfastly adhere to the religion which was taught by Saint Peter to the Romans, which is *the sole Deity of the Father, the Son, and Holy Ghost*, under an equal majesty; and we authorize the followers of this doctrine to assume the title of Catholic Christians." If Rome under Damasus and the teachings of Jerome was the seat of orthodoxy, Constantinople was the headquarters of Arianism. We in our times have no conception of the interest which all classes took in the metaphysics of theology. Said one of the writers of the day: "If you desire a man to change a piece of silver, he informs you wherein the Son differs from the Father; if you ask the price of a loaf, you are told in reply that the Son is inferior to the Father; if you inquire whether the bath is ready, the answer is that the Son was made out of nothing." The subtle questions pertaining to the Trinity were the theme of universal conversation, even amid the calamities of the times.

Theodosius, as soon as he had finished his campaign against the Goths, summoned the Arian archbishop of Constantinople, and demanded his subscription to the Nicene Creed or his resignation. It must be remembered that the Arians were in an overwhelming majority in the city, and occupied the principal churches. They complained of the injustice of removing their metropolitan, but the emperor was inflexible; and Gregory Nazianzen, the friend of Basil, was promoted to the vacant See, in the midst of popular grief and rage. Six weeks afterwards Theodosius expelled from all the churches of his dominions, both of bishops and of presbyters, those who would not subscribe to the Nicene Creed. It was a great reformation, but effected without bloodshed.

Moreover, in the year 381 he assembled a general council of one hundred and fifty bishops at his capital, to finish the work of the Council of Nice, and in which Arianism was condemned. In the space of fifteen years seven imperial edicts were fulminated against those who maintained that the Son was inferior to the Father. A fine equal to two thousand dollars was imposed on every person who should receive or promote an Arian ordination. The Arians were forbidden to assemble together in their churches, and by a sort of civil excommunication they were branded with infamy by the magistrates, and rendered incapable of civil offices of trust and emolument. Capital punishment even was inflicted on Manicheans.

So it would appear that Theodosius inaugurated religious persecution for honest opinions, and his edicts were similar in spirit to those of Louis XIV against the Protestants, – a great flaw in his character, but for which he is lauded by the Catholic historians. The eloquent Fléchier enlarges enthusiastically on the virtues of his private life, on his chastity, his temperance, his friendship, his magnanimity, as well as his zeal in extinguishing heresy. But for him, Arianism might possibly have been the established religion of the Empire, since not only the dialectical Greeks, but the sensuous Goths, inclined to that creed. Ulfilas, in his conversion of those barbarians, had made them the supporters of Arianism, not because *they* understood the subtile distinctions which theologians had made, but because it was the accepted and fashionable faith of Constantinople. Spain, however, through the commanding influence of Hosius, adhered to the doctrines of Athanasius, while the eloquence of the commanding intellects of the age was put forth in behalf of Trinitarianism. The great leader of Arianism had passed away when Augustine dictated to the Christian world from the little town of Hippo, and Jerome transplanted the monasticism of the East into the West. At Tours Martin defended the same cause that Augustine had espoused in Africa; while at Milan, the court capital of the West, the venerable Ambrose confirmed Italy in the Latin creed. In Alexandria the fierce Theophilus suppressed Arianism with the same weapons that he had used in extirpating the worship of Isis and Osiris. Chrysostom at Antioch was the equally strenuous advocate of the Athanasian Creed. We are struck with the appearance of these commanding intellects in the last days of the Empire, – not statesmen and generals, but ecclesiastics and churchmen, generally agreed in the interpretation of the faith as declared by Paul, and through whose counsels the emperor was unquestionably governed. In all matters of religion Theodosius was simply the instrument of the great prelates of the age, – the only great men that the age produced.

After Theodosius had thus established the Nicene faith, so far as imperial authority, in conjunction with that of the great prelates, could do so, he closed the final contest with Paganism itself. His laws against Pagan sacrifices were severe. It was death to inspect the entrails of victims for sacrifice; and all other sacrifices, in the year 392, were made a capital offence. He even demolished the Pagan temples, as the Scots destroyed the abbeys and convents which were the great monuments of Mediaeval piety. The revenues of the temples were confiscated. Among the great works of ancient art which were destroyed, but might have been left or converted into Christian use, were the magnificent temple of Edessa and the serapis of Alexandria, uniting the colossal grandeur of Egyptian with the graceful harmony of Grecian art. At Rome not only was the property of the temples confiscated, but also all privileges of the priesthood. The Vestal virgins passed unhonored in the streets. Whoever permitted any Pagan rite – even the hanging of a chaplet on a tree – forfeited his estate. The temples of Rome were not destroyed, as in Syria and Egypt; but as all their revenues were confiscated, public worship declined before the superior pomps of a sensuous and even idolatrous Christianity. The Theodosian code, published by Theodosius the Younger, A.D. 438, while it incorporated Christian usages and laws in the legislation of the Empire, did not, however, disturb the relation of master and slave; and when the Empire fell, slavery still continued as it was in the times of Augustus and Diocletian. Nor did Christianity elevate imperial despotism into a wise and beneficent rule. It did not change perceptibly the habits of the aristocracy. The most vivid picture we have of the vices of the leading classes of Roman society are painted by a contemporaneous Pagan historian, – Ammianus Marcellinus, – and many a Christian matron adorned herself with the false and colored hair, the ornaments, the rouge, and the silks of the Pagan women of the time of Cleopatra. Never was luxury more enervating, or magnificence more gorgeous, but without refinement, than in the generation that preceded the fall of Rome. And coexistent with the vices which prepared the way for the conquests of the barbarians was the wealth of the Christian clergy, who vied with the expiring Paganism in the splendor of their churches, in the ornaments of their altars, and in the imposing ceremonial of their worship. The bishop became a great worldly potentate, and the strictest union was formed between the Church and State. The greatest beneficent change which the Church effected was in relation to divorce, – the facility for which disgraced the old Pagan civilization; but Christianity invested marriage with the utmost solemnity, so that it became a holy and indissoluble sacrament, – to which the Catholic Church, in the days of deepest degeneracy has ever clung, leaving to the Protestants the restoration of this old Pagan custom of divorce, as well as the encouragement and laudation of a material civilization.

The spirit of Paganism never has been exorcised in any age of Christian progress and triumph, but has appeared from time to time in new forms. In the conquering Church of Constantine and Theodosius it adopted Pagan emblems and gorgeous rites and ceremonies; in the Middle Ages it appeared in the dialectical contests of the Greek philosophers; in our times in the deification of the reason, in the apotheosis of art, in the inordinate value placed on the enjoyments of the body, and in the splendor of an outside life. Names are nothing. To-day we are swinging to the Epicurean side of the Greeks and Romans as completely as they did in the age of Commodus and Aurelian; and none may dare to hurl their indignant protests without meeting a neglect and obloquy sometimes more hard to bear than the persecutions of Nero, of Trajan, of Leo X., of Louis XIV.

If Theodosius were considered aside from his able administration of the Empire and his patronage of the orthodox leaders of the Church, he would be subject to severe criticism. He was indolent, irascible, and severe. His name and memory are stained by a great crime, – the slaughter of from seven to fifteen thousand of the people of Thessalonica, – one of the great crimes of history, but memorable for his repentance more than for his cruelty. Had Theodosius not submitted to excommunication and penance, and given every sign of grief and penitence for this terrible deed, he would have passed down in history as one of the cruellest of all the emperors, from Nero downwards; for nothing can excuse, or even palliate, so gigantic a crime, which shocked the whole civilized world, – a crime more inexcusable than the slaughter of Saint Bartholomew or the massacre which followed the revocation of the edict of Nantes.

Theodosius survived that massacre about five years, and died at Milan, 395, at the age of fifty, from a disease which was caused by the fatigues of war, which, with a constitution undermined by self-indulgence, he was unable to bear. But whatever the cause of his death it was universally lamented, not from love of him so much as from the sense of public dangers which he alone had the power to ward off. At his death his Empire was divided between his two feeble sons, – Honorius and Arcadius, and the general ruin which everybody began to fear soon took place. After Theodosius, no great and warlike sovereign reigned over the crumbling and dismembered Empire, and the ruin was as rapid as it was mournful.

The Goths, released from the restraints and fears which Theodosius imposed, renewed their ravages; and the effeminate soldiers of the Empire, who formerly had marched with a burden of eighty pounds, now threw away the heavy weapons of their ancestors, even their defensive armor, and of course made but feeble resistance. The barbarians advanced from conquering to conquer. Alaric, leader of the Goths, invaded Greece at the head of a numerous army. Degenerate soldiers guarded the pass where three hundred Spartan heroes had once arrested the Persian hosts, and fled as Alaric approached. Even at Thermopylae no resistance was made. The country was laid waste with fire and sword. Athens purchased her preservation at an enormous ransom. Corinth, Argos, and Sparta yielded without a blow, but did not escape the doom of vanquished cities. Their palaces were burned, their families were enslaved, and their works of art were destroyed.

Only one general remained to the desponding Arcadius, – Stilicho, trained in the armies of Theodosius, who had virtually intrusted to him, although by birth a Vandal, the guardianship of his children. We see in these latter days of the Empire that the best generals were of barbaric birth, – an impressive commentary on the degeneracy of the legions. At the approach of Stilicho, Alaric retired at first, but collecting a force of ten thousand men penetrated the Julian Alps, and advanced into Italy. The Emperor Honorius was obliged to summon to his rescue his dispirited legions from every quarter, even from the fortresses of the Rhine and the Caledonian wall, with which Stilicho compelled Alaric to retire, but only on a subsidy of two tons of gold. The Roman people, supposing that they were delivered, returned to their circuses and gladiatorial shows. Yet Italy was only temporarily delivered, for Stilicho, – the hero of Pollentia, – with the collected forces of the whole western Empire, might still have defied the armies of the Goths and staved off the ruin another generation, had not imperial jealousy and the voice of envy removed him from command. The supreme guardian of the western Empire, in the greatest crisis of its history, himself removes the last hope of Rome. The frivolous senate which Stilicho had saved, and the weak and timid emperor whom he guarded, were alike demented. *Quos Deus vult perdere, prius dementat.* In an evil hour the brave general was assassinated.

The Gothic king observing the revolutions at the palace, the elevation of incompetent generals, and the general security in which the people indulged, resolved to march to a renewed attack. Again he crossed the Alps, with a still greater army, and invaded Italy, destroying everything in his path. Without obstruction he crossed the Apennines, ravaged the fertile plains of Umbria, and reached the city, which for four hundred years had not been violated by the presence of a foreign enemy. The walls were then twenty-five miles in circuit, and contained so large a population that it affected indifference. Alaric made no attempt to take the city by storm, but quietly and patiently enclosed it with a cordon through which nothing could force its way, – as the Prussians in our day invested Paris. The city, unprovided for a siege, soon felt all the evils of famine, to which pestilence was naturally added. In despair, the haughty citizens condescended to sue for a ransom. Alaric fixed the price of his retreat at the surrender of all the gold and silver, all the precious movables, and all the slaves of barbaric birth. He afterwards somewhat modified his demands, but marched away with more spoil than the Romans brought from Carthage and Antioch.

Honorius intrenched himself at Ravenna, and refused to treat with the magnanimous Alaric. Again, consequently, he marched against the doomed capital; again invested it; again cut off supplies. In vain did the nobles organize a defence, – there were no defenders. Slaves would not fight, and a degenerate rabble could not resist a warlike and superior race. Cowardice and treachery opened the gates. In the dead of night the Gothic trumpets rang unanswered in the streets. The old heroic virtues were gone. No resistance was made. Nobody fought from temples and palaces. The queen of the world, for five days and nights, was exposed to the lust and cupidity of despised barbarians. Yet a general slaughter was not made; and as much wealth as could be collected into the churches of St. Peter and St. Paul was spared. The superstitious barbarians in some degree respected churches. But the spoils of the city were immense and incalculable, – gold, jewels, vestments, statues, vases, silver plate, precious furniture, spoils of Oriental cities, – the collective treasures of the world, – all were piled upon the Gothic wagons. The sons and daughters of patrician families became, in their turn, slaves to the barbarians. Fugitives thronged the shores of Syria and Egypt, begging daily bread. The Roman world was filled with grief and consternation. Its proud capital was sacked, since no one would defend it. "The Empire fell," says Guizot, "because no one belonged to it." The news of the capture "made the tongue of old Saint Jerome to cling to the roof of his mouth in his cell at Bethlehem. What is now to be seen," cried he, "but conflagration, slaughter, ruin, – the universal shipwreck of society?" The same words of despair came from Saint Augustine at Hippo. Both had seen the city in the height of its material grandeur, and now it was laid low and desolate. The end of all things seemed to be at hand; and the only consolation of the great churchmen of the age was the belief in the second coming of our Lord.

The sack of Rome by Alaric, A.D. 410, was followed in less than half a century by a second capture and a second spoliation at the hands of the Vandals, with Genseric at their head, – a tribe of barbarians of kindred

Germanic race, but fiercer instincts and more hideous peculiarities. This time, the inhabitants of Rome (for Alaric had not destroyed it, – only robbed it) put on no airs of indifference or defiance. They knew their weakness. They begged for mercy.

The last hope of the city was her Christian bishop; and the great Leo, who was to Rome what Augustine had been to Carthage when that capital also fell into the hands of Vandals, hastened to the barbarian's camp. The only concession he could get was that the lives of the people should be spared, – a promise only partially kept. The second pillage lasted fourteen days and nights. The Vandals transferred to their ships all that the Goths had left, even to the trophies of the churches and ancient temples; the statues which ornamented the capital, the holy vessels of the Jewish temple which Titus had brought from Jerusalem, imperial sideboards of massive silver, the jewels of senatorial families, with their wives and daughters, – all were carried away to Carthage, the seat of the new Empire of the Vandals, A.D. 455, then once more a flourishing city. The haughty capital met the fate which she had inflicted on her rival in the days of Cato the censor, but fell still more ingloriously, and never would have recovered from this second fall had not her immortal bishop, rising with the greatness of the crisis, laid the foundation of a new power, – that spiritual domination which controlled the Gothic nations for more than a thousand years.

With the fall of Rome, – yet too great a city to be wholly despoiled or ruined, and which has remained even to this day the centre of what is most interesting in the world, – I should close this Lecture; but I must glance rapidly over the whole Empire, and show its condition when the imperial capital was spoiled, humiliated, and deserted.

The Suevi, Alans, and Vandals invaded Spain, and erected their barbaric monarchies. The Goths were established in the south of Gaul, while the north was occupied by the Franks and Burgundians. England, abandoned by the Romans, was invaded by the Saxons, who formed permanent conquests. In Italy there were Goths and Heruli and Lombards. All these races were Germanic. They probably made serfs or slaves of the old population, or were incorporated with them. They became the new rulers of the devastated provinces; and all became, sooner or later, converts to a nominal

Christianity, the supreme guardian of which was the Pope, whose authority they all recognized. The languages which sprang up in Europe were a blending of the Roman, Celtic, and Germanic. In Spain and Italy the Latin predominated, as the Saxon prevailed in England after the Norman conquest. Of all the new settlers in the Roman world, the Normans, who made no great incursions till the time of Charlemagne, were probably the strongest and most refined. But they all alike had the same national traits, substantially; and they entered upon the possessions of the Romans after various contests, more or less successful, for two hundred and fifty years.

The Empire might have been invaded by these barbarians in the time of the Antonines, and perhaps earlier; but it would not have succumbed to them. The Legions were then severely disciplined, the central power was established, and the seeds of ruin had not then brought forth their wretched fruits. But in the fifth century nothing could have saved the Empire. Its decline had been rapid for two hundred years, until at last it became as weak as the Oriental monarchies which Alexander subdued. It fell like a decayed and rotten tree. As a political State all vitality had fled from it. The only remaining conservative forces came from Christianity; and Christianity was itself corrupted, and had become a part of the institutions of the State.

It is mournful to think that a brilliant external civilization was so feeble to arrest both decay and ruin. It is sad to think that neither art nor literature nor law had conservative strength; that the manners and habits of the people grew worse and worse, as is universally admitted, amid all the glories and triumphs and boastings of the proudest works of man. "A world as fair and as glorious as our own," says Sismondi, "was permitted to perish." Rome, Alexandria, Antioch, Athens, met the old fate of Babylon, of Tyre, of Carthage. Degeneracy was as marked and rapid in the former, notwithstanding all the civilizing influences of letters, jurisprudence, arts, and utilitarian science, as in the latter nations, – a most significant and impressive commentary on the uniform destinies of nations, when those virtues on which the strength of man is based have passed away. An observer in the days of Theodosius would very likely have seen the churches of Rome as fully attended as are those in New York itself to-day; and he would have seen a more magnificent city, – and yet it fell. There is no cure for a corrupt and rotten civilization. As the farms of the old Puritans of Massachusetts and Connecticut are gradually but surely passing into the hands of the Irish, because the sons and grandsons of the old New-England farmer prefer the uncertainties and excitements of a demoralized city-life to laborious and honest work, so the possessions of the Romans passed into the hands of German barbarians, who were strong and healthy and religious. They desolated, but they reconstructed.

The punishment of the enervated and sensual Roman was by war. We in America do not fear this calamity, and have no present cause of fear, because we have not sunk to the weakness and wickedness of the Romans, and because we have no powerful external enemies. But if amid our magnificent triumphs of science and art, we should accept the Epicureanism of the ancients and fall into their ways of life, then there would be the same decline which marked them, – I mean in virtue and public morality, – and there would be the same penalty; not perhaps destruction from external enemies, as in Persia, Syria, Greece, and Rome, but some grievous and unexpected series of catastrophes which would be as mournful, as humiliating, as ruinous, as were the incursions of the Germanic races. The operations of law, natural and moral, are uniform. No individual and no nation can escape its penalty. The world will not be destroyed; Christianity will not prove a failure, – but new forces will arise over the old, and prevail. Great changes will come. He whose right it is to rule will overturn and overturn: but "creation shall succeed destruction; melodious birth-songs will come from the fires of the burning phoenix," assuring us that the progress of the race is certain, even if nations are doomed to a decline and fall whenever conservative forces are not strong enough to resist the torrent of selfishness, vanity, and sin.

AUTHORITIES

The following are original authorities: Claudien; Jerome; Ammianus Marcellinus; Gregory Nazianzen; Socrates; Sozomen; Zosimus;

Augustine, "De Civitate Dei" ["City of God"]
Epistles of Ambrose
Paulinus, *Life of Ambrose*
Sulpicius Severus, *Life of Martin of Tours*
Theodoret, *Theodosian Code*

The following are modern authorities:

Flécier's *Life of Theodosius*
Gibbon's *Decline and Fall*
Milmans's *History of Christianity*
Neander; Sheppard's *Fall of Rome*
Tillemont's *History of the Emperors*

Chapter 10

LEO THE GREAT: FOUNDATION OF THE PAPACY

A.D. 390-461

With the great man who forms the subject of this Lecture are identified those principles which lay at the foundation of the Roman Catholic power for fifteen hundred years. I do not say that he is the founder of the Roman Catholic Church, for that is another question. Roman Catholicism, as a polity, or government, or institution, is one thing; and Roman Catholicism, as a religion, is quite another, although they have been often confounded. As a government, or polity, it is peculiar, – the result of the experience of ages, adapted to society and nations in a certain state of progress or development, with evils and corruptions, of course, like all other human institutions. As a religion, although it superadded many dogmas and rites which Protestants do not accept, and for which they can see no divine authority, – like auricular confession, the deification of the Virgin, indulgences for sin, and the infallibility of the Pope, – still, it has at the same time defended the cardinal principles of Christian faith and morality; such as the personality and sovereignty of God, the divinity of Christ, salvation in consequence of his sufferings and death, immortality, the final judgment, the necessity of a holy life, temperance, humility, patience, and the virtues which were taught upon the Mount and enforced by the original disciples and apostles, whose writings are accepted as inspired.

In treating so important a subject as that represented by Leo the Great, we must bear in mind these distinctions. While Leo is conceded to have been a devout Christian and a noble defender of the faith as we receive it, – one of the lights of the early Christian Church, numbered even among the Fathers of the Church, with Augustine and Chrysostom, – his special claim to greatness is that to him we trace some of the first great developments of the Roman Catholic power as an institution. More than any other one man, he laid the foundation-stone of that edifice which alike sheltered and imprisoned the European nations for more than a thousand years. He was not a great theologian like Augustine, or preacher like Chrysostom, but he was a great bishop like Ambrose, – even far greater, inasmuch as he was the organizer of new forces in the administration of his important diocese. In fact he was a great statesman, as the more able of the popes always aspired to be. He was the associate and equal of princes.

It was the sublime effort of Leo to make the Church the guardian of spiritual principles and give to it a theocratic character and aim, which links his name with the mightiest moral movements of the world; and when I speak of the Church I mean the Church of Rome, as presided over by men who claimed to be the successors of Saint Peter, – to whom they assert Christ had given the supreme control over all other churches as His vicars on the earth. It was the great object of Leo to substantiate this claim, and root it in the minds of the newly converted barbarians; and then institute laws and measures which should make his authority and that of his successors paramount in all spiritual matters, thus centring in his See the general oversight of the Christian Church in all the countries of Europe. It was a theocratic aspiration, one of the grandest that ever entered into the mind of a man of genius, yet, as Protestants now look at it, a usurpation, – the beginning of a vast system of spiritual tyranny in order to control the minds and consciences of men. It took several centuries to develop this system, after Leo was dead. With him it was not a vulgar greed of power, but an inspiration of genius, – a grand idea to make the Church which he controlled a benign and potent influence on society, and to prevent civilization from being utterly crushed out by the victorious Goths and Vandals. It is the success of this idea which stamps the Church as the great leading power of Mediaeval Ages, – a power alike majestic and venerable, benignant yet despotic, humble yet arrogant and usurping.

But before I can present this subtle contradiction, in all its mighty consequences both for good and evil, I must allude to the Roman See and the condition of society when Leo began his memorable pontificate as the precursor of the Gregories and the Clements of later times. Like all great powers, it was very gradually developed. It was as long in reaching its culminating greatness as that temporal empire which controlled the ancient world. Pagan Rome extended her sway by generals and armies; Mediaeval Rome, by her prelates and her principles.

However humble the origin of the Church of Rome, in the early part of the fifth century it was doubtless the greatest See (or *seat* of episcopal power) in Christendom. The Bishop of Rome had the largest number of dependent bishops, and was the first of clerical dignitaries. As early as A.D. 250, – sixty years before Constantine's conversion, and during the times of persecution, – such a man as Cyprian, metropolitan Bishop of Carthage, yielded to him the precedence, and possibly the presidency, because his See was the world's metropolis. And when the seat of empire was removed to the banks of the Bosporus, the power of the Roman Bishop, instead of being diminished, was rather increased, since he was more independent of the emperors than was the Bishop of Constantinople. And especially after Rome was taken by the Goths, he alone possessed the attributes of sovereignty. "He had already towered as far above ordinary bishops in magnificence and prestige as Caesar had above Fabricius."

It was the great name of ROME, after all, which was the mysterious talisman that elevated the Bishop of Rome above other metropolitans. Who can estimate the moral power of that glorious name which had awed the world for a thousand years? Even to barbarians that proud capital was sacred. The whole world believed her to be eternal; she alone had the prestige of universal dominion. This queen of cities might be desolated like Babylon or Tyre, but her influence was indestructible. In her very ruins she was majestic. Her laws, her literature, and her language still were the pride of nations; they revered her as the mother of civilization, clung to the remembrance of her glories, and refused to let her die. She was to the barbarians what Athens had been to the Romans, what modern Paris is to the world of fashion, what London ever will be to the people of America and Australia, – the centre of a proud civilization. So the bishops of such a city were great in spite of themselves, no matter whether they were remarkable as individuals or not. They were the occupants of a great office; and while their city ruled the world, it was not necessary for them to put forth any new claims to dignity or power. No person and no city disputed their pre-eminence. They lived in a marble palace; they were clothed in purple and fine linen; they were surrounded by sycophants; nobles and generals waited in their ante-chambers; they were the companions of princes; they controlled enormous revenues; they were the successors of the high pontiffs of imperial domination.

Yet for three hundred years few of them were eminent. It is not the order of Providence that great posts, to which men are elected by inferiors, should be filled with great men. Such are always feared, and have numerous enemies who defeat their elevation. Moreover, it is only in crises of imminent danger that signal abilities are demanded. Men are preferred for exalted stations who will do no harm, who have talent rather than genius, – men who have business capacities, who have industry and modesty and agreeable manners; who, if noted for anything, are noted for their character. Hence we do not read of more than two or three bishops, for three hundred years, who stood out pre-eminently among their contemporaries; and these were inferior to Origen, who was a teacher in a theological school, and to Jerome, who was a monk in an obscure village. Even Augustine, to whose authority in theology the Catholic Church still professes to bow down, as the schools of the Middle Ages did to Aristotle, was the bishop of an unimportant See in Northern Africa. Only Clement in the first century, and Innocent in the fourth loomed up above their contemporaries. As for the rest, great as was their dignity as bishops, it is absurd to attribute to them schemes for enthralling the world. No such plans arose in the bosom of any of them. Even Leo I. merely prepared the way for universal domination; he had no such deep-laid schemes as Gregory VII or Boniface VIII. The primacy of the Bishop of Rome was all that was conceded by other bishops for four hundred years, and this on the ground of the grandeur of his capital. Even this was disputed by the Bishop of Constantinople, and continued to be until that capital was taken by the Turks.

But with the waning power, glory, and wealth of Rome, – decimated, pillaged, trodden under foot by Goths and Vandals, rebuked by Providence, deserted by emperors, abandoned to decay and ruin, – some expedient or new claim to precedency was demanded to prevent the Roman bishops from sinking into mediocrity. It was at this crisis that the pontificate of Leo began, in the year 440. It was a gloomy period, not only for Rome, but for civilization. The queen of cities had been repeatedly sacked, and her treasures destroyed or removed to distant cities. Her proud citizens had been sold as slaves; her noble matrons had been violated; her grand palaces had been levelled with the ground; her august senators were fugitives and exiles. All kinds of calamities overspread the earth and decimated the race, – war, pestilence, and famine. Men in despair hid themselves in caves and monasteries. Literature and art were crushed; no great works of genius appeared. The paralysis of despair deadened all the energies of civilized man. Even armies lost their vigor, and citizens refused to enlist. The old mechanism of the Caesars, which had kept the Empire together for three hundred years after all vitality had fled, was worn out. The general demoralization had led to a general destruction. Vice was succeeded by universal violence; and that, by universal ruin. Old laws and restraints were no longer of any account. A civilization based on material forces and Pagan arts had proved a failure. The whole world appeared to be on the eve of dissolution. To the thoughtful men of the age everything seemed to be involved in one terrific mass of desolation and horror. "Even Jerome," says a great historian, "heaped together the awful passages of the Old Testament on the capture of Jerusalem and other Eastern cities; and the noble lines of Virgil on the sack of Troy are but feeble descriptions of the night which covered the western Empire."

Now Leo was the man for such a crisis, and seems to have been raised up to devise some new principle of conservation around which the stricken world might rally. "He stood equally alone and superior," says Milman, "in the Christian world. All that survived of Rome – of her unbounded ambition, of her inflexible will, and of her belief in her title to universal dominion – seemed concentrated in him alone."

Leo was born, in the latter part of the fourth century, at Rome, of noble parents, and was intensely Roman in all his aspirations. He early gave indications of future greatness, and was consecrated to a service in which only talent was appreciated. When he was nothing but an acolyte, whose duty it was to light the lamps and attend on the bishop, he was sent to Africa and honored with the confidence of the great Bishop of Hippo. And he was only deacon when he was sent by the Emperor Valentinian III to heal the division between Aëtius and Albinus, – rival generals, whose dissensions compromised the safety of the Empire. He was absent on important missions when the death of Sixtus, A.D. 440, left the Papacy without a head. On Leo were all eyes now fixed, and he was immediately summoned by the clergy and the people of Rome, in whom the right of election was vested, to take possession of the vacant throne. He did not affect unworthiness like Gregory in later years, but accepted at once the immense responsibility.

I need not enumerate his measures and acts. Like all great and patriotic statesmen he selected the wisest and ablest men he could find as subordinates, and condescended himself to those details which he inexorably exacted from others. He even mounted the neglected pulpit of his metropolitan church to preach to the people, like Chrysostom and Gregory Nazianzen at Constantinople. His sermons are not models of eloquence or style, but are practical, powerful, earnest, and orthodox. Athanasius himself was not more evangelical, or Ambrose more impressive. He was the especial foe of all the heresies which characterized the age. He did battle with all who attempted to subvert the Nicene Creed. Those whom he especially rebuked were the Manicheans, – men who made the greatest pretension to intellectual culture and advanced knowledge, and yet whose lives were disgraced not merely by the most offensive intellectual pride, but the most disgraceful vices; men who confounded all the principles of moral obligation, and who polluted even the atmosphere of Rome by downright Pagan licentiousness. He had no patience with these false philosophers, and he had no mercy. He even complained of them to the emperor, as Calvin did of Servetus to the civil authorities of Geneva (which I grant was not to his credit); and the result was that these dissolute and pretentious heretics were expelled from the army and from all places of trust and emolument.

Many people in our enlightened times would denounce this treatment as illiberal and persecuting, and justly. But consider his age and circumstances. What was Leo to do as the guardian of the faith in those dreadful times? Was he to suffer those who poisoned all the sources of renovation which then remained to go unrebuked and unpunished? He may have said, in his defence, "Shall I, the bishop of this diocese, the appointed guardian of faith and morals in a period of alarming degeneracy, – shall I, armed with the sword of Saint Peter, stop to draw the line between injuries inflicted by the tongue and injuries inflicted by the hand? Shall we defend our persons, our property, and our lives, and take no notice of those who impiously and deliberately would destroy our souls by their envenomed blasphemies? Shall we allow the wells of water which spring up to everlasting life to be poisoned by the impious atheists and scoffers, who in every age set themselves up against Christ and His kingdom, and are only allowed by God Almighty to live, as the wild beasts of the desert or scorpions and serpents are allowed to live? Let them live, but let us defend ourselves against their teeth and fangs. Are the overseers of God's people, in a world of shame, to be mere philosophical Gallios, indifferent to our higher interests? Is it a Christian duty to permit an avalanche of evils to overwhelm the Church on the plea of toleration? Shall we suffer, when we have the power to prevent it, a pandemonium of scoffers and infidels and sentimental casuists to run riot in the city which is intrusted to us to guard? Not thus will we be disloyal to our trusts. Men have souls to save, and we will come to the rescue with any weapons we can lay our hands upon. The Church is the only hope of the world, not merely in our unsettled times, but for all ages. And hence I, as the guardian of those spiritual principles which lie at the root of all healthy progress in civilization, and all religious life, will not tamely and ignobly see those principles subverted by dangerous and infidel speculations, even if they are attractive to cultivated but irreligious classes."

Such may have been the arguments, it is not unreasonable to suppose, which influenced the great Leo in his undoubted persecutions, – persecutions, we should remember, which were then indorsed by the Catholic Church. They would be condemned in our times by all enlightened men, but they were the only remedy known in that age against dangerous opinions. So Leo put down the Manicheans and preserved the unity of the faith, which was of immeasurable importance in the sea of anarchies which at that time was submerging all the traditions of the past.

Leo also distinguished himself by writing a treatise on the Incarnation, – said to be the ablest which has come down to us from the primitive Church. He was one of those men who believed in theology as a series of divine declarations, to be cordially received whether they are fully grasped by the intellect or not. These declarations pertain to most momentous interests, and hence transcend in dignity any question which mere philosophy ever attempted to grasp, or physical science ever brought forward. In spite of the sneers of the infidels, or the attacks of *savans*, or the temporary triumph of false opinions, let us remember they have endured during the mighty conflicts of the last eighteen hundred years, and will endure through all the conflicts of ages, – the might, the majesty, and the glory of the kingdom of Christ. Whoever thus conserves truths so important is a great benefactor, whether neglected or derided, whether despised or persecuted.

In addition to the labors of Leo to preserve the integrity of the received faith among the semi-barbaric western nations, his efforts were equally great to heal the disorders of the Church. He reformed ecclesiastical discipline in Africa, rent by Arian factions and Donatist schismatics. He curtailed the abuses of metropolitan tyranny in Gaul. He sent his legates to preside over the councils of Ephesus and Chalcedon. He sat in judgment between Vienna and Arles. He fought for the independence of the Church against emperors and barbaric chieftains. He encouraged literature and missions and schools and the spread of the Bible. He was the paragon of a bishop, – a man of transcendent dignity of character, as well as a Father of the Church Universal, of whom all Christendom should be proud.

Among Leo's memorable acts as one of the great lights of his age was the part he was called upon to perform as a powerful intercessor with barbaric kings. When Attila with his swarm of Mongol conquerors appeared in Italy, – the "scourge of God," as he was called; the instrument of Providence in punishing the degenerate rulers and people of the falling Empire, – Leo was sent by the affrighted emperor to the barbarian's camp to make what terms he could. The savage Hun, who feared not the armies of the emperor, stood awe-struck, we are told, before the minister of God; and, swayed by his eloquence and personal dignity, consented to retire from Italy for the hand of the princess Honoria. And when afterwards Genseric, at the head of his Vandals, became master of the capital, he was likewise influenced by the powerful intercession of the bishop, and consented to spare the lives of the Romans, and preserve the public buildings and churches from conflagration. Genseric could not yield up the spoil of the fallen capital, and his soldiers transported to Carthage, the seat of the new Vandal kingdom, the riches and trophies which illustrious generals had won, – yea, the treasures of three religions; the gods of the capitoline temple, the golden candlesticks which Titus brought from Jerusalem, and the sacred vessels which adorned the churches of the Christians, and which Alaric had spared.

Figure 13. Invasion of the Huns into Italy. *After the painting by V. Checa.*

Thus far the intrepid bishop of Rome – for he was nothing more – calls forth our sympathy and admiration for the hand he had in establishing the faith and healing the divisions of the Church, for which he earned the title of Saint. He taught no errors like Origen, and pushed out no theological doctrines into a jargon of metaphysics like Athanasius. He was more practical than Jerome, and more moderate than Augustine.

But he instituted a claim, from motives of policy, which subsequently ripened into an irresistible government, on which the papal structure as an institution or polity rests. He did not put forth this claim, however, until the old capital of the Caesars was humiliated, vanquished, and completely prostrated as a political power. When the Eternal City was taken a second time, and her riches plundered, and her proud palaces levelled with the dust; when her amphitheatre was deserted, her senatorial families were driven away as fugitives and sold as slaves, and her glory was departed, – nothing left her but recollections and broken columns and ruined temples and weeping matrons, ashes, groans, and lamentations, miseries and most bitter sorrows, – then did her great bishop, intrepid amid general despair, lay the foundation of a new empire, vaster in its influence, if not in its power, than that which raised itself up among the nations in the proudest days of Vespasian and the Antonines.

Leo, from one of the devastated hills of Rome, – once crowned with palaces, temples, and monuments, – looked out upon the Christian world, and saw the desolation spoken of by Jeremy the prophet, as well as by the Cumaean sibyl: all central power hopelessly prostrated; law and justice by-words; provinces wasted, decimated, and anarchical; literature and art crushed; vice, in all its hateful deformity, rampant and multiplying itself; false opinions gaining ground; Christians adopting the errors of Paganism; soldiers turned into banditti; the contemplative hiding themselves in caves and deserts; the rich made slaves; barbarians everywhere triumphant; women shrieking in terror; bishops praying in despair, – a world disordered, a pandemonium of devils let loose, one terrific and howling mass of moral and physical desolation such as had never been seen since Noah entered into the ark.

Amid this dreary wreck of the old civilization, which had been supposed to be eternal, what were Leo's designs and thoughts? In this mournful crisis, what did he dream of in his sad and afflicted soul? To flee into a monastery, as good men in general despair and wretchedness did, and patiently wait for the coming of his Lord, and for the new dispensation? Not at all: he contemplated the restoration of the eternal city, – a new creation which should succeed destruction; the foundation of a new power which should restore law, preserve literature, subdue the barbarians, introduce a still higher civilization than that which had perished, – not by bringing back the Caesars, but by making himself Caesar; a revived central power which the nations should respect and obey. That which the world needed was this new central power, to settle difficulties, depose tyrants, establish a common standard of faith and worship, encourage struggling genius, and conserve peace. Who but the Church could do this? The Church was the last hope of the fallen Empire. The Church should put forth her theocratic aspirations. The keys of Saint Peter should be more potent than the sceptres of kings. The Church should not be crushed in the general desolation. She was still the mighty power of the world. Christianity had taken hold of the hearts and minds of men, and raised its voice to console and encourage amid universal despair. Men's thoughts were turned to God and to his vicegerents. He was mighty to save. His promises were a glorious consolation. The Church should arise, put on her beautiful garments, and go on from conquering to conquer. A theocracy should restore civilization. The world wanted a new Christian sovereign, reigning by divine right, not by armies, not by force, – by an appeal to the future fears and hopes of men. Force had failed: it was divided against itself. Barbaric chieftains defied the emperors and all temporal powers. Rival generals desolated provinces. The world was plunging into barbarism. The imperial sceptre was broken. Not a diadem, but a tiara, must be the emblem of universal sovereignty. Not imperial decrees, but papal bulls, must now rule the world. Who but the Bishop of Rome could wear this tiara? Who but he could be the representative of the new theocracy? He was the bishop of the metropolis whose empire never could pass away. But his city was in ruins. If his claim to precedency rested on the grandeur of his capital, he must yield to the Bishop of Constantinople. He must found a new claim, not on the greatness and antiquity of his capital, but on the superstitious veneration of the Christian world, – a claim which would be accepted.

Now it happened that one of Leo's predecessors had instituted such a claim, which he would revive and enforce with new energy. Innocent had maintained, forty years before Leo, that the primacy of the Roman See was derived from Saint Peter, – that Christ had delegated to Peter supreme power as chief of the apostles; and that he, as the successor of Saint Peter, was entitled to his jurisdiction and privileges. This is the famous *jus divinum* principle which constitutes the corner-stone of the papal fabric. On this claim was based the subsequent encroachments of the popes. Leo saw the force of this claim, and adopted it and intrenched himself behind it, and became forthwith more formidable than any of his predecessors or any living bishop; and he was sure that so long as the claim was allowed, no matter whether his city was great or small, his successors would become the spiritual dictators of Christendom. The dignity and power of the Roman bishop were now based on a new foundation. He was still venerable from the souvenirs of the Empire, but more potent as the successor of the chief of the apostles. Ambrose had successfully asserted the independent spiritual power of the bishops; Leo seized that sceptre and claimed it for the Bishop of Rome.

Protestants are surprised and indignant that this haughty and false claim (as they view it) should have been allowed; it only shows to what depth of superstition the Christian world had already sunk. What an insult to the reason and learning of the world! What preposterous arrogance and assumption! Where are the proofs that Saint Peter was really the first bishop of Rome, even? And if he were, where are the Scripture proofs that he had precedency over the other apostles? And more, where do we learn in the Scriptures that any prerogative could be transmitted to successors? Where do we find that the successors of Peter were entitled to jurisdiction over the whole Church? Christ, it is true, makes use of the expression of a "rock" on which his Church should be built. But Christ himself is the rock, not a mortal man. "Other foundation can no man lay than that is laid, which is Jesus Christ," – a truth reiterated even by Saint Augustine, the great and acknowledged theologian of the Catholic Church, although Augustine's views of sin and depravity are no more relished by the Roman Catholics of our day than the doctrines of Luther himself, who drew his theological system, like Calvin, from Augustine more than from any other man, except Saint Paul.

But arrogant and unfounded as was the claim of Leo, – that Peter, not Christ, was the rock on which the Church is founded, – it was generally accepted by the bishops of the day. Everything tended to confirm it, especially the universal idea of a necessary unity of the Church. There must be a head of the Church on earth, and who could be lawfully that head other than the successor of the apostle to whom Christ had given the keys of heaven and hell?

But this claim, considering the age when it was first advanced, had the inspiration of genius. It was most opportune. The Bishop of Rome would soon have been reduced to the condition of other metropolitans had his dignity rested on the greatness of his capital. He now became the interpreter of his own decrees, – an arch-pontiff ruling by divine right. His power became indefinite and unlimited. Just in proportion to the depth of the religious sentiment of the newly converted barbarians would be his ascendancy over them; and the Germanic races were religious peoples like the early Greeks and Romans. Tacitus points out this sentiment of religion as one of their leading characteristics. It was not the worship of ancestors, as among the Aryan races until Grecian and Roman civilization was developed. It was more like the worship of the invisible powers of Nature; for in the rock, the mountain, the river, the forest, the sun, the stars, the storms, the rude Teutonic mind saw a protecting or avenging deity. They easily transferred to the Christian clergy the reverence they had bestowed on the old priests of Odin, of Freya, and of Thor. Reverence was one of the great sentiments of our German ancestors. It was only among such a people that an overpowering spiritual despotism could be maintained. The Pope became to them the vicegerent of the great Power which they adored. The records of the race do not show such another absorbing pietism as was seen in the monastic retreats of the Middle Ages, except among the Brahmans and Buddhists of India. This religious fervor the popes were to make use of, to extend their empire.

And that nothing might be wanted to cement their power which had been thus assured, the Emperor Valentinian III – a monarch controlled by Leo – passed in the year 445 this celebrated decree: –

"The primacy of the Apostolic See having been established by the merit of Saint Peter, its founder, the sacred Council of Nice, and the dignity of the city of Rome, we thus declare our irrevocable edict, that all bishops, whether in Gaul or elsewhere, shall make no innovation without the sanction of the Bishop of Rome; and, that the Apostolic See may remain inviolable, all bishops who shall refuse to appear before the tribunal of the Bishop of Rome, when cited, shall be constrained to appear by the governor of the province."

Thus firmly was the Papacy rooted in the middle of the fifth century, not only by the encroachments of bishops, but by the authority of emperors. The papal dominion begins, as an institution, with Leo the Great. As a religion it began when Paul and Peter preached at Rome. Its institution was peculiar and unique; a great spiritual government usurping the attributes of other governments, as predicted by Daniel, and, at first benignant, ripening into a gloomy tyranny, – a tyranny so unscrupulous and grasping as to become finally, in the eyes of Luther, an evil power. As a religion, as I have said, it did not widely depart from the primitive creeds until it added to the doctrines generally accepted by the Church, and even still by Protestants, those other dogmas which were means to an end, – that end the possession of power and its perpetuation among ignorant people. Yet these dogmas, false as they are, never succeeded in obscuring wholly the truths which are taught in the gospel, or in extinguishing faith in the world. In all the encroachments of the Papacy, in all the triumphs of an unauthorized Church polity, the flame of true Christian piety has been dimmed, but not extinguished. And when this fatal and ambitious polity shall have passed away before the advance of reason and civilization, as other governments have been overturned, the lamp of piety will yet burn, as in other churches, since it will be fed by the Bible and the Providence of God. Governments and institutions pass away, but not religions; certainly not the truths originally declared among the mountains of Judea, which thus far have proved the elevation of nations.

It is then the government, not the religion, which Leo inaugurated, with which we have to do. And let us remember in reference to this government, which became so powerful and absolute, that Leo only laid the foundation. He probably did not dream of subjecting the princes of the earth except in matters which pertained to his supremacy as a spiritual ruler. His aim was doubtless spiritual, not temporal. He had no such deep designs as Hildebrand and Innocent III cherished. The encroachments of later ages he did not anticipate. His doctrine was, "Render unto Caesar the things which are Caesar's, and unto God the things which are God's." As the vicegerent of the Almighty, which he felt himself to be in spiritual matters, he would institute a guardianship over everything connected with religion, even education, which can never be properly divorced from it. He was the patron of schools, as he was of monasteries. He could advise kings: he could not impose upon them his commands (except in Church matters), as Boniface VIII sought to do. He would organize a network of Church functionaries, not of State officers; for he was the head of a great religious institution. He would send his legates to the end of the earth to superintend the work of the Church, and rebuke princes, and protest against wars; for he had the religious oversight of Christendom.

Now when we consider that there was no central power in Europe at this time, that the barbaric princes were engaged in endless wars, and that a fearful gloom was settling upon everything pertaining to education and peace and order; that even the clergy were ignorant, and the people superstitious; that everything was in confusion, tending to a worse confusion, to perfect anarchy and barbaric license; that provincial councils were no longer held; that bishops and abbots were abdicating their noblest functions, – we feel that the spiritual supremacy which Leo aimed to establish had many things to be said in its support; that his central rule was a necessity of the times, keeping civilization from utter ruin.

In the first place, what a great idea it was to preserve the unity of the Church, – the idea of Cyprian and Augustine and all the great Fathers, – an idea never exploded, and one which we even in these times accept, though not in the sense understood by the Roman Catholics! We cannot conceive of the Church as established by the apostles, without recognizing the necessity of unity in doctrines and discipline. Who in that age could conserve this unity unless it were a great spiritual monarch? In our age books, universities, theological seminaries, the press, councils, and an enlightened clergy can see that no harm comes to the great republic which recognizes Christ as the invisible head. Not so fifteen hundred years ago. The idea of unity could only be realized by the exercise of sufficient power in one man to preserve the integrity of the orthodox faith, since ignorance and anarchy covered the earth with their funereal shades.

The Protestants are justly indignant in view of subsequent encroachments and tyrannies. But these were not the fault of Leo. Everything good in its day is likely to be perverted. The whole history of society is the history of the perversion of institutions originally beneficent. Take the great foundations for education and other moral and intellectual necessities, which were established in the Middle Ages by good men. See how these are perverted and misused even in such glorious universities as Oxford and Cambridge. See how soon the primitive institutions of apostles were changed, in order to facilitate external conquests and make the Church a dignified worldly power. Not only are we to remember that everything good has been perverted, and ever will be, but that all governments, religious and civil, seem to be, in one sense, expediencies, – that is, adapted to the necessities and circumstances of the times. In the Bible there are no settled laws definitely laid down for the future government of the Church, – certainly not for the government of States and cities. A government which was best for the primitive Christians of the first two centuries was not adapted to the condition of the Church in the third and fourth centuries, else there would not have been bishops. If we take a narrow-minded and partisan view of bishops, we might say that they always have existed since the times of the apostles; the Episcopalians might affirm that the early churches were presided over by bishops, and the Presbyterians that every ordained minister was a bishop, – that elder and bishop are synonymous. But that is a contest about words, not things. In reality, episcopal power, as we understand it, was not historically developed till there was a large increase in the Christian communities, especially in great cities, where several presbyters were needed, one of whom presided over the rest. Some such episcopal institution, I am willing to concede, was a necessity, although I cannot clearly see the divine authority for it. In like manner other changes became necessary, which did not militate against the welfare of the Church, but tended to preserve it. New dignities, new organizations, new institutions for the government of the Church successively arose. All societies must have a government. This is a law recognized in the nature of things. So Christian society must be organized and ruled according to the necessities of the times; and the Scriptures do not say what these shall be, – they are imperative and definite only in matters of faith and morals. To guard the faith, to purify the morals according to the Christian standard, overseers, officers, rulers are required. In the early Church they were all brethren. The second and third century made bishops. The next age made archbishops and metropolitans and patriarchs. The age which succeeded was the age of Leo; and the calamities and miseries and anarchies and ignorance of the times, especially the rule of barbarians, seemed to point to a monarchical head, a more theocratic government, – a government so august and sacred that it could not be resisted.

And there can be but little doubt that this was the best government for the times. Let me illustrate by civil governments. There is no law laid down in the Bible for these. In the time of our Saviour the world was governed by a universal monarch. The imperial rule had become a necessity. It was tyrannical; but Paul as well as Christ exhorted his followers to accept it. In process of time, when the Empire fell, every old province had a king, – indeed there were several kings in France, as well as in Germany and Spain. The prelates of the Church never lifted up their voice against the legality of this feudo-kingly rule. Then came a revolt, after the Reformation, against the government of kings. New England and other colonies became small republics, almost democracies. On the hills of New England, with a sparse rural population and small cities, the most primitive form of government was the best. It was virtually the government of townships. The selectmen were the overseers; and, following the necessities of the times, the ministers of the gospel were generally Independents or Congregationalists, not clergy of the Established Church of Old England. Both the civil and the religious governments which they had were the best for the people. But what was suited to Massachusetts would not be fit for England or France. See how our government has insensibly drifted towards a strong central power. What must be the future necessities of such great cities as New York, Philadelphia, and Chicago, – where even now self-government is a failure, and the real government is in the hands of rings of politicians, backed by foreign immigrants and a lawless democracy? Will the wise, the virtuous, and the rich put up forever with such misrule as these cities have had, especially since the Civil War? And even if other institutions should gradually be changed, to which we now cling with patriotic zeal, it may be for the better and not the worse. Those institutions are the best which best preserve the morals and liberties of the people; and such institutions will gradually arise as the country needs, unless there shall be a general shipwreck of laws, morals, and faith, which I do not believe will come. It is for the preservation of these laws, morals, and doctrines that all governments are held responsible. A change in the government is nothing; a decline of morals and faith is everything.

I make these remarks in order that we may see that the rise of a great central power in the hands of the Bishop of Rome, in the fifth century, may have been a great public benefit, perhaps a necessity. It became corrupt; it forgot its mission. Then it was attacked by Luther. It ceased to rule England and a part of Germany and other countries where there were higher public morals and a purer religious faith. Some fear that the rule of the Roman Church will be re-established in this country. Never, – only its religion. The Catholic Church may plant her prelates in every great city, and the whole country may be regarded by them as missionary ground for the re-establishment of the papal polity. But the moment this polity raises its head and becomes arrogant, and seeks to subvert the other established institutions of the country or prevent the use of the Bible in schools, it will be struck down, even as the Jesuits were once banished from France and Spain. Its religion will remain, – may gain new adherents, become the religion of vast multitudes. But it is not the faith which the Roman Catholic Church professes to conserve which I fear. That is very much like that of Protestants, in the main. It is the institutions, the polity, the government of that Church which I speak of, with its questionable means to gain power, its opposition to the free circulation of the Bible, its interference with popular education, its prelatical assumptions, its professed allegiance to a foreign potentate, though as wise and beneficent as Pio Nono or the reigning Pope.

In the time of Leo there were none of these things. It was a poor, miserable, ignorant, anarchical, superstitious age. In such an age the concentration of power in the hands of an intelligent man is always a public benefit. Certainly it was wielded wisely by Leo, and for beneficent ends. He established the patristic literature. The writings of the great Fathers were by him scattered over Europe, and were studied by the clergy, so far as they were able to study anything. All the great doctrines of Augustine and Jerome and Athanasius were defended. The whole Church was made to take the side of orthodoxy, and it remained orthodox to the times of Bernard and Anselm. Order was restored to the monasteries; and they so rapidly gained the respect of princes and good men that they were richly endowed, and provision made in them for the education of priests. Everywhere cathedral schools were established. The canon law supplanted in a measure the old customs of the German forests and the rude legislation of feudal chieftains. When bishops quarreled with monasteries or with one another, or even with barons, appeals were sent to Rome, and justice was decreed. In after times these appeals were settled on venal principles, but not for centuries. The early Mediaeval popes were the defenders of justice and equity. And they promoted peace among quarrelsome barons, as well as Christian truth among divines. They set aside, to some extent, those irascible and controversial councils where good and great men were persecuted for heresy. These popes had no small passions to gratify or to stimulate. They were the conservators of the peace of Europe, as all reliable historians testify. They were generally very enlightened men, – the ablest of their times. They established canons and laws which were based on wisdom, which stood the test of ages, and which became venerable precedents.

The Catholic polity was only gradually established, sustained by experience and reason. And that is the reason why it has been so permanent. It was most admirably adapted to rule the ignorant in ages of cruelty and crime, – and, I am inclined to think, to rule the ignorant and superstitious everywhere. Great critics are unanimous in their praises of that wonderful mechanism which ruled the world for one thousand years.

Nor did the popes, for several centuries after Leo, grasp the temporal powers of princes. As political monarchs they were at first poor and insignificant. The Papacy was not politically a great power until the time of Hildebrand, nor a rich temporal power till nearly the era of the Reformation. It was a spiritual power chiefly, just such as it is destined to become again, – the organizer of religious forces; and, so far as these are animated by the gospel and reason, they are likely to have a perpetuated influence. Who can predict the end of a spiritual empire which shows no signs of decay? It is not half so corrupt as it was in the time of Boniface VIII., nor half so feeble as in the time of Leo X. It is more majestic and venerable than in the time of Luther. Nor are Protestants so bitter and one-sided as they were fifty years ago. They begin to judge this great power by broader principles; to view it as it really is, – not as "Antichrist" and the "scarlet mother," but as a venerable institution, with great abuses, having at heart the interests of those whom it grinds down and deceives.

But, after all, I do not in this Lecture present the Papacy of the eleventh century or the nineteenth, but the Papacy of the fifth century, as organized by Leo. True, its fundamental principles as a government are the same as then. These principles I do not admire, especially for an enlightened era. I only palliate them in reference to the wants of a dark and miserable age, and as a critic insist upon their notable success in the age that gave them birth.

With these remarks on the regimen, the polity, and the government of the Church of which Leo laid the foundation, and which he adapted to barbarous ages, when the Church was still a struggling power and Christianity itself little better than nominal, – long before it had much modified the laws or changed the morals of society; long before it had created a new civilization, – with these remarks, acceptable, it may be, neither to Catholics nor to Protestants, I turn once more to the man himself. Can you deny his title to the name of Great? Would you take him out of the galaxy of illustrious men whom we still call Fathers and Saints? Even Gibbon praises his exalted character. What would the Church of the Middle Ages have been without such aims and aspirations? Oh, what a benevolent mission the Papacy performed in its best ages, mitigating the sorrows of the poor, raising the humble from degradation, opposing slavery and war, educating the ignorant, scattering the Word of God, heading off the dreadful tyranny of feudalism, elevating the learned to offices of trust, shielding the pious from the rapacity of barons, recognizing man as man, proclaiming Christian equalities, holding out the hopes of a future life to the penitent believer, and proclaiming the sovereignty of intelligence over the reign of brute forces and the rapacity of ungodly men! All this did Leo, and his immediate successors. And when he superadded to the functions of a great religious magistrate the virtues of the humblest Christian, – parting with his magnificent patrimony to feed the poor, and proclaiming (with an eloquence unusual in his time) the cardinal doctrines of the Christian faith, and setting himself as an example of the virtues which he preached, – we concede his claim to be numbered among the great benefactors of mankind. How much worse Roman Catholicism would have been but for his august example and authority! How much better to educate the ignorant people, who have souls to save, by the patristic than by heathen literature, with all its poison of false philosophies and corrupting stimulants! Who, more than he and his immediate successors, taught loyalty to God as the universal Sovereign, and the virtues generated by a peaceful life, – patriotism, self-denial, and faith? He was a dictator only as Bernard was, ruling by the power of learning and sanctity. As an original administrative genius he was scarcely surpassed by Gregory VII. Above all, he sought to establish faith in the world. Reason had failed. The old civilization was a dismal mockery of the aspirations of man. The schools of Athens could make Sophists, rhetoricians, dialecticians, and sceptics. But the faith of the Fathers could bring philosophers to the foot of the Cross. What were material conquests to these conquests of the soul, to this spiritual reign of the invisible principles of the kingdom of Christ?

So, as the vicegerents of Almighty power, the popes began to reign. Ridicule not that potent domination. What lessons of human experience, what great truths of government, what principles of love and wisdom are interwoven with it! Its growth is more suggestive than the rise of any temporal empires. It has produced more illustrious men than any European monarchy. And it aimed to accomplish far grander ends, – even obedience to the eternal laws which God has decreed for the public and private lives of men. It is invested with more poetic interest. Its doctors, its dignitaries, its saints, its heroes, its missions, and its laws rise up before us in sublime grandeur when seriously contemplated. It failed at last, when no longer needed. But it was not until its encroachments and corruptions shocked the reason of the world, and showed a painful contrast to those virtues which originally sustained it, that earnest men arose in indignation, and declared that this perverted institution should no longer be supported by the contributions of more enlightened ages; that it had become a tyrannical and dangerous government, to be assailed and broken up. It has not yet passed away. It has survived the Reformation and the attacks of its countless enemies. How long this power of blended good and evil will remain we cannot predict. But one thing we do know, – that the time will come when all governments shall become the kingdoms of our Lord and Saviour Jesus Christ; and Christian truth alone shall so permeate all human institutions that the forces of evil shall be driven forever into the immensity of eternal night.

With the Pontificate of Leo the Great that dark period which we call the "Middle Ages" may be said to begin. The disintegration of society then was complete, and the reign of ignorance and superstition had set in. With the collapse of the old civilization a new power had become a necessity. If anything marked the Middle Ages it was the reign of priests and nobles. This reign it will be my object to present in the Lectures which are to fill the next volume of this Work, together with subjects closely connected with papal domination and feudal life.

AUTHORITIES

The following are original authorities: Neander; Socrates; Theodoret; Zosimus.

Alexander de Saint Chéron's *Histoire du Pontificat de Saint Leo le Grande*, [*History of the Pontificate of Saint Leo the Great*]

Arendt's *Leo der Grosse und seine Zeit* [*Leo the Great and his time*]

Beugot's *Histoire de la Destruction du Paganism*. [*History of the Destruction of Paganism*].

Biographie Universelle [*Universal Biography*]

Butler, *Lives of the Saints*

Dumoulin, *Vie et Religion de deux Papes Léon I. et Grégoire I.* [*Life and Religion of two Popes Leo I. and Gregory I.*]

Encyclopaedia Britannica

Fleury, *Ecclesiastical History*

Gibbon, *Decline and Fall*

Maimbourg, *Histoire du Pontificat de Saint Léon* [*History of the Pontificate of Saint Leo*].

Milman's *Latin Christianity*

Tillemont, *Histoire des Empereurs* [*History of the Emperors*]

Works of Leo, edited by Quesnel

INDEX

A

Alaric, 180, 188, 189, 190, 203
ambition, 12, 18, 22, 24, 27, 29, 31, 37, 42,
    49, 70, 99, 114, 134, 200
Ambrose, 83, 90, 109, 129, 132, 133, 134,
    135, 136, 137, 138, 139, 140, 141, 142,
    143, 145, 146, 147, 148, 149, 156, 182,
    183, 185, 194, 196, 200, 206
Antonines, 58, 192, 204
aristocracy, 27, 28, 30, 33, 36, 37, 38, 39,
    40, 41, 42, 43, 44, 45, 130, 186
Arius, 78, 79, 82, 84, 136, 166
asceticism, 68, 88, 90, 120, 153, 158, 160
Asiatic supremacy, v, 1
assassination, 43, 50, 63
Assyria, 7, 10, 18, 22
Athanasius, 52, 75, 79, 80, 82, 84, 89, 109,
    131, 135, 136, 152, 163, 165, 166, 169,
    185, 200, 204, 213
Augustine, 52, 80, 90, 91, 96, 109, 111, 113,
    119, 132, 134, 135, 136, 148, 152, 153,
    154, 155, 156, 157, 159, 161, 162, 163,
    164, 165, 166, 167, 168, 169, 170, 171,
    183, 185, 191, 194, 196, 198, 204, 206,
    209

authorities, 22, 45, 58, 64, 84, 105, 126,
    135, 149, 172, 193, 201, 216

B

Babylonia, 2, 7, 17
barbarians of Germany, 50
barbaric kings, 203
battle of Adrianople, 71
battle of Pharsalia, 40
Bishop of Hippo, 163, 167, 200
Bishop of Rome, 197, 199, 205, 206, 207,
    208, 212

C

Cambyses, 7, 8, 9, 21
cathedral, 59, 119, 122, 123, 133, 146, 147,
    213
Catholic Church, 115, 134, 140, 156, 162,
    164, 166, 187, 195, 198, 202, 206, 212
Celestius, 165
character of Cyrus, 2
Christian graces, 111
Christian legislation, 73

Christian preachers, 108
Christian theology, v, 151, 167
Christianity enthroned, v, 65
Chrysostom, v, 89, 107, 111, 113, 115, 116, 117, 119, 120, 121, 122, 123, 124, 125, 126, 132, 134, 140, 148, 184, 186, 196, 200
Cicero, 25, 27, 28, 30, 37, 41, 42, 43, 44, 45, 91, 95, 96, 101, 109, 110, 112, 119, 124, 125, 153, 169
Commodus, 51, 52, 57, 175, 178, 187
conquest of Babylon, 15
Constantine, v, 20, 24, 50, 52, 65, 69, 70, 71, 72, 73, 74, 75, 76, 77, 79, 82, 83, 88, 131, 133, 139, 147, 176, 177, 182, 184, 187, 197
Constantine the Great, v, 65
conversion to Christianity, 73
Council of Nice, 82, 139, 185, 208
Council of the Oaks, 123
Croesus, 11, 12, 13, 14, 15
Cyrus the Great, v, 1

D

death, 14, 21, 25, 41, 43, 50, 51, 54, 57, 67, 73, 77, 83, 88, 103, 109, 110, 111, 112, 116, 125, 133, 136, 144, 148, 158, 166, 173, 175, 180, 181, 183, 186, 188, 195, 200
death of Valens, 181
Diocletian, 50, 66, 69, 71, 75, 83, 176, 183, 186
division of the Empire, 183
doctrine of the Trinity, 77, 82, 163
doctrines of Augustine, 213
Donatists, 161, 162, 164

E

education, 7, 25, 48, 54, 61, 86, 91, 92, 99, 112, 113, 133, 152, 209, 210, 212, 213
elected Consul, 29
enemies, 32, 34, 38, 41, 42, 43, 50, 52, 68, 93, 121, 123, 125, 137, 147, 167, 174, 176, 180, 181, 193, 198, 216
epictetus, 47, 52, 53, 54, 55, 61
Episcopal authority, v, 129
Eutropius, 121
external glories, 63

F

fall of Rome, 187, 191, 194
fame, 11, 20, 26, 27, 31, 34, 44, 48, 50, 52, 70, 73, 79, 92, 102, 104, 111, 116, 124, 147, 156, 169, 172
family, 3, 7, 10, 21, 25, 28, 48, 51, 88, 108, 119, 133, 148, 178
fate of Croesus, 14
Faustina, 51, 52, 137, 140
female friendship, 85
foundation of Constantinople, 71
foundation of the Papacy, v, 195

G

Galerius, 70
Gibbon, 52, 57, 58, 60, 64, 76, 84, 105, 123, 149, 174, 177, 194, 214, 217
glory of Rome, v, 47
Goths, 71, 90, 132, 144, 177, 178, 179, 180, 181, 183, 184, 185, 188, 189, 191, 197, 199
grace, 93, 96, 103, 109, 115, 136, 158, 163, 165, 167, 168, 169

H

historical puzzle, 45

I

imperialism, v, 23, 31, 37, 38, 39, 41, 43, 44
influence, 5, 24, 28, 47, 51, 54, 61, 68, 75,
    79, 80, 90, 96, 107, 108, 112, 113, 117,
    118, 119, 123, 125, 126, 131, 133, 148,
    149, 153, 160, 162, 169, 170, 184, 185,
    197, 204, 214

J

jus divinum principle, 206

L

latter Days of Rome, v, 173
Leges Juliae, 30, 45
Leo the Great, v, 195, 196, 208, 216
Licinius, 70, 71

M

Manicheans, 136, 153, 154, 156, 160, 164,
    185, 200, 202
marriage, 12, 29, 37, 86, 156, 174, 187
martyrdoms, 66
Maxentius, 70, 73
Maximin, 70, 71
Median empire, 8, 11
meditations, 50, 52, 53, 55, 56, 64

N

Nicene Creed, 80, 184, 200

P

Paganism, 67, 69, 74, 84, 85, 87, 88, 89,
    104, 126, 167, 170, 173, 183, 186, 187,
    204, 216
Papacy, 200, 208, 214
parentage, 53, 152
Paula, v, vii, 85, 87, 90, 92, 94, 95, 97, 99,
    100, 101, 102, 103, 104, 105, 155, 159
Pelagianism, 169
Pelagians, 136, 164, 165, 166, 169
Persia, 2, 4, 6, 7, 8, 9, 10, 11, 12, 13, 15, 17,
    21, 22, 153, 193
Persian Empire, 14, 17, 22
Pontifex Maximus, 29, 79, 139
posthumous influence, 140
Praetor, 29
predestination, 168
profession, 27, 28, 112, 113, 155, 158

R

religious toleration, 139
return to Africa, 159
Roman world, 23, 48, 50, 58, 60, 107, 111,
    120, 151, 174, 178, 190, 192
Rubicon, 38, 40

S

sacred eloquence, v, 107, 115
Saint Ambrose, v, 129, 148
Saint Augustine, v, 148, 151, 164, 170, 172,
    190, 206
Saint Jerome, 85, 90, 104, 105, 126, 155,
    190
seeds of ruin, 45, 111, 192
Senate, 27, 28, 29, 30, 31, 32, 35, 36, 37,
    38, 39, 42, 44, 62, 71, 108

sermons, 115, 117, 119, 125, 148, 149, 170, 200
servitude of the will, 168
soliloquies, 169
sovereignty of God, 195
Spain, 23, 29, 39, 40, 41, 48, 58, 79, 143, 177, 181, 182, 185, 191, 211, 212
Stilicho, 189

T

teacher of rhetoric, 148, 156
the City of God, 169
the Cross, 67, 97, 157, 165, 215
the Roman Senate, 25, 70
Theodosius the Great, v, 173, 177
theologian, 79, 82, 84, 129, 135, 148, 160, 164, 196, 206

theological discussion, 77, 140, 165
Theophilus of Alexandria, 119

U

unity of the Church, 162, 163, 207, 209

V

virtues, 3, 6, 7, 8, 15, 20, 51, 68, 73, 83, 86, 88, 90, 96, 98, 99, 116, 129, 168, 178, 180, 181, 185, 190, 192, 196, 215, 216

X

Xerxes, 5, 20, 21

The Philosophy of Natural Theology

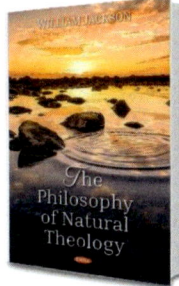

AUTHOR: William Jackson

SERIES: World Philosophy

BOOK DESCRIPTION: This book, originally published in 1876, was written in confutation of the Materialism of its time by arguments derived from Evidences of Intelligence, Design, Contrivance, and Adaptation of Means to Ends, in the Universe, and especially in Man considered in his Moral Nature, his Religious Aptitudes, and his Intellectual Powers; and in all Organic Nature.

HARDCOVER ISBN: 978-1-53613-829-0
RETAIL PRICE: $195

Philosophy of Mind

EDITORS: Russell J. Jenkins and Walter E. Sullivan

SERIES: World Philosophy

BOOK DESCRIPTION: In this book, the authors present current research in the study of the philosophy of the mind.

HARDCOVER ISBN: 978-1-62257-215-1
RETAIL PRICE: $145

The Varieties of Religious Experience: A Study in Human Nature

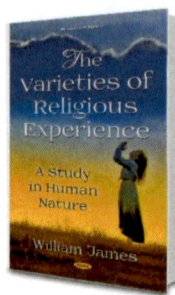

Author: William James

Series: Religion and Society

Book Description: In 1901, William James was appointed as Gifford Lecturer on Natural Religion at the University of Edinburgh. This book is composed of the lectures he gave during that time.

Hardcover ISBN: 978-1-53614-870-1
Retail Price: $250